Teamworking in Mental Health

Also by Steve Onyett

CASE MANAGEMENT IN MENTAL HEALTH

Teamworking in Mental Health

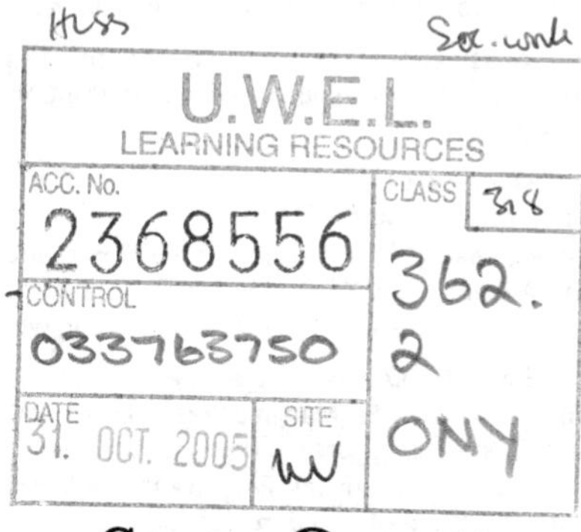

Steve Onyett

Consultant Editor: Jo Campling

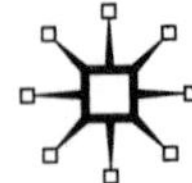

First published 2003 by
PALGRAVE MACMILLAN
Houndmills, Basingstoke, Hampshire RG21 6XS and
175 Fifth Avenue, New York, N.Y. 10010
Companies and representatives throughout the world

PALGRAVE MACMILLAN is the global academic imprint of the Palgrave Macmillan division of St. Martin's Press, LLC and of Palgrave Macmillan Ltd. Macmillan® is a registered trademark in the United States, United Kingdom and other countries. Palgrave is a registered trademark in the European Union and other countries.

ISBN 0–333–76375–0

This book is printed on paper suitable for recycling and made from fully managed and sustained forest sources.

A catalogue record for this book is available from the British Library.

10 9 8 7 6 5 4 3 2
12 11 10 09 08 07 06 05 04

Printed and bound in Great Britain by
J. W. Arrowsmith Ltd, Bristol

For my team players
of the future – Jacob, Isaac and Elena

Contents

List of Boxes, Figures and Tables

Boxes

Figures

Tables

Acknowledgements

A number of people devoted time to reviewing draft material. I am particularly indebted to Steve Morgan, Mo Hutchison, John Wells, Dawn Wakeling and Michael Bainbridge for contributing their time and expertise. I am also grateful to Jo Campling for her support and guidance over this project.

The author and publishers wish to thank the following for permission to reproduce copyright material:

M. A. West, C. S. Borrill and K. L. Unsworth, 'Team Effectiveness in Organisations' in C. L. Cooper and I. T. Robertson, *International Review of Industrial and Organisational Psychology*. (1988 @ John Wiley & Sons) Reproduced with permission of John Wiley & Sons Limited and Professor Michael West.

M. Slade, 'Needs Assessment' in *British Journal of Psychiatry*, **165**, 293–6. Reproduced with permission of Dave Jago, Head of Publications, The Royal College of Psychiatrists.

Risk indicators in Box 5 reproduced with permission of Steve Morgan.

Every effort has been made to trace the copyright holders but if any have been inadvertently overlooked the publishers will be pleased to make the necessary arrangements at the first opportunity.

Acronym Buster

A&E	Accident and emergency department
ACT	Assertive community treatment
BPS	British Psychological Society
CMD	Continuous medical development
CMHC	Community mental health centre
CMHN	Community mental health nurse
CMHT	Community mental health team
CPA	Care programme approach
CPD	Continuous professional development
FTE	Full-time equivalent
GP	General practitioner based in primary care
MHPIG	Mental Health Policy Implementation Guide
MRF	Multi-rater feedback
NHSE	National Health Service Executive
NIMBY	Not in my backyard
NIMHE	National Institute for Mental Health in England
NSF	National Service Framework
PCT	Primary care trust
SCMH	Sainsbury Centre for Mental Health
SSI	Social Services Inspectorate

Introduction: What is this Book about?

When a person has mental health problems that arise from their social environment and their individual ability to cope, some coordinated effort is usually needed to improve the situation. This effort involves the individual themselves, the people that are nearest and dearest to them, and some input from services. This demands teamwork.

Teamworking needs to involve the users of services as active participants in the team process. This book examines such teamworking as the cornerstone of effective mental health service provision. As well as looking at the practicalities of clinical work in a team context, this book explores the role of teams in a social, political and policy context. Why? Not everybody wants the same thing out of mental health services. Indeed, not even the members of any one team will necessarily be in pursuit of the same outcomes, or have the same values about what constitutes a good service. Individual team members will be caught in the midst of the tensions between managers and staff, users and staff, different disciplines, health and social care, primary and specialist care, in-patient and community care, and advocates of medical versus psychosocial interventions. Many other such tensions could be described. This book argues that those who are aware of the social and political context in which they are working are more likely to stay effective, and maintain higher morale. It is also important that they understand the interests and roles that other stakeholders are pursuing. It is only through these individuals being effective that teamworking can benefit service users.

When is a team a team?

Teams should be used when teamworking is required. The required work group can be defined as 'three or more people employed by an organisation who see themselves as a group, are seen by others in the organisation as a group and who depend on each other for resources . . . to accomplish a task or set of tasks' (Shea and Guzzo, 1987: 327). The type and level of dependence between team members is important. There is no consensus on the extent of differentiation and interdependence between roles within mental health teams. Indeed, it is the source of lively debate (Brown *et al.*, 2000). Nor have community mental health teams (CMHTs) been proficient in defining the outcomes that they are aiming to achieve (Onyett *et al.*, 1995). Thus, formal definitions used in the wider social and organisational psychology literature on work teams do not accurately describe those organisations named and recognised as mental health teams. However, as we become more sophisticated about the nature of teamworking it is important that we continue to aspire to this rigour in defining teams and teamworking, otherwise we will not be in a position to accurately assess whether we are achieving effective teamworking or not.

What does 'teamworking' mean in practice?

In the past we have accepted that teamworking is merely what is described as teamworking. Indeed, in order to differentiate multidisciplinary *teams* from mere *networks* of practitioners that work in a multidisciplinary fashion, a national study of CMHTs in England explicitly included the *recognition* of the service as a CMHT by senior managers in its research criteria (Onyett *et al.*, 1994). This recognition may be a key defining criteria for many teams. Øvretveit (1986) noted how: 'Just calling a group of practitioners a team has become a way in which managers and planners avoid the real problems and work needed to coordinate an increasingly complex range of services in the community'.

The Shea and Guzzo (1987) definition above highlighted team-member interdependence as intrinsic to teamworking. The issue of interdependence between team members can be further explored by looking at the different levels of integration of practice achieved through teams.

Multidisciplinary mental health teams have been defined as 'a group of practitioners with different professional training, employed by more than one agency, who meet regularly to coordinate their work providing services to one or more clients in a defined area' (Ovretveit, 1993: 9). Opie (1997) regards this as merely *inter-disciplinary* teamworking whereby members operate from within their particular disciplinary orientations but undertake some joint collaborative work. She defines *multi-disciplinary* teamworking as 'where members, operating out of their disciplinary bases, work parallel to each other, their primary objective being that of coordination' (263). She further defines *trans-disciplinary* teamworking as the achievement of a significantly higher level of work integration where professional values and terminology are scrutinised and the team is able to develop a common language. Deciding what kind of team you are will require candid reflection on how team members work together and share a common way of construing and responding to mental health problems.

A focus on doing, not definition

Ovretveit (1986, 1993) described teams along three dimensions: structure, process and integration. *Structure* refers to the composition of the team and how it is managed. *Process* describes how the team receives referrals and works with service users over time. *Integration* refers to the 'closeness' of working between members. Ovretveit (1993) contrasted 'network-association teams' with 'formal teams'. The former are networks of practitioners coming together on a voluntary basis, each managed by their own professional line management. In contrast, formal teams require a team leader and collective responsibility for specified objectives.

Ovretveit's categories have provided a useful framework for service development, but the actual features of the organisation and operation of mental health teams appear not to lend themselves to meaningful categorization when you look at what they *actually* do, rather than what they *aim* to do (Onyett *et al.*, 1994). The Golden Rule with mental health teams is not to be dazzled by what they call themselves and their stated aims. For example, large-scale research efforts evaluating the effectiveness of intensive community team provision for people with severe and long-term mental health problems have found that the interventions in question were not nearly intensive enough (for example, Marshall *et al.*, 1999; Ridgely *et al.*, 1996). It is therefore justified that we take a permissive definition of mental health teams, but remain aware that in order to achieve specific outcomes teams will need to be tightly defined, designed and managed.

The description of teams and government policy

This book should be read alongside the detailed guidance in the Mental Health Policy Implementation Guide (MHPIG) (Department of Health, 2001a; 2002a,b,c), which describes the service models within the National Service Framework for Mental Health (NSF; Department of Health, 1999). This guidance describes a range of teams, such as assertive outreach teams, crisis resolution teams, early intervention teams and community mental health teams. Since this provides such rich detail this book will merely describe these teams in outline while focusing on those aspects of teamworking that transcend specific service models. The Mental Health Policy Implementation Guide (2001) describes the following kinds of teams:

Assertive community treatment (ACT) teams serve people with severe mental health problems who have complex health and social care needs. The government guidance above refers to these teams as 'assertive outreach' teams. This is unhelpful, as 'assertive outreach' has also been used to describe the practice of taking services to where people need them in their own environment. It is also a key feature of some of the other service models described below. What is important about ACT is the *intensity* of service provision provided in community settings in order to achieve effective working relationships with people with whom this can be a challenge.

Some teams have eschewed the phrase 'assertive' as it places too much emphasis on the potentially coercive nature of intrusive community treatment, and so have favoured the phrase 'intensive' or 'active' community treatment. The acronym 'ACT' is used throughout this book because of its widespread currency.

Crisis resolution (or 'home treatment') teams provide a 24-hour service to users in their own homes to avoid hospital admissions where possible and provide the maximum opportunity to resolve crises in the contexts in which they occur.

Early intervention teams also work proactively but specifically seek to serve people in the early stages of developing psychotic symptoms in order to reduce their longer-term dependency on services and promote better outcomes.

Community mental health teams (CMHTs) or primary care liaison teams. The Mental Health Policy Implementation Guide stated that

> CMHTs, in some places known as Primary Care Liaison Teams, will continue to be a mainstay of the system. CMHTs have an important, indeed integral, role to play in supporting service users and families in community settings. They should provide the core around which newer service elements are developed. The responsibilities of CMHTs may change over time with the advent of new services, however they will retain an important role. They, alongside primary care will provide the key source of referrals to the newer teams. They will also continue to care for the majority of people with mental illness in the community (Department of Health, 2001: 6–7).

In essence then, CMHTs appear to be that crucial part of the whole service system that is left when the other newer service models have become operational. The Mental Health Policy Implementation Guidance update on CMHTs (Department of Health, 2002a) is therefore not prescriptive about team structure but rather focuses on the functions that the team should achieve:

1 Giving advice on the management of mental health problems by other professionals – in particular advice to primary care and a triage function enabling appropriate referral.
2 Providing treatment and care for those with time-limited disorders who can benefit from specialist interventions.
3 Providing treatment and care for those with more complex and enduring needs.

People with 'time limited disorders [who can] be referred back to their GPs after a period of weeks or months' are described as the major client group of CMHTs and would be served through functions 1 and 2 above. However, another role of CMHTs is to 'reduce stigma, ensure that care is delivered in the least restrictive and disruptive manner possible'. It is questionable whether involvement in a dedicated team process is the least stigmatising way to serve such individuals where they could be better served through individual practice-based counselling or therapy (Gask *et al.*, 2000; Mellor-Clark, 2000). The NHS Plan also requires that by 2004 there will be two new staff groups working in primary care: graduates helping GPs to manage common mental health problems, and new 'Gateway' workers responding to people requiring immediate help.

The MHPIG highlights that 'Rehabilitation and Recovery Teams' may fulfil the third function. Where there are complex issues such as difficulty establishing effective working relationships with users, and multiple diagnoses, this function is also likely to be fulfilled by the local ACT team.

When is a CMHT not a CMHT?

The Mental Health Policy Implementation Guide (2002a) provides recommendations for CMHTs that acknowledge that many of the functions will be carried out in other ways. At the same time, some argue that reconfiguring services to accord with these newer models is inappropriate where existing teams have already evolved to fulfil the required functions effectively (for example, Thornicroft *et al.*, 1999; Tyrer, 1998a; Tyrer *et al.*, 2001). This is partly supported by Simmonds *et al.*'s (2001) review of CMHTs, which found them to be achieving many of the outcomes claimed for the newer service models (see Chapter 3). In practice, such CMHTs may be difficult to distinguish from the more 'functional' teams. In many local circumstances this is just as it should be as teams have evolved to reflect local needs and circumstances. It is notable that mature UK ACT teams tend to stress their continuity of practice with existing CMHTs rather than differences (Burns and Firn, 2002).

In this context it has to be questioned whether it is helpful to restrict the term CMHT to a specific *type* of team. Any team providing coordinated multidisciplinary input in community settings through a team process is by definition a 'community mental health team'. I therefore use the phrase to describe all the service models above that can be said to be teams working in the community. This has the advantage of diluting some of the tribal rivalry that can exist between 'CMHTs' and 'Functional' teams (Burns and Firn, 2002; Onyett, 1992). They are all CMHTs and they should all be functional. A team that is not functional should not be offering a service.

The answer to the question, 'When is a CMHT not a CMHT?' is therefore 'When it is not a team at all'. In other words, those situations where the needs of the client do not require that people from different disciplines and agencies work with each other through a defined team process. Teamworking where it is not actually needed quickly degrades and just gives teams a bad name.

It is unhelpful to be too rigid about having a range of specific types of teams fulfilling specific functions for the residents of a given locality. We do need to be clear about the range of functions that need to be delivered locally. These include early intervention, assertive outreach for people who are difficult to engage, home treatment for people in crisis, services addressing the needs of people with dual diagnoses, culturally appropriate services for black and minority ethnic communities, and services for homeless people and mentally disordered offenders. All these services need to be able to address peoples' housing, income, occupational and social needs.

How these functions are delivered should be informed by research on service models, the specific components of their implementation that appear to be effective, and the evidence for their effectiveness. We need to consider how teamworking *across the patch* provides the right range of functions for service users. All teams need to be 'functional' and their teamworking within the locality will include a range of service configurations, the design of which needs to be informed by the available evidence, but also by local needs assessment, existing strengths, and the unique geographical and demographic characteristics of the patch. The design of CMHTs fulfilling these functions may and should vary depending on their history and context. They will, however, share some key common elements that are required to support individual practitioners in their work with people with complex needs. This book focuses on these common elements.

It is important to recognise that not all teamworking takes place in the community. Even the most intensive community service is unlikely to completely eliminate the need for in-patient care. Most of the principles outlined in this book are equally applicable to in-patient teams. Continuity of practice between the hospital and the community is critical, and it is encouraging to see the increased emphasis on joint working between in-patient and crisis resolution teams (Department of Health, 2002b).

A route-map through the chapters

This introduction has established some basic concepts and the scope of the book. Chapter 1 explores issues concerning team effectiveness, embedded within a discussion of the functions of mental health services from the perspective of a range of different groups, such as users, carers, staff and society in general. Tensions between the interests of these groups are further explored when looking at the historical and social policy context for team development in Chapter 2.

Chapter 3 poses the question, 'What's so great about teamworking anyway?' Has teamworking evolved as the dominant way of providing mental health services because it is so evidently effective or are CMHTs merely some ill-conceived historical accident? What is the evidence that teams have achieved their stated objectives?

A major problem of team design has been a failure to fully explore their strategic context and how they are designed to respond to clearly defined needs. Chapter 4 considers the broader issues of the design of teams to respond to particular categories of needs in particular circumstances (for example, rural environments). Chapter 5 explores other key design considerations such as team size, location and composition. The frequent references to 'the CMHT survey' here refer to Onyett *et al.*'s (1994) comprehensive survey of CMHTs in England. Although other mapping exercises have taken place since then, this study remains the only comprehensive source of data available.

Chapter 6 further explores the cornerstone of effective provision: establishing effective collaborative working relationships between staff, service users and their social networks. The care coordinator role within teams is described as a vehicle for this relationship.

The final three chapters look more closely at aspects of the leadership and management of the process of teamworking. Chapter 7 explores issues of power, authority, responsibility and accountability and how these shape leadership and management roles within teams. Chapter 8 looks more closely at how the team manages its most precious resource: the mental health and effectiveness of its members. The concluding chapter again places teams in a broader context by looking at the issue of continuous change for service improvement.

What you will not get from this book

This book is written primarily with clients of working age with mental health problems in mind. Issues relating to the particular needs of other client groups will not be covered, although the principles of teamworking, leadership, management and service improvement will be applicable.

Readers exploring this topic are making increasing use of on-line resources. For this reason I have not included case examples of effective teams as full descriptions with up-to-date contact details are available on-line. See, for example, the web site of the National Institute for Mental Health in England at *www.nimhe.org.uk* and the practice database available through the Sainsbury Centre for Mental Health web site at *www.scmh.org.uk.* There is no substitute for researching the practices of teams operating in contexts like your own and going to visit them.

Finally, it is important to stress that good teamworking provides only a platform for effective relationships between users, carers and staff. To achieve significant clinical change, that platform needs to support the implementation of effective clinical interventions. Those interventions have not been reviewed here, and would be the subject of a whole other book. Excellent books have already been written (see for example, BPS (2000) for a useful orientation to the literature). This book will therefore focus on the effectiveness of teams rather than individual clinical interventions, and this is where our discussion starts in Chapter 1.

CHAPTER 1

Describing Effective Teams

The only reason for being interested in teams at all is to examine their potential for achieving positive outcomes for users and other key stakeholders in ordinary service environments. But what constitutes effectiveness? This chapter explores this question from the perspective of users, carers, staff, policy-makers, politicians and the wider society. While these perspectives will never be wholly aligned I argue that focusing on effective working relationships between staff and service users provides a way of working with these tensions in the best possible way. Before examining these various stakeholder perspectives on what effectiveness means, let's look at the social psychological model of team effectiveness that underpins the structure of this book.

A model for team effectiveness

West (1994) considered team effectiveness to have three main components:

- *Task effectiveness*: the extent to which the team is successful in achieving its task-related objectives.
- *Mental health*: the well-being, growth and development of team members.
- *Team viability*: the probability that the team will continue to work together and function effectively.

Teams are only likely to be viable over the long term if they are both effective in meeting their objectives and can attend to the well-being of their members. For example, the Daily Living Programme was an innovative service that nonetheless proved to be unsustainable because of poor morale and lack of support from key stakeholders (Audini *et al.*, 1994).

West developed his model of team effectiveness with particular emphasis on 'reflexivity'. He argued that teams are effective to the extent that they reflect upon their objectives, strategies and processes, as well as their environments, and adapt these aspects of their worlds accordingly (West *et al.*, 1998). In contrast to other models of team effectiveness, which focus on more static processes, this formulation captures the dynamic nature of 'complex decision-making teams'. These are teams fulfilling seven criteria:

- *They operate in uncertain, unpredictable environments.* Chapter 2 will review the ever-changing social policy context in which teams operate.
- *They work with uncertain and unpredictable technology.* For CMHTs, the uncertain nature of risk assessment and management is a key example.
- *It is unclear how tasks should be performed on a day-to-day basis.* CMHTs are perhaps unique in that not only is there a contested evidence-base for much that is provided to users, but also there are often ideological schisms within the team concerning the very nature of mental distress and its care and treatment.
- *Team member interdependence is high.* Where teams are targeted on people with the complex health and social care needs, there is an obvious need for team members with different backgrounds to combine their efforts to achieve successful outcomes.
- *Autonomy and control for the teams are relatively high.* It is only with the advent of the NSF that a high level of prescription has become evident. How this policy is translated into practice remains to be seen. The experience of previous highly prescribed policy imperatives, such as the care programme approach (CPA), would suggest that change will only occur where practitioners are in support of the change (Bindman *et al.*, 1999).
- *The tasks that the team are required to perform are complex.* Work in mental health teams may require high levels of technical knowledge, for example, in terms of the application of complex psychological theory, the effects and side effects of prescribed drugs, and unravelling the vagaries of the benefits system. In addition, practitioners may experience ethical and intellectual

tensions, for example, regarding their roles as caring professionals responding to need alongside their increasingly explicit role as an agent of social control.

- *There are multiple components of effectiveness, and the team is responsible to multiple constituents.* This chapter describes the many different outcomes that different stakeholder groups seek from CMHTs.

West's model of group reflexivity is particularly applicable to knowledge-based teams of professionals with diverse backgrounds such as CMHTs (West, 1996). He describes two dimensions of reflexivity as part of the achievement of team effectiveness:

- *Task reflexivity*: demonstrated in the team's ability to achieve the team's objectives. For example, critiques of CMHTs have focused on their tendency to neglect people with the most severe and long-term mental health problems (for example, Patmore and Weaver, 1991a; Sayce *et al.*, 1991). Subsequent guidance has emphasised successful targeting as the key task of CMHTs (Department of Health, 1996, 1999, 2001a). Later in this book we will explore those features of team design that promote the successful achievement of this objective.
- *Social reflexivity*: demonstrated in the team's ability to promote the well-being of its members. Factors influencing morale among team members will be explored below and in Chapter 8.

Effectiveness in the eye of the beholder

It is important that mental health practitioners, users and carers, fully understand the difficult and contradictory nature of work in mental health. Since different interest groups may define effectiveness in different ways, it is also important to maintain an awareness of the power relationships that exist between staff and service users, and among the other key interest groups involved in mental health service provision. These interest groups include users, managers, the variety of provider agencies, the criminal-justice system, the commissioners of services, local and national politicians, carers and the wider public. This analysis should include a clear understanding of the potential for good and harm involved in receiving mental health services. Without this it is difficult to achieve a critically constructive perspective on the role of CMHTs.

This is not the place for a full exploration of the sociology of mental health services (see instead Pilgrim and Rogers, 1999). This discussion will merely summarise some of the different expectations of various stakeholders in order to explore common interests and unavoidable tensions.

Our starting point is to consider how an expressed need on the part of service users is seen as a legitimate focus for intervention. Most commentators view need as being negotiated between users, professional mental health service staff and other key stakeholders such as the authorities that pay for services. In other words there is (1) a professional/service provider/commissioner view of need, (2) what users seek from services and, (3) an area of negotiated need that is the overlap between (1) and (2) (Slade, 1994; see Figure 1). What constitutes a legitimate need is therefore influenced by basic human values about what services should achieve for people, the respective powers of the agencies involved in negotiation, and the absolute level of resources that are available to meet the demand. This is determined by similar processes of negotiation at higher levels. The NHS and Community Care Act (1990) defined need as 'the requirement of individuals to enable them to achieve,

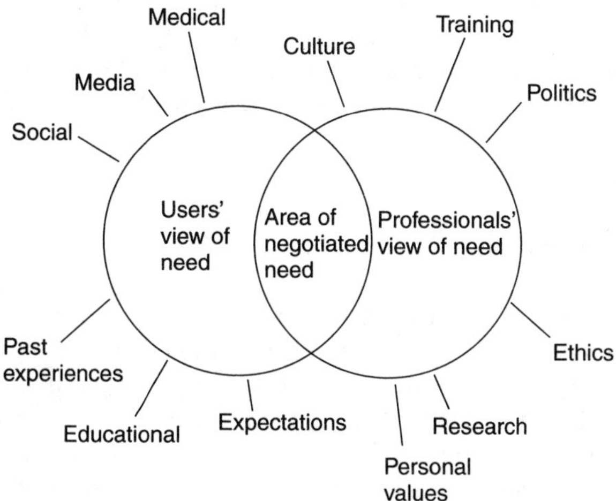

Figure 1 *Factors influencing perceptions of need*

maintain or restore an acceptable level of social independence or quality of life'. What is acceptable clearly bears upon our level of expectation.

We shall start with a user perspective, and then explore the role of mental health services as a provider of therapeutic input, practical help, social control and surveillance. We shall also examine the ways in which these expectations serve to produce social policy, and create issues for staff.

User perspectives on effectiveness

The following provides only a broad-brush account of key messages that occur consistently when asking users about what is sought from mental health services. It does not substitute for your own local inquiries into what the current and potential users of your services perceive as important. Being responsive to the needs of users requires sensitivity to changing needs, and recognising that people with different problems, backgrounds and cultures require different responses. Users do not represent a single culture or community. Different groups have different needs of services and find that services respond differently to them.

In that we are all users, or potential users of mental health services, the outcomes sought by service users will be familiar to everyone. Figure 2 illustrates how the needs that CMHTs might address form part of what mental health services as a whole should help people achieve, which in turn is informed by what all of us need to live fulfilling, effective lives.

Strategies for living

Maslow (1954) described a hierarchy of needs ranging from basic needs for sustenance and safety, through needs for belonging and love, and the promotion of one's self esteem, through to the ultimate goal of 'self-actualisation' wherein one's potential is realised and self-fulfilment is achieved. Many of these key themes are echoed in the user-led Strategies for Living study (Faulkner, 2000). Mental health service users described living well as involving the achievement of a feeling of being accepted, achieving a sense of belonging,

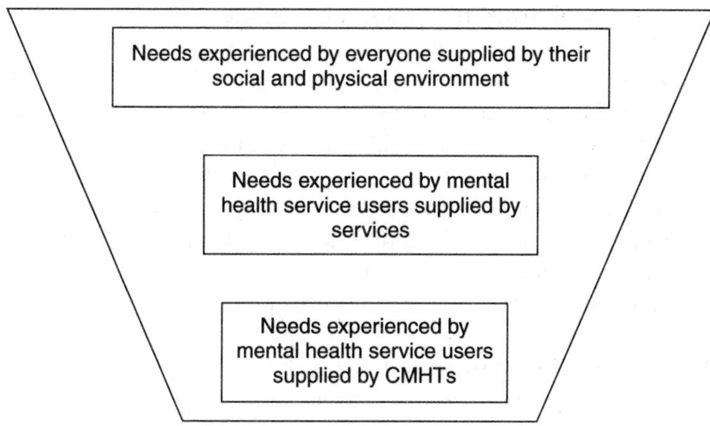

Figure 2 *Addressing needs from different sources*

feeling supported, achieving purpose and meaning in life, experiencing peace and relaxation, being able to think positively, finding personal expression, distraction and control over one's life.

Good personal relationships were seen as the key to fulfilling these ends. This included relationships developed with friends, families and partners, with professionals and through involvement in voluntary sector projects. The relationships needed to provide emotional support which itself entailed the need for acceptance of the individual in their totality, and for the relationship to offer love, physical affection and understanding. Relationships provided companionship with people who one could talk to and with whom one could share experiences and interests. They gave life meaning by providing a sense of belonging, a sense of purpose and someone to live for. Relationships also provided practical support, a fulfilling home life, and financial support.

Aside from the achievement of effective relationships, the study highlighted other strategies for living such as religious and spiritual pursuits, physical exercise, and hobbies. Having enough money, and achieving the right medication was also highlighted as important to effective survival. It is important to note that this study found that the required supports were normally drawn from sources other than mainstream services.

What users seek from mental health services

The Audit Commission (1994) commissioned a review of user surveys that looked more narrowly at what users seek from services. Users particularly sought help with finding employment and finance, including access to the welfare benefits to which they were entitled. The remarkable consistency of reports from users about the importance of social factors such as housing, finance and occupation is reflected in the equally consistent failure of services to afford these aspects adequate attention (Carpenter and Sbaraini, 1997).

The review also highlighted the need for more 24-hour crisis facilities offering out-of hours contact, non-hospital crisis centres, and more voluntary sector and user-run services. There was also a demand for increased sensitivity to ethnic and cultural needs, and users having more rights, and respect from service providers. Rights included improved equality of access to services, and access to advocacy when required. Users sought greater involvement in decision-making, both in their own care and in service management and development. Users sought staff who listened.

The importance of information was evident. This included details of treatment options available, the effects and side effects of medication, and the range of services available. It was also important for people to be aware of the rules and expectations on admission, complaints procedures and their expected length of stay in hospital. Users wanted to be made aware of the roles and responsibilities of staff, rules of confidentiality and their rights to a second opinion.

Other changes that users saw as likely to improve care included better collaboration and cooperation between agencies, better liaison with local interest groups (for example, those concerned with minority ethnic groups), more efficient handling of complaints, the use of crisis cards, more help for carers and more user-only forums.

In order to develop a tool to evaluate CMHT effectiveness, Richards and Rees (1998) mapped what a range of stakeholders expected CMHTs to achieve. The stakeholders involved in developing these effectiveness criteria included users, carers, advocates, practitioners, policy-makers, managers, and researchers. The study highlighted the importance of CMHT workers' ability to build relationships based on friendliness and trust with users and carers. The first contact with services was seen as an important point for the subsequent development of a good quality relationship. Staff needed to be able to address users' emotional responses with sensitivity and consistency.

This study also highlighted the need for users to be involved in decision-making about both their own care, and in evaluation and service development. Having a clearly identified individual within the team was important to promote this accessibility. Accessibility meant achieving a clear point of contact, short waiting times, and a rapid response.

It is also important to stress that users did not want to be involved with the CMHT for the sake of it. They had an expectation that the CMHT would be effective in improving their quality of life, clinical symptoms and social life. This, in turn, required interventions that could be expected to work.

Enabling users to make informed choices was seen as a way of promoting users' autonomy, and required both the provision of choice and information about what was available. Information needed to be well-researched, unbiased and effectively presented in verbal and written form.

What do carers seek from mental health services?

There is often a danger of lumping user and carer interests together as if they represent a single-interest group. While they will share many of the same concerns, particularly concerning their involvement in services and the accessibility and choice of provision, there may also be differences in emphasis.

Outcomes sought by people with caring roles include (Audit Commission, 1994; National Schizophrenia Fellowship, 1995):

- Receiving enough advice and information to support the person experiencing mental distress in the best possible way.
- Someone to talk to, for example, a named team member for carers who will avoid professional jargon (Carpenter and Sbaraini, 1997). This support needs to be available out of normal working hours.
- Having emotional support when necessary.

- Being able to work.
- Being as financially secure as possible.
- Getting a break from caring responsibilities.
- To be able to sustain a social network and avoid isolation.
- Being valued and respected by services.
- Seeing the person they support receiving high quality services that meet their needs.
- Having a voice, both in terms of individual advocacy and also at a strategic level.

In terms of general service priorities, carers highlight the need for daytime occupation with flexible hours and a focus on employment skills, and special support for users who have had frequent hospital re-admissions. They also highlight the need for 24-hour access, alternatives to hospital, including home treatment or crisis resolution, early intervention to prevent crises, a range of residential provision with different levels of staff support, and more self-help schemes. The importance attached to self-help schemes and other resources aimed at furthering independence would appear to undermine the oft-encountered stereotype of carers as over-anxious and over-protective.

What do staff seek from work in mental health services?

Members of any organisation act in pursuit of individual and collective goals that may deviate from the formally stated aims of the organisation. It cannot be assumed that the function of CMHT membership for CMHT members is to produce outcomes valued by service users or carers, or indeed to achieve any of the effectiveness criteria highlighted above. It is just as plausible to argue that the function of team membership may be to earn a living, to fulfil a need to help people, or to exercise a desire to achieve social control of people experienced as socially and morally alien to oneself.

The research does, however, suggest that team members derive job satisfaction and a sense of reward from clinical work, particularly where they are able to be effective in their work (Heim, 1991; Onyett *et al.*, 1995; Payne and Firth-Cozens, 1999). This remains true even where that clinical work is a source of stress. Barriers to effectiveness, such as lack of resources, work overload and bureaucracy are key sources of pressure (Edwards *et al.*, 2000; Onyett *et al.*, 1995).

Onyett *et al.* (1995) found that teamworking itself was the most frequently cited source of reward among 445 CMHT members. Respondents valued being in a team with supportive colleagues and working well together in a committed, cohesive and sometimes humorous way. For example, the consultant psychiatrist who cited: 'Relationships with colleagues – mutual support, respect and fun', as a source of reward and the occupational therapist who felt 'The atmosphere of the team is very supportive and open and we all share a slightly off-key sense of humour.' The UK 'Care in the Community' demonstration programme (Knapp *et al.*, 1992) also found the most frequently cited areas of satisfaction were relationships with colleagues (cited by 93 per cent of their sample) and Borrill *et al.* (2000) found team membership to be associated with improved mental health among staff in their large-scale study of team effectiveness.

Other sources of reward that were highlighted in the Onyett *et al.* (1995) study included opportunities for innovation, variety, challenge and training. One community mental health nurse (CMHN) valued the 'team's continued commitment to in-service training – stops you going stale'. Other valued tasks included inter-agency work, group work, supervising others, project work and management. Some people made particular mention of the benefits of community work, such as the nurse who valued 'supporting people in the community – not being divorced from the social realities', or the CMHN who valued exposure to 'the broad-range of life situations encountered in the client group'.

Herzberg *et al.* (1959) regarded the avoidance of dissatisfaction with extrinsic factors of the job such as pay and security as a more basic, lower-order need than the achievement of satisfaction through intrinsic factors of the job such as a sense of achievement or meaning from one's work. Koelbel *et al.* (1991) found that social service, variety, and opportunities to use one's abilities were major sources of satisfaction among nurse practitioners. Dissatisfaction was expressed with pay, promotion, policies and practices, recognition and supervision and relationships. Similarly, Knapp *et al.* (1992) found the main sources of dissatisfaction were income and promotion prospects.

It is possible to conclude that staff are most concerned to achieve a sense of intrinsic satisfaction through being able to feel effective in their work. This allows people to derive some meaning and social value from their work, even when it is stressful. While it is also important to avoid extrinsic sources of dissatisfaction (like low pay and status) when considering what staff seek from their work, it is important to ensure that the work environment allows staff to be maximally effective in order to promote the mental health of both staff and service users.

What does society expect from mental health services? – The tension between care and control

Staff, users and their carers form part of the societies in which we live and the cultures that characterise them. As Rose (1996a: 353) observes:

> While our political, professional, moral and cultural authorities still speak happily of 'society', the very meaning and ethical salience of this term is under question as 'society' is perceived as dissociated into a variety of ethical and cultural communities with incompatible allegiances and incommensurable obligations.

Mental health services sit within these cultures, and act to maintain the interests of certain groups. Mental health services are certainly concerned with helping troubled individuals in whatever way possible. However, they also demonstrate a role in controlling behaviours that are deemed socially unacceptable. Furthermore, since the goals of mental health service interventions are often shaped by prevailing cultural norms and definitions of normality, mental health service provision also serves to maintain and shape social values.

There has been an explosion of popular interest in counselling and psychotherapy. The remit of mental health services has now expanded to include a much wider range of mental distress. For many people it may provide a secular alternative source of meaning and relief from unhappiness that was formerly achieved by religious observance. One might predict that this would make the barrier between 'mental illness' and 'normality' more blurred and permeable thereby reducing stigma. A less benign interpretation is that this expansion in a therapy industry serves to 'pathologise' that which might formally have been considered normal human misery or distress by creating new medical categories of questionable validity.

A culture that is overconcerned with the management of risk also extends the remit of mental health expertise from diagnosis of dangerousness or vulnerability among people confined in institutions, to evaluation of failures of self-management in community encounters. These may arise from failures to budget, cook, maintain tenancies or cope with family relationships (Rose, 1996b). Rather than aspire to achieve recovery of roles among mental health users, the emphasis shifts to 'management' of risk within these various domains of the user's life. Users are already highlighting concerns about the role of intensive community team treatment in exercising this level of control and surveillance (Smith *et al.*, 1999a).

This cultural concern with management of risk also has implications for staff. We are all to a greater or lesser degree potentially a risk to others or ourselves in these ordinary life domains. Yet this culture inculcates a fear of accountability and blame among mental health practitioners for events that they feel to be out of their control.

Stigma is an enduring feature of mental health problems. People with a psychiatric history fare worse than other disabled people when returning to work. Only 13 per cent are in employment compared with over a third of disabled people generally (Office of National Statistics, 1998). Sayce and Measey (1999) highlight that this cannot be accounted for by the nature of the mental health problems themselves as mental distress is not a reliable predictor of work capacity (Anthony *et al.*, 1995) and unemployment rates can be significantly reduced when people are offered real jobs but with intensive and flexible support (Bond *et al.*, 1997; Crowther *et al.*, 2001). Read and Baker (1996) in a large-scale survey of users reported that 34 per cent had been sacked or forced to resign from employment. Unsurprisingly, Link *et al.* (1997) found that 75 per cent of serious mentally distressed people would not tell a prospective employer about their psychiatric history.

Sayce and Measey (1999) also highlight the problems that people with mental health problems have in accessing housing in the community of their choice. There was an increase in NIMBY ('Not in my backyard') campaigns in the 1990s that often resulted in delays in implementation or the relocation of mental health projects, and occasionally attacks on residents and staff. Read and Baker (1996) reported that 26 per cent of their sample had moved home because of harassment, 47 per cent had been abused or harassed in public and 14 per cent subject to physical assault. They also found that access to key opportunities such as life insurance, mortgages or holidays could also be threatened by revelation of a psychiatric diagnosis. Indeed, even access to basic medical care is threatened with users reporting difficulty and delays getting tests for physical problems because the complaints are initially interpreted as manifestations of their mental health problems. This is of great concern, particularly in view of the high rates of heart disease and other major illnesses among people with mental health problems (Department of Health, 1994a).

There has been a marked social policy shift with the New Labour Government of the late 1990s towards recognising the importance of social inclusion. Landmark features include the New Deal for disabled people concerning employment opportunities, an emphasis on achieving effective partnerships between key agencies to reduce exclusion through local 'Action Zones' for health and education, and the establishment of a Disability Rights Commission. However, this has gone hand in hand with policies that continue to emphasise containment and concealment of people with the most publicly unacceptable manifestations of mental distress, as well as providing psychiatrists with a new mandate for social control.

The urge towards containment and minimisation of risk was manifest in government proposals to introduce compulsory treatment in the community and detain people deemed dangerous and diagnosed as having a severe personality disorder, regardless of whether they are regarded as treatable, and whether they have committed a crime (Department of Health/Home Office, 2000). So while there is a new emphasis on social inclusion, new social policies reveal a parallel and more enduring concern with social control and segregation. The commitment to community-based provision and the integration of service users into communities with the full rights of any other citizens seems at best questionable in this context. Thomas *et al.* (1996) argue that this is because, while the location of care has changed for many, the language of psychiatry and the theory that underpins it has remained the same. They argue that psychiatry has always been founded on a social policy of exclusion rather than advances in medical science. They point out that:

> Isolating the insane from society [through the asylum system] grew out of the Romantic belief in a Utopian society which regarded urbanisation and industrialisation responsible for the growth of insanity (sic). This isolation was linked to a search for medical causes of mental illness, as asylum care isolated the insane from the effects of poverty, overcrowding, alcohol misuse, violence, prostitution and other forms of abuse that characterised industrial urban life. Yet paradoxically this sequestration, and the emerging concept of mental illness, devalued the importance of social factors in relation to insanity. Psychiatrists studied mental illness devoid of any social context, producing a schism between the social reality of mental illness and the interpretation of sufferers experiences. (Thomas *et al.*, 1996: 401)

Despite the emergence of social psychiatry and the development of 'community care', the broader picture is of a deepening of this schism. The 'social reality' for many users is increased economic polarisation and poverty, particularly among minority ethnic groups (Joseph Rowntree Foundation, 1995). The UK has closely followed America's passage into a post-industrial economy characterised by upward distribution of income, cuts in benefit entitlements and a loss of low-cost housing stock. At the same time the trend in the two main American psychiatric journals from 1969 to 1990 was away from psychological and sociological formulations and towards biological perspectives, (Pincus *et al.*, 1993).

Concerns about medicalisation of distress and neglect of social factors do not reflect a belief that politicians, and the practitioners and managers who have to implement social policy, are personally malign or politically ignorant. Indeed, we have seen above how most practitioners appear to value their relationships with users as individuals. Nonetheless, there is a tension between care and social control that has long characterised work in mental health services. Mental health workers operate as members of a culture and understanding this culture offers insights into some of the social forces that shape our work.

Mossman cites a 'mythologised individualism' (Merelman, 1989) as the contemporary manifestation of these themes. This holds the individual to be virtuous, and naturally free while the collective (or 'society') has the connotation of being constraining, centralising, corrupting, repressive or even evil. This theme has become central to political rhetoric and policy and an important part of popular culture. Examples of the impact on political discourse on both sides of the Atlantic can be found in the hardening attitudes towards welfare, campaigns to address corruption in the working of central government, and claims to reduce the influence of central government to an optimal minimum. The UK has adopted the political imperative, embraced by both major parties, to keep personal taxation to a minimum in order that individuals can exercise maximum choice on how to spend their income. Individualism is also manifest in the emphasis on marrying individual rights with personal responsibilities. In an international context, the cultural triumph of individualism over collectivism has also been powerfully embodied in the expansion of liberal market economies and the collapse of Eastern bloc, so-called 'socialist', totalitarian regimes.

Indeed the UK has seen the most dramatic rhetorical emblem of individualism with Margaret Thatcher's statement that: 'There is no such thing as Society. There are individual men and women, and there are families' (*Woman's Own*, 31 October, 1987). This reinforces a pre-existing tendency among mental health services. As Handy (1990) pointed out, 'the mental health system has a tendency to locate the sources of people's problems within either organic dysfunctions or psychological dysfunctions within the individual or their immediate family...and by so doing it implicitly denies the relationship between social conditions and human experience'.

Mossman (1997) argued that by acting on the premise that socio-economic problems require an individualised professional response, mental health services are affirming their social function of defining and controlling non-criminal deviance. Expansion of social control is premised on the idea that the behaviour of mentally distressed people is an exception to normality, mainly by dint of being biologically induced, and so they become categorically different. This in turn validates a policy of exclusion and confinement.

One way in which psychiatry serves to maintain the 'mythologised individualism' of post-industrial societies is to provide, as it always has done, the means by which the people that violate categories and threaten personal safety or property can be redefined out of 'legal personhood'. This has found dramatic expression in the proposals referred to above where people without a formal 'mental illness' but instead a 'severe personality disorder' may be subject to detention on the basis of assessed risk, even if they have not committed criminal acts.

Mossman's (1997) focus on individualism links to the notion of 'healthism' whereby health and sickness are both polarised and moralised such that attainment of health, (and increasingly the associated physical beauty), becomes a socially valued and individual goal to which all should aspire. Sickness is thus forgivable only when it is temporary and resolvable within a biomedical model of health (Carpenter, 1994). Where cure is not available the state of 'illness' becomes stigmatising and leads to a 'spoiled identity' (Goffman, 1961).

Members of CMHTs are both members of societies in which these themes are evident, and individuals charged with managing deviance on society's behalf. The expectations of them are enormous. The National Service Framework for Mental Health (NSF; Department of Health, 1999) places considerable emphasis on ensuring that staff are competent to assess the risk of suicide by providing training for staff in specialist mental health services in risk assessment and management as a priority. The last of the seven standards within the framework states that, 'assertive outreach is in place for all individuals who may fail to take their prescribed medication and would then be at risk of depression, severe mental illness or suicide; for those who have a tendency to drop out of contact with services; and for those who are not well engaged with services' (79). The expectation is that by April 2002 assertive outreach will be in place for all service users on enhanced care programmes who are at risk of losing contact. Compulsory treatment in the community was proposed as a way of ensuring that contact would be maintained and that prescribed treatment administered. As the agents of community supervision, CMHT members are charged with responsibility for the maintenance of public confidence in the policy of community care, a function acknowledged by the Department of Health to be part of the rationale for increased coercion (Atkinson, 1996).

At the same time the NSF exhorted service providers to 'ensure health and social services promote mental health and reduce the discrimination and social exclusion associated with mental health problems'. CMHTs and their members are thus charged both with responsibility for social control of deviance and community integration.

Managing the tensions

The enduring strength of the cultural determinants of mental health policy and practice goes some way towards explaining why, despite endless policy shifts, the experience of services by users remains very much the same. How might the tensions between the interests of the groups described be addressed in a way that might improve outcomes for people that use services? How might CMHTs work with individuals and agencies to make things different?

Achieving profound change through local initiatives

The policy context for socially inclusive practice has never been more favourable. The NSF, with its emphasis on mental health promotion, provided an impetus towards greater partnership working locally between health, social services, education, employment agencies and other key stakeholders concerned with the quality of life of people with mental health problems. Subsequent guidance on mental health promotion also provided an invaluable resource for strategy formation and case examples (NHS Executive, 2001). Clinical governance, the framework for continuous quality improvement in the NHS, (Department of Health, 1998b) introduced a national performance framework that places the experience of users and carers at the centre of service development. The guidance on auditing care planning under the care programme approach stressed audit from the user perspective and the need to include assessment and care planning with respect to employment, education, accommodation, income and leisure (Department of Health, 2001b).

However, translating policy into practice requires consideration of the issue of power and conflict. It is easy to exaggerate the level of consensus within systems. Critical theorists stress that the social order is often negotiated from structurally determined positions of unequal strength that frequently work against the interests of users and employees. Handy (1990) stated that:

> The nature of power relationships is often poorly perceived by members of an organisation or society and may be subject to systematic distortions by dominant power holders whose structural position in society gives

> them an enhanced ability to make their own sectional interests appear to others as universal ones (359).

The changes required to make services truly user-led, based on users' needs and accountable to users are *profound*, which as Senge *et al.* (1999) point out means 'moving towards the fundamental'. It is the level of change that has been sought by the UK user movement since the first patients' councils and advocacy projects were developed in the mid-1980s. Inasmuch as the fundamental nature of mental health services is not easy to observe from within, there is an inevitable element of 'consciousness raising' required among users, staff, carers and other key players about power relationships and the cultural forces described above.

It is therefore important (a) that an ongoing and informed dialogue takes place through every media available on the nature of mental health services, their social role, and how mental health and social inclusion may be promoted, and (b) that access to the means to influencing that dialogue is open, easy and fair. This has implications at a local level with respect to shaping involvement in the processes concerned with one's own care and in the planning and development of local services, and in terms of broader public education about mental health and illness. Sayce and Measey (1999) argued that such local approaches to promoting social inclusion are likely to be more effective than large national education campaigns. CMHTs have a large role in achieving this local action.

Profound change requires not just doing different things, but rather building capacity to do things in a new way, which in turn requires new ways of thinking. One aim of this book is that members of teams will think differently about their work, and in a way that is more psychologically and sociologically informed. The hopeful and informed ideology embodied within the recovery approach (see Carling and Allott, 2000) is important in this regard and is described in Chapter 6. This profound change in thinking can be brought about through practical means such as team-based training or review, particularly where this provides fresh insights into the perspective of users by involving them in the training and team development process. It is also important to achieve a shared sense of the possible among local stakeholders. Sayce and Measey (1999) and NHS Executive (2001) provide many example of clinicians, voluntary organisations and user groups that are working together to break down obstacles to inclusion. For example, Perkins *et al.* (1997) have introduced policies within their NHS Trust that debar discrimination in employment and provide support to promote the employment of staff who use mental health services as members of mental health teams. The Bradford Home Treatment team provides a valuable early example of this approach (Bracken and Cohen, 1999). Voluntary organisations are also active in supporting people to get involved in work, education, religious activities and leisure pursuits. Mind has produced guidelines for local service providers on how to prevent and resolve NIMBY campaigns through working constructively with local communities (Sayce and Willmot, 1997).

Equipped with such examples of best practice, team members are better placed to advocate for the interests of users locally and work alongside them in supporting the kinds of relationships where they come to be seen as contributors to their communities rather than burdens or victims.

At the dawn of this millennium the alignment of user concerns and policy imperatives concerning social inclusion was unprecedented. The challenge is now for these imperatives to be underpinned by adequate resources, for urges towards inclusion to prevail over imperatives concerned with risk management and coercion, and for users, carers and local providers to work in effective local partnerships to produce meaningful change.

Effective relationships between users and staff as the foundation

We have seen how users are concerned to feel understood and listened to so that the support they receive is of practical and personal value. They want to improve the quality of their lives and feel able to be included within ordinary community life. Similarly, staff value feeling effective in their work and benefit from the personal contact they have with users through their clinical work. At the same time, employing and funding organisations, politicians and the public at large are concerned with avoiding adverse events and ensuring risk is effectively managed. The evidence reviewed in Chapter 6 will suggest that an emphasis on the establishment of effective relationships between staff and service users will be important in managing these tensions. If relationships are valued by service users, they promote effective involvement with services, improve clinical and social outcomes, improve the management of clinical risk and may attenuate some of the more oppressive aspects of mental health service provision.

Conclusion

This opening chapter has explored the issue of effectiveness from a stakeholder perspective and foreshadowed some issues to be explored in more detail later, such as team design to achieve valued outcomes for users and the mental health of staff, the centrality of effective relationships, and the need for staff to be aware of their context in order to function as reflective and effective practitioners.

Effective working relationships between staff and service users do not in themselves create good mental health services. They provide a necessary, if not a sufficient condition for an environment in which users, their social networks and staff can work together to achieve the best outcomes given the prevailing conditions. The effective assessment, planning, service delivery and the continuity of contact required for on-going provision, monitoring of outcomes and review all require that staff and service users have good reason to want to stay working together. It is a paradox then that perhaps the most important aspect of *teams* for the provision of services for people with severe and long-term mental health problems is the extent to which they are able to promote successful *individual* relationships between users and staff.

CHAPTER 2

The Historical and Policy Context for Mental Health Teamworking

Why describe social policy?

Few would suggest that policy is based simply upon a rational process of assimilating research and field experience, which is then debated and used to allocate resources and shape practice. Social policy is incremental, ambiguous and self-contradictory in practice and the outcome of high-level political compromises, (Pettigrew *et al.*, 1988). Research itself has a complex relationship with policy-making. Berridge and Thom (1996) demonstrate two-way influence between policy and research, with policy and prevailing political ideologies shaping the way research is framed, interpreted and used to the extent that sometimes research can function as a 'front', legitimating actions which particular interests want to achieve. Policy has a political role in providing a visible response to public demand (for example, following high-profile media coverage of homicides carried out by service users, despite the lack of evidence of risk to the general public) regardless of whether or not the policy is actually implemented.

The relationship of policy to implementation is similarly complex. The care programme approach and care management policies described below offer examples of policies that were difficult in practice and were shaped by resistance from powerful stakeholders. Indeed, they provide an example of how their reception in the field itself moulded further social policy refinement, illustrating a two-way flow of influence between policy-makers and those charged with implementation.

The purpose of this chapter is therefore to amplify the tensions evident in the opening chapter about what constitutes effective and desirable service development among different groups. It does this by looking at the current policy context for CMHTs, how it came about, and the implications for implementation.

The National Service Framework and the NHS plan

At the Labour Party's Annual Conference in October 1999, the long-awaited National Service Framework for Mental Health (NSF; Department of Health, 1999) was announced. It signalled a major development in social policy aimed at driving up quality and removing 'the wide and unacceptable variations in provision' (6). It also provided a clear statement of national standards to be achieved by all local health and social care communities with a strong emphasis on firm performance management underpinned by a mixture of national and local milestones. It was the first national guidance to have been explicitly developed with the support of an external reference group that included users and carers, among a wide variety of other stakeholders.

In 2000, the Labour Government introduced a new 'NHS Plan' (Department of Health, 2000) that committed extra annual investment to 'fast forward' the NSF. Further longer-term targets were established for 2004 including a further 50 assertive outreach teams in addition to the target of 170 to be in place by April 2001; 335 crisis resolution/home treatment teams; 500 more community mental health staff to respond to people requiring immediate help; and early intervention teams to work with young people experiencing their first episode of psychosis.

The following discussion will amplify some key underlying themes that inform the local context for service development: the imperative to integrate health and social care, and the developing of the care programme approach and care management into an integrated system. For people with complex health and social care needs, who are particularly difficult to serve, this system will be implemented through assertive community treatment (ACT) teams. We will therefore look at the role of ACT with respect to the tensions between care and control described earlier and the implications of this for local implementation.

The integration of health and social care

One explicit rationale for the development of CMHTs is the effective targeting and coordination of resources (Department of Health, 1996). It is important to remain mindful of the fact that this concern is very long standing, and that CMHTs are only the last in a long line of attempted solutions. The very creation of the NHS was based upon post-war all-party recognition that hospital and general practitioner services were under-resourced, inefficient, poorly managed and unevenly distributed. Each major structural reorganisations of the NHS (from 1974 to the abolition of the NHS Executive in 2001) aimed to introduce more rational planning mechanisms in the face of increasing consumer demands. These demands are driven by demographic changes, heightened expectations of medical technology, screening and preventative programmes and particularly, in the case of mental health service users, an increasingly vociferous user movement.

The first community mental health centres (CMHCs) emerged in the UK in the 1970s. Part of the role of CMHCs, that has endured with present-day CMHTs, was to integrate health and social care by bringing together health and social services staff.

There was a rapid increase in the numbers of CMHCs to around 80 in 1988 (Sayce *et al.*, 1991). Over the same period they had moved from being largely ancillary to mainstream psychiatric services to a more central role, often providing a base for a multidisciplinary team that offered outpatient and day care to populations upward of around 50,000. A review of British CMHCs in the mid-1980s highlighted a range of different approaches but a shared commitment to moving the 'centre of gravity' of psychiatric services from institutional settings to a more accessible local environment (McAusland, 1985). They often placed great emphasis on health promotion and community development work.

The mid-1980s also saw the commissioning of an influential study of CMHCs by the Department of Health and Social Security (Patmore and Weaver, 1991a). This study specifically sought to examine whether the American CMHCs' neglect of people with the most severe and complex health and social care needs had been repeated in the UK. This was found to be the case, although this was almost inevitable given that six of the 10 CMHCs sampled were specifically aiming to be 'comprehensive', in that they planned to serve the entire mental health service needs of a geographically-defined local population. Nonetheless, their conclusion was corroborated by Sayce *et al.*'s (1991) study of a more broadly defined sample of CMHCs. They found that CMHCs tended to define their aims extremely broadly with only a very small proportion (19 per cent) reporting that long-term treatment and support was a major aim of the service. Instead they were tending to interpret the provision of a 'comprehensive' service as offering a comparatively limited range of provision to a very broad range of people.

The Audit Commission (1986) highlighted the obstacles to coordinating health and social care that had to be overcome at that time. These included a shortfall in investment in services for people leaving hospital, immense variations among local authorities in their expenditure on services for people with mental health problems, and failures of joint planning between health and social services.

From case to care management

The 1986 Audit Commission report first advocated 'case managers' with budgetary autonomy as a way of circumventing problems in inter-organisational collaboration. This mirrored the US National Institute of Mental Health model of a 'systems agent' or case manager who would coordinate services at the individual level in order to provide continuity of care and a consistent relationship for users. In order to appropriately prioritise services for people with severe and long-term mental health problems, 'community support systems' were established in the USA from 1974 with greater emphasis on case management coordinating a comprehensive system of service provision within which specific services could be tailored to individual need. They embodied ten essential functions or components (Stroul, 1989):

1 Identification of the target population, whether in hospitals or in the community, and outreach to offer appropriate services to those willing to participate.

2 Assistance in applying for entitlements.
3 Crisis stabilisation in the least restrictive setting possible, with hospitalisation available when other options are insufficient.
4 Psychosocial rehabilitation services, including but not limited to (1) goal-orientated rehabilitation training in community living in natural settings wherever possible; (2) opportunities to improve employability; (3) appropriate living conditions in an atmosphere that encourages improvements in functioning; and (4) opportunities to develop social skills, interests, and leisure time activities that promote a sense of community participation and worth.
5 Supportive services of indefinite duration, including supportive living and working arrangements, and other such services for as long as they are needed.
6 Medical and psychiatric care.
7 Support for families, friends and community members.
8 Involvement of concerned community members in planning and offering housing or work opportunities.
9 Protection of users' rights, both in hospitals and in the community.
10 Case management to ensure continuous availability of appropriate assistance.

It is notable that when originally conceived in the USA, case management was only one of several service components deemed necessary for successful provision. The literature on case management has suggested that in resource-rich contexts, case management becomes almost redundant since users are able to negotiate their own access to relevant provision (Onyett, 1998). On the other hand, case management is equally ineffective if there are inadequate resources for housing, meaningful occupation and other supports.

The content of this framework was echoed in the UK with the specifications for a comprehensive mental health service enshrined in the 'Spectrum of Care' guidance (Department of Health, 1996), and subsequently the NSF. Prior to this, the 'Caring for People' White Paper (Cm 849, 1989) introduced case management into social services, as part of the purchaser-provider split necessary to introduce market conditions into health and social care. The objectives of case management stressed meeting individual care needs through the most effective use of resources, and promoting users' independence by enabling people to live in the community wherever possible (Department of Health, 1990a). The White Paper also introduced a distinction between health and social care, without offering much guidance as to their respective definitions. A typical approach was to examine the elements of provision and decide whether they were predominantly health or social care. Health authorities asked to be remunerated by local authorities for residential care provided in health facilities and local authorities sought to be remunerated for any nursing care provided in local authority premises.

At practice level, health and social care proved very difficult to separate. A case manager for older adults on the Isle of Sheppey epitomised the cynicism of the time among practitioners, commenting that, 'the only difference between a health care bath and a social care bath is that you put Dettol in one and bubble bath in the other!' Her comment was remarkably prescient in that for domiciliary care 'bathing' was indeed officially defined as health care and 'washing' as social care (Carpenter, 1994).

The guidance emphasised that case managers should not be involved in service provision themselves, or manage provider agencies (Department of Health, 1990a). This was in order to avoid conflicts of interest when assessing need and monitoring the effects of service provision as part of the new purchasing role for case managers. The 1990 NHS and Community Care Act transferred the social security element of residential care to local authorities. Case managers had the task of assessing need and designing 'packages of care'. In order to promote a new 'mixed economy of care', 85 per cent of this resource had to be spent on purchasing residential and domiciliary services from the private sector.

Early models of case management in the USA also emphasised the importance of coordination of services as a means to achieving positive outcomes for service users. Stein (1992) highlighted the radical limitations of such an approach arguing that coordination is effective only insofar as there are resources to deploy and agencies with an interest in collaborating. Where this is lacking, as it usually is, he stressed that mental health workers need to be able to step into the breach as providers when no other option is available. Mueser *et al.*'s (1998) review of case management services also described how brokerage models evolved into more clinically-based approaches, such as ACT and intensive case management, when it became apparent that case managers needed high levels of clinical skill in order to involve people in care and support, assess their needs and then intervene effectively. This conclusion is reinforced by the disappointing outcomes of case management (or 'keyworking' under the UK system) when operated merely as a means of service coordination and follow-up outside of a multidisciplinary team context (Franklin *et al.*, 1987; Marshall *et al.*, 1995; Tyrer *et al.*, 1995).

Subsequent guidance renamed case management as 'care management', apparently in the face of user concerns about being described as 'cases' that had to be 'managed' (Department of Health/ Social Services Inspectorate, 1991). Evaluation of care management has highlighted concerns about investment in assessment processes at the expense of other aspects of the care management process, problems in achieving truly needs-led assessment and reliance on menus of existing provision (Hudson, 1996). There has also been a tendency to fail to record service shortfalls, enormous variations in the operationalisation of eligibility criteria, poor individual service planning processes, inadequate information systems, and poor inter-agency working (ibid.). Critiques of care management have particularly lamented the removal of social workers from multidisciplinary teams and their redeployment in more remote middle-management roles (Marshall, 1996).

The care programme approach

The care programme approach (CPA) can be traced back to the inquiry into the homicide by Sharon Campbell, a former service user, which provoked a media campaign castigating the policy of community care. As Peck and Parker (1998) commented: 'Mental health policy was moving from being driven by abuse of patients in hospital to being driven by disasters involving mentally ill people in the community' (245). In reality, there is no evidence of an increase in the numbers of homicides committed by people with severe mental health problems, and indeed there was a decline in their contribution to the total number of homicides committed in England and Wales between 1957 and 1995 (Taylor and Gunn, 1999).

Nonetheless it was evident that improvement in mental health services needed to be made. The CPA was conceived to serve all psychiatric in-patients considered for discharge, and all new users involved with specialist psychiatric services from April 1991. It demanded that arrangements for support outside of hospital were made prior to discharge. Consultant psychiatrists and their colleagues were to decide whether such support was feasible within available resources. Health care needs were to be regularly reviewed and arrangements made with local social services departments to ensure the assessment of social needs. A clear link to care management was therefore required although the guidance gave hospital-based keyworkers responsibility for ensuring that appropriate arrangements were in place.

Although attention to assessment and planning prior to discharge was welcomed, a number of concerns arose over the CPA such as the power it gave hospital-based psychiatrists (Sayce, 1990). The CPA was originally felt to be too ambitious in demanding that it be applied to all users of specialist mental health services, rather than just those with the most complex needs. Subsequent guidance introduced three tiers of graduated complexity which, by the end of the 1990s, had collapsed into just two tiers: enhanced and standard (NHSE/SSI, 1999).

Care management guidance stressed the coordinating and purchasing role in social care while, at the same time, exhorting close partnerships with health services (Department of Health/Social Services Inspectorate, 1991). In practice, much confusion surrounded the relationship of the CPA to care management. Both shared the same core tasks, stressed the involvement of users and carers, were concerned with the coordinated assessment of health and social care needs, and had convergent client groups. The stated purposes of supervision registers, a subsequent elaboration of the CPA, provide an example of the confused introduction of these two initiatives: they include providing a care plan that aims to reduce risk, regularly reviewing care needs, maintaining contact with users, providing a point of reference for relevant and authorised health and social services staff, planning for the facilities and resources necessary to meet need and identifying those patients who should receive the highest priority for care, and active follow up (NHS Management Executive, 1994a). These functions had all been previously described as the remit of care management (Department of Health/Social Services Inspectorate, 1991). Finally, the definitive Government guidance on the implementation of the CPA, 'Building Bridges' came to assert full integration.

> For people subject to the CPA, in essence the key worker and care management functions are the same. Both involve coordinating the delivery of an agreed care plan. One way of looking at the CPA is as a specialist variant of care management... In well integrated systems, it is quite possible for the care management function to extend in whole or part to health services as well, and for health professionals to be designated as care managers (Department of Health, 1995a).

Ironically the same point about the diverse range of people who could assume the care management role was expressed in the earliest care (then 'case') management guidance (Department of Health, 1990a) before the introduction of the CPA. We will never know how much time and energy could have gone into improved provision had mental health service provision been firmly located with social services as the lead agency, thus avoiding the need for a separate, health-led CPA.

Complete integration was finally achieved through joint NHSE/SSI (1999) guidance on 'care coordination', the recommended term for the role that integrated the care manager role with keyworking under the CPA. It stressed that: 'The CPA is Care Management for those of working age in contact with specialist mental health and social care services' (1999: 8), and that: 'It is critical that the care coordinator should have the authority to coordinate the delivery of the care plan and that this is respected by all those involved in delivering it, regardless of agency of origin' (22). It is therefore a more powerful role than that typically exercised by keyworkers under the old CPA arrangements.

The 1999 Health Act provided new opportunities for health and local authorities to pool budgets, reach agreements over lead commissioning, and integrate provision. One concrete example of integrated provision is the NSF target that the percentage of CMHTs that have integrated health and social services staff within a single management structure will increase by 50 per cent between 1999–2000 and April 2002. The NSF suggests that local elected members and non-executives of NHS trusts, primary care groups, primary care teams and health authorities should facilitate these closer partnerships, perhaps through cross membership of local authorities and NHS boards. Achieving such an integrated context for teams is explored in Chapter 4, and the resulting care coordinator role is discussed in Chapter 6.

The continued emphasis on safety for users and the general public

As part of the implementation of the CPA, all provider units providing mental health care were required to set up supervision registers from April 1994 which 'identify and provide information on patients who are, or are liable to be, at risk of committing serious violence or suicide or of serious self neglect, whether existing patients or newly accepted by the secondary psychiatric services' (NHS Management Executive, 1994a). Supervision registers provoked an unusually united chorus of dissent from a wide range of interest groups such as Mind (Harrison, 1994) and the Royal College of Psychiatrists (Caldicott, 1994). By 1995, implementation remained patchy with a third of consultants having no one registered (Vaughan, 1996). Lack of compliance with registration was particularly widespread among London consultants (ibid.). Two years later, a national survey revealed that implementation of the CPA and supervision registers continued to be patchy and not related to population-based estimates of need (Bindman *et al.*, 1999).

The subsequent introduction of supervised aftercare followed concerns that the CPA had not been an effective enough vehicle for social control and monitoring in the community expressed as a result of a series of high profile Government inquiries (Department of Health, 1994c). Subsequent calls for community treatment orders by the Royal College of Psychiatrists and the introduction of the Mental Health (Supervised discharge) Bill in 1994 appeared to be prompted by landmark events that were construed by the media as indicating significant failures of community care. Perhaps most notable of these was the mauling of a service user after he climbed into London Zoo's lions' den. The resulting Bill included a 'power of enforcement' to comply with treatment for those deemed at risk.

In 1999, the UK's Secretary of State for Health announced that: 'Community care has failed' following a series of homicide inquiries that highlighted the shortcoming of community mental health services. *Our Healthier Nation* (Cm 4386, 1999) demanded a reduction in the suicide rate by at least one fifth by 2010. Reductions in suicide also form the seventh and most encompassing standard within the NSF effectively elevating it to the ultimate high-level performance indicator for mental health services.

Supervised discharge has been left to wither on the vine by practitioners, with only a handful of users being subject to it (Peck and Parker, 1998). Supervision registers were also quietly abolished with the introduction of the NSF (with the local proviso that enhanced care coordination should be fully operational). Nonetheless, proposals for compulsory community treatment have re-emerged (Department of Health/Home Office, 2000) and there remain heightened fears among practitioners of a 'blame culture' where individual practitioners will be expected to be personally accountable for so-called failures of community care. It is important to look at experience elsewhere in order to predict the implications for CMHT practitioners should such procedures become law. In the USA, concern has arisen among practitioners over the lack of enforcement mechanisms for community treatment orders, individual practitioners' accountability for the outcome of interventions, poor monitoring of the deployment of orders, and great variation in what users were forcibly committed to do (Hiday, 1996). While there was sometimes a treatment plan, it usually focused on medication. Practitioners protested about the amount of paperwork and the court appearances involved in outpatient commitment orders noting that: 'Instead they often attempt to persuade reluctant patients to accept voluntary treatment, but their methods of persuasion may be viewed as coercive by both observers and patients' (Hiday, 1996: 35). Over half the users in a survey of 'severely mentally ill out-patients' reported that pressure to accept outpatient treatment included threats of hospitalisation or deprivation of a resource such as housing or disability benefits (Lucksted and Coursey, 1995). Rogers (1993) identified similarly high levels of coercion to accept in-patient treatment among users who had been admitted 'voluntarily' in the UK.

The history of social policy surrounding the CPA has validated early concerns that the approach could act as a vehicle for the extension of coercive psychiatric practice from the psychiatric hospital into the community (Sayce, 1990; White and Brooker, 1990). It is possible that less emphasis on 'treatment' and social control would have been apparent had care management originally been the sole vehicle for individual service planning for people with severe and long-term mental health problems. However, it is important to recognise that concerns about the medicalisation of difference and the denial of dignity and choice were being voiced before the introduction of the CPA. As Pelican observed in 1991, 'care management can be seen to be reproducing the values and reality of the total institution in the community: psychiatric imperialism in a marriage of convenience to the rhetoric of autonomy, dignity and choice'. It is therefore critical that care coordination is developed on the basis of a set of values that demonstrate a concern with users' choice, control and autonomy in practice. This requires that the implications of the social control aspect of the care coordinator's role are fully recognised and dealt with appropriately.

Assertive community treatment, risk and coercion

Assertive community treatment (ACT) is the deployment of a CMHT to serve a defined group of long-term users by providing assertive outreach *in situ*. It is the model that is proposed when guidance refers to 'assertive outreach' (see Introduction). Key features are that users are visited at home, and that contact is maintained during the user's involvement with other parts of the service or other providers, for example when they are admitted to inpatient services. Services aim to help users manage the symptoms of their mental distress, improve their material and social environment and train in activities of daily living, social relations and work skills. Caseloads are low in order to achieve such intensive individualised services.

Although the arguments for implementing ACT can be made on a variety of grounds (see Chapter 3), the NSF tended to frame ACT as part of a risk reduction and crisis prevention strategy rather than as a way of providing users with better quality care on their own terms. Indeed, the most explicit standard for ACT concerns suicide prevention. In its concern to effectively manage risk, the NSF demands that, 'assertive outreach is in place for all individuals who may fail to take their prescribed medication and would then be at risk of depression, severe mental illness or suicide; for those who have a tendency to drop out of contact with services; and for those who are not well engaged with services' (79). The expectation was that, by April 2001, assertive outreach would be in place for all service users on enhanced care programmes who were at risk of losing contact. Under the care programme approach, all mental health service users should, 'receive care which optimises engagement, anticipates or prevents a crisis, and reduces risk', and have a copy of a written care plan which includes contingency plans in crises.

Although such measures represent good practice it is also important to be mindful of the ways in which an overconcern with managing or reducing risk can lead to provision that users experience as overcontrolling or coercive. A frequently cited example from the USA is the withholding of welfare payments unless users accept treatment. This is defended on the grounds that welfare payments form part of a social contract between the individual and the state aimed at achieving the basic functioning of individuals, (for example, with respect to paying rent, buying food, and so on). Staff justify this approach by construing benefits as not the user's 'real' money and that maintaining their involvement in services allows users to go out and earn a proper income. The practice of managing the user's income appears to be widespread with 82 per cent of the 303 ACT teams surveyed by Deci *et al.* (1995) providing 'financial management' of users' income.

Diamond (1996: 58) notes that another form of coercion is the licence that 'keyworkers' can assume to communicate with the user's whole social network.

> This communication, even when done with the client's permission, allows enormous pressure to be applied for the client to take medication, stay in treatment, live in a particular place, or 'follow the plan' in any number of ways. This pressure can be almost as coercive as the hospital in controlling behaviour, but with fewer safeguards.

Spindel and Nugent (1999) also raise concern about the role of ACT in collaborating with other agencies to enforce treatment, particularly medication. They cite Solomon and Draine's (1995a) study of ACT in comparison with standard case management for people released from jail. They question whether the fact that more ACT users returned to jail (60 per cent) than the case-managed users (40 per cent) may be attributable to the fact that staff collaborated with probation and parole officers to reincarcerate users when they were found to be non-compliant. They state:

> It is notable that most subjects in their study reflected jail populations, and included a disproportionate number of black males. The clients in

> this study were not incarcerated because they had committed new crimes. They were incarcerated because they defied the social controls which were placed upon them (Solomon and Draine, 1995a: 3).

The outcome literature on ACT will be explored in more detail in Chapter 3. In general, while there is much to recommend it in terms of both outcomes achieved, savings on hospital care and user and carer satisfaction, it nonetheless risks becoming highly coercive unless implemented carefully.

The allocation and adequacy of resources

The allocation and adequacy of resources for service provision also influences the coercive nature of services. Coercion often becomes applied as a short-term solution to long-term problems concerning lack of resources. Services become crisis-driven, overly concerned with social control, and delivered in a manner that precludes the development of good quality relationships and collaborative work with service users. As Diamond (1996: 61) noted: 'When effective community based treatments are available, the effectiveness of community-based coercion increases but the need for such coercion is less'.

Tensions over whether to focus resources on people with the common mental health problems presenting in primary care, (such as mild depression, anxiety and relationship problems) versus the smaller numbers of people with severe and longer-term mental health problems were exacerbated by the introduction of GP fundholding as part of the internal market at the beginning of the 1990s. In 2001, the 'Shifting the Balance of Power' (Department of Health, 2001c) reforms reorganised the NHS to support increased devolution of commissioning powers to primary care organisations. How they exercise this role will be crucial. Importantly, the NSF reaffirmed the priority afforded to people with the most complex and severe problems by stating:

> First priority will continue to be addressing gaps in current services for people with severe and enduring mental illness . . . In areas where specialist mental health services are able to meet local needs for severe mental illness, the most cost-effective focus will now be on people with common mental health problems (7).

It is, however, unlikely that development will occur in this serial fashion, particularly where PCTs have an increasingly powerful role in purchasing and providing mental health services. Gatekeeping access to resources to maintain a focus on people with complex health and social care needs may also be made more difficult by the NSF requirement for 24-hour access to specialist mental health care (Marshall, 1999). However, investing locally to intervene as early as possible with people who are likely to become users of services is likely to improve outcomes for users in the longer term and result in a less coercive and crisis-driven service (Drake *et al.*, 2000).

The design and operation of CMHTs will be highly contingent on local processes for the prioritising of local needs, which will in turn impact on practice. The key issue of prioritising client groups is returned to in more detail in Chapter 4.

Going forward by starting from where we are

The challenge of implementation was given full recognition within the NSF, as informed by the bitter experience of trying to introduce effective evidence-based practice and previous centrally-driven initiatives such as the CPA.

The NSF stressed that the 'local health and social care community' should be the focus of change. In practice, these communities are defined by the populations served by PCTs, and come together for the purposes of local planning in 'Local Implementation Teams' which include purchasers and providers of care alongside a range of other stakeholders including users and carers.

The NSF also placed great emphasis on processes for performance management. This is not new to mental health services. However, the NHS Plan and subsequent 'modernisation' reviews emphasised the connection of local performance management to performance management frameworks for the NHS and local authority care as a whole. Performance management is also underpinned by new accountability structures through clinical governance that holds individuals at the top of organisations liable for failure to improve quality (Department of Health, 1998b).

The expectations of CMHTs in this context are considerable. They are charged with the task of resolving inter-agency and interdisciplinary tensions as a means to achieving social inclusion, cultural change, and the implementation of Government policy. Not only are they the gatekeepers to specialist care services but also they are the suppliers of services to primary care and the agents of a revitalised interest in community development work and mental health promotion (Peck, 1995). They also have a key role in clinical risk management and the delivery of evidence-based interventions.

Despite enormous policy and organisational changes, perhaps the most significant impression from the user movement is the *lack* of shift from a model of provision dominated by medical interests (Hutchison, 1999). A paucity of resources risks maintaining this situation as services remain crisis-driven, unnecessarily coercive and dominated by drug administration in the absence of the time, and often the expertise to do anything differently.

It is possible that CMHTs may have served in part to maintain this status quo. The burgeoning CMHC movement provided non-medics with an opportunity to avoid the medical hegemony of the hospital and the ward round by providing a new setting for 'rituals' of referral, allocation, assessment and review (Peck, 1994). This enabled innovation to take place without fundamentally challenging the dominance of hospitals and their doctors in terms of both clinical practice and financial commitment. Since the 1990 reforms, the role of CMHTs as a refuge from the 'medical model' has steadily declined as CMHTs became the mainstream for psychiatric practice in community settings. They are now the setting for a revitalised interest in new models of care, such as the recovery approach, which draw upon evidence concerning the importance of valued social roles, such as employment while also emphasising user self-determination and positive risk-taking.

To move forward from where we are now means recognising that CMHTs have come of age in their role as the cornerstone of local mental health provision and that a range of stakeholders need to invest in their success through well-managed local processes for planning and implementation. To mature gracefully into adulthood, they will need to establish working methods based upon ideologies of care that locate service-user interests at the centre of planning and implementation of care. The NSF, the Mental Health Policy Implementation Guide, and the National Institute for Mental Health for England all advocate this. If it is to be realised in practice, a sound foundation of shared values at local level is required to inform practice as well as an approach to local development that is innovative while building from strengths. New and existing services need to be developed with an eye to the previous history of CMHTs, including the earlier implementation of the more recent service models. However, it is important that our attention does not get consumed by concerns about service models while the more fundamentally problematic nature of mental health service provision evident in current CMHTs, such as the tension between care and control described in this and the last chapter remains unaddressed.

Increasingly these issues have to be addressed in a team context with an explicit focus on the aims and values of the team. Importantly, approaches to modernising services such as 'collaboratives' and 'process redesign' all stress the need to start with the user experience as the foundation from which to develop services (see *www.modernnhs.nhs.uk*). This also means building on the strengths of local services as they are currently experienced by service users. But what are these strengths? The next chapter will take a critical look at the claims made for teamworking in mental health.

CHAPTER 3

So What's so Great about Teamworking?

The previous chapter showed how social policy developments have placed teamworking at the centre of mental health service delivery. How has this come about? Can we assume that working in teams is going to be more effective than staff working in isolation or as part of looser networks? Why is teamworking sometimes seen as problematic by those that are asked to do it?

This chapter reviews the stated advantages and disadvantages of teamworking and then looks at how mental health teamworking is experienced by staff. We then examine the social and organisational psychological literature on the effectiveness of work groups in order to evaluate some of the core assumptions on which teamworking is based. This will highlight some of the requirements for effective teamworking.

Having looked at work groups in general, we will then shift our attention to the outcome literature on different models of CMHT working. This will allow us to explore some of the features of teams that are associated with the achievement of an effective service for people with severe mental health problems.

What are the advantages and disadvantages of teamworking in mental health?

A number of assertions are often made about the merits and demerits of teamworking. Looking at the role of teams in organisations generally, Mohrman *et al.*'s (1995) review found that working in teams enabled organisations to rapidly develop and deliver high quality products and services cost effectively, allowed the organisation to learn and retain learning more effectively, promoted innovation through the cross-fertilisation of ideas, achieved better integration of information and saved time by having tasks undertaken concurrently.

Opie (1997) reviewed some of the stated advantages and problems associated with teamworking in health care teams while drawing few conclusions about the evidence-base for these assertions. Stated advantages included the development of quality care for users through the achievement of coordinated and collaborative inputs from different disciplines; improved, better informed and holistic care planning; higher productivity; the development of joint initiatives; increased staff satisfaction and professional stimulation; and consequently, more effective use of resources. She also, however, highlighted a range of reported problems including inadequate or absent organisational support; unclear goals; lack of clear structures and directions; the dominance of particular ways in which the current reality was described to the exclusion of others; the existence of tensions between professions resulting in potentially unsafe practices; the absence of training in teamwork; the absence of orientation programmes for new members joining the team; lack of inter-professional trust resulting in complicated power relations between professions; an over-abundance of or, alternatively, an absence of conflict; staff coming and going with little continuity; the team's failing to examine the team's processes, and team discussions which, far from addressing user goals, marginalise them and contribute to users' disempowerment. Many of these issues echo critiques of CMHT working (for example, Galvin and McCarthy, 1994; Paxton, 1995).

The King's Fund and King's College London systematically explored the actual experiences of staff working in community mental health teams using a series of facilitated workshops. In these workshops, staff from a variety of disciplines were asked to generate accounts of their own roles and identities within community health services and those of each of the other disciplines. This initiative highlighted a prevailing adherence to uni-professional cultures among staff bolstered by the absence of an alternative strong and shared philosophy of community mental health services (Norman and Peck, 1999). Inter-professional collaboration was further impeded by:

- Ambiguous roles and responsibilities of staff.
- Lack of agreement about what working together means. For example, did it mean conferring, cooperating, or ensuring that there were multiple inputs to work with any one individual user?

- Different health and social care organisations having different structures, competing priorities and agendas.
- Problematic power relationships arising from different cultures, philosophies, educational requirements, status and backgrounds of different disciplines.
- Professional protectionism, job insecurity and concern about dilution of professional skills or identity.
- Ideological differences underpinned by different values and assumptions.
- Conflicting models of care from which workers derive their objectives and working methods.

However, the initiative also identified factors that were felt to promote interdisciplinary collaboration in health care among the participants. These included:

- Shared understanding of each other's cultures, roles and responsibilities, and methods of working.
- Direct and regular contact between those providing care. This was promoted by named care coordinators, contacts or link workers and clear systems for referral.
- Understanding the aims and methods of working of the organisations involved in collaboration.
- Good communication systems leading to trust between users, carers and health care workers.
- Access to practical local information about services and contacts.
- Individual commitment by all workers to a collaborative approach that is supported by management.
- Organisational structures that support inter-agency collaboration (for example, joint planning, commissioning and review committees) and, within this, individuals with the shared vision, inter-personal skills and knowledge required to make collaboration effective.
- Change champions and groups to push forward interdisciplinary/inter-agency initiatives.
- National policies that promote a coordinated approach supported by adequate resources.

Another key problem identified by the initiative was a 'loss of faith' among CMHT staff arising from a perceived emphasis on 'conformance criteria', such as the implementation of the CPA and associated paperwork resulting in 'centralised bureaucratic systems of service delivery'. This 'loss of faith' formed part of a wider mistrust of managerialist solutions among practitioners. This served to undermine the meaning that clinicians derived from their work because managerialist solutions were seen as unrelated to achieving positive outcomes for service users.

We saw in the first two chapters that CMHTs exist in a turbulent conflux of different interests among a variety of stakeholders. Many of the problems that Opie and the King's Fund/King's College initiative identified are manifestations of problems in the relationships between users and staff, staff and their managers, and between individual staff and disciplines. Teams are the manifestation of this complex web of relationships, and how 'good' or 'bad' a team is will reflect this. For this reason Hosking and Morley (1991) argued for a move away from considering groups as bounded entities, and stressed that there may be multiple and complex ways in which individuals experience '*degrees of groupness*' described by cognitive, social, and political processes within and between groups. These processes comprise recurrent interactions and continuing relationships between people. These relationships are based upon more or less continuous relationship building and support, including the negotiation of values and influence. The issues of values and influence will be returned to when considering leadership and management in Chapter 7, and the achievement of service improvement in Chapter 9.

What does the research say about effective teamworking?

Being definitive about team effectiveness in mental health is complicated by the range of interests and relationships represented, and the varying degrees of 'groupness' described above. It is nonetheless useful to look at the wider organisational psychology literature when thinking about community mental health team design. Borrill *et al.* (2000) examined 113 CMHTs as part of a larger scale Department of Health-funded study of health care teams in the NHS. This comprehensive programme used a wide range of quantitative and qualitative measures, multiple sources of data, validated measures, cross-sectional and longitudinal data and had a large sample of teams.

Using the stakeholder-derived formulation of effectiveness described in Chapter 1 (Richards and Rees, 1998), the team effectiveness study found that better functioning CMHTs had clearer objectives, higher levels of participation, a stronger commitment to quality and better support for innovation. Their members also had better mental health. These broad findings also applied to the other health care teams studied.

A typical effective CMHT had few part-time workers, enjoyed a positive team climate (in terms of vision, high participation, an expectation of excellence and support for innovation), had a single, clear leader, and tended to have relatively low stress levels. As reflected in the wider organisational psychology literature, the biggest contributor to poor functioning of teams was unclear team objectives. This was associated with the absence of a clear team leader or coordinator or where there was conflict about leadership.

Although this study underlined the potential for effective CMHTs, the notion of an inevitable 'synergy' arising when people are organised into groups has to be questioned. West (1994) concluded that individuals working alone in general produce more ideas, and better quality ideas, when compared with individuals brainstorming in groups. His review also concluded that, overall, the performance of teams is about 75 per cent as effective as the performance of the aggregate of individuals working alone, but that in relation to decision-making, group performance is generally superior to the average member of the group, but often inferior to that of its most competent member. It is evident then that team effectiveness cannot be assumed and that its study must be grounded in an understanding of the tasks that the team has to perform, and some consideration of the knowledge, skills and experience that individuals bring to the team. We cannot assume teams will be effective unless we specifically design them to be effective, and recruit and train their members accordingly.

The range of factors at the individual, group, organisational and wider environmental levels that may influence effectiveness are vast (see West *et al.*, 1998 for review) and it is difficult to abstract the key elements of team performance that will produce positive outcomes in any given setting. There is no single theory that can encompass and deal simultaneously with the complexity of factors that can affect group task effectiveness (Hackman, 1990). However, some core concepts have considerable implications for CMHT design.

Figure 3 (based upon West *et al.*, 1998) provides a structure for thinking about team effectiveness in terms of inputs, processes and outputs. Although it merely represents one way of construing the important elements, it provides a route map for coverage of later topics in the book. The elements inter-relate in complex ways. For example, while having a clear task is an important team input, translating that into a clear vision and ideology for the team invokes a number of processes including good communication, clear leadership and an identification with the team among its members. CMHT outputs in terms of innovation and performance will be described later in this chapter. Inputs are considered as contextual factors and aspects of team design in chapters 4 and 5. Care coordination as a vehicle for social and therapeutic interventions is covered in Chapter 6 and team processes and their management are considered in Chapter 7. Issues of staff well-being and the measures to promote the long-term viability of the team are considered in Chapters 8 and 9.

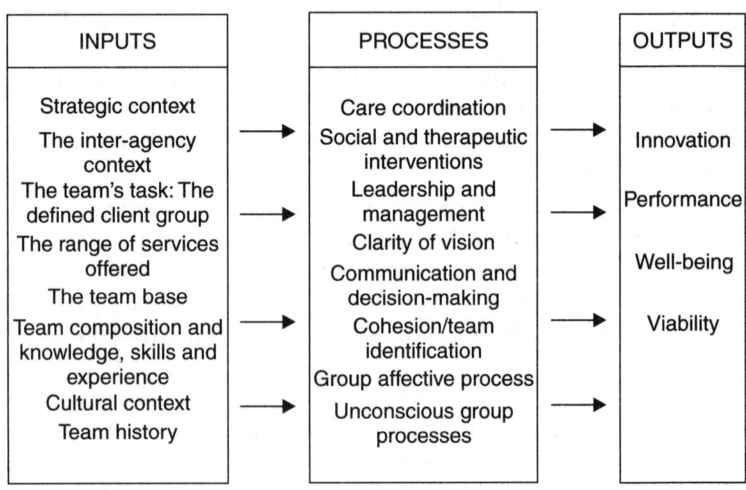

Figure 3 *Team inputs, processes and outputs*
Source: West *et al.*, 1998.

Approaches to teamworking in mental health

This discussion looks at the ways in which teams have been designed to offer different levels of team integration, before taking a more detailed exploration of team design and process.

From a user's perspective, teamworking is essentially about how many members of the team they personally have contact with. This will in turn have implications for how the team conducts its allocation and decision-making processes, and how staff are organised to work with users and their carers over time.

The 'team approach'

Patmore and Weaver (1991a) placed great emphasis on the extent to which different approaches to teamworking affect opportunities for service users to form relationships with more than one worker. They stressed the importance of multi-worker relationships in order to inform care planning and case review. As one CMHC worker commented: 'How can you discuss patients fully in a multidisciplinary team unless others are familiar with a person? Without that you would end up doing it badly or not doing it at all' (Patmore and Weaver, 1991b).

The adoption of a 'team approach' is one key element that is said to differentiate ACT from case management. Although applied with different levels of stringency in different teams, this approach asserts that service users should have a relationship with all the members of the team, rather than a single worker in a care coordinator role. Advantages claimed included improved continuity of care, peer support and consultation, and reduced stress for staff. The 'team approach' to teamworking was advocated by Bond *et al.* (1988) in their evaluations of the 'Thresholds' service in Chicago, and was subsequently implemented by the Tulip project in Haringey, London. In these services, all team members formed a relationship with all users of the service such that all staff were effectively interchangeable. An evaluation of the Tulip project generally demonstrated the stated advantages of a team approach. There was good engagement with users, in that few lost contact with the service (Gauntlett *et al.*, 1996). There was also high job satisfaction and low burnout among staff. However, some workers missed the opportunities to develop individual responsibility for a holistic approach to their work with users. Others encountered practical difficulties, for example, in establishing effective liaison with other agencies.

It is also important to be aware of negative feelings about the 'team approach' among users. Some users of the Tulip service preferred to develop individual relationships with fewer staff. They complained of having to tell the same story to different team members and experienced a lack of continuity among staff in the way they managed tasks over time. Workers forgot tasks and users had problems remembering the names of everyone visiting them. Spindel and Nugent (1999) criticised the American ACT evaluations in the same vein:

> The client obtaining services from an ACT team must establish meaningful working relationships with a team rather than just one person. It is well documented that the success of any professional intervention depends more on the quality of the relationship between the professional and the service recipient than on any other factor, including service model... It is much more difficult, if not impossible, for any human being to establish warm, supportive, and trusting relationships with a 'team' (7).

Spindel and Nugent (1999) also argued that the whole team approach creates a very negative image of mental health service users, and that this in itself creates a barrier to achieving a valued lifestyle. They argued that it implies that 'a client is so abnormal, bad, or different that a whole team of people is needed to work with him or her... Far from seeing a person as having strengths, and creating a context for their empowerment, this kind of overprofessionalised, stigmatising approach may destroy what little self-worth, sense of belonging, and hope a client has' (8). The professionalised nature of the team response may also risk usurping natural supports provided by community, family and friends. Spindel and Nugent argued that teams are also not easy for family and friends to work with, and that high profile professional responses may lead others to drop out of their involvement assuming that the team is 'taking care of it'.

The all-singing, all-dancing keyworker approach

At the other end of the teamworking continuum is the so-called 'generic' keyworker approach where individual workers supply all one-to-one contact themselves. Patmore and Weaver (1991c) observed this among the English CMHCs of the late eighties, and saw it as an attempt to avoid defining skill mix thereby perpetuating the myth that everybody was equally competent to work with a wide range of issues. They observed an informal rule that if you assessed an individual you either became their keyworker yourself or turned the referral down on behalf of the team. This encouraged reluctance to take up unattractive referrals for assessment because you knew that other workers would not get involved.

One implication of this arrangement was that the only opportunity for users to get to know staff other than their keyworker came through collective service contacts like group therapy, day centres or social drop-ins. Patmore and Weaver (1991b) found these opportunities tended to be geared towards people with 'relatively minor stress problems, whom the CMHC workers found particularly interesting' (34). There was thus an emphasis on anxiety management groups, verbal psychotherapy groups, relaxation classes and groups for people withdrawing from benzodiazepines.

Other ways of achieving multi-worker contacts

Patmore and Weaver (1991a) found that CMHCs only developed significant multi-worker resources for people with severe and long-term mental health problems when planners had required them to include a day centre. They found that that this led to more multi-worker contacts for service users even where a 'generic' keyworker role was in operation. Attached day services promoted joint working and continuity of support. For example, when a member of staff was unavailable to a user, another team member could intervene who was familiar with the user because of day unit activities.

In CMHTs without day units, Patmore and Weaver found that keyworkers for people with severe and long-term mental health problems often used non-CMHT staff, such as hostel-workers, as co-workers rather than a member of the CMHT. Other teams have found this to be advantageous in promoting inter-agency continuity and communication and in avoiding ghettoising user contacts into a single agency (Onyett, 1998; Waldron, 1981).

In general, the need for flexibility and the avoidance of dogma is paramount. The overriding principle of adjusting the service response to meet the needs of individual service users should also apply to the model of teamworking adopted. Indeed, it is perhaps most productive to think of *the user as the central team member* and then design the rest of the 'team' around them as a functioning network where each element has a relevant task to perform. Within this team, there should be at least one person that the user feels they can establish a positive working relationship with. As Spindel and Nugent state: 'It is... perfectly natural that some case managers may gravitate to particular clients and vice versa. This is a reasonable outcome, since it stimulates a more trusting relationship, when client and case manager have an affinity for each other' (1999: 8). This is likely to work where the whole team is focused on, and values work with people with severe mental health problems, and where the team as a whole can maintain an awareness of each member's caseloads. It becomes problematic when it encourages staff to spend most of their time working with people who are perceived as being more socially rewarding. This underlines the need for the team as a whole to be able to reflect on its work on the basis of valid and useful information, and then honestly address any issues of inequity (see Chapters 8 and 9). One of the major advantages of working as a team is that the team hosts particular ideologies and ways of working that values work with people with severe mental health problems; an ideology that can be developed and sustained through continued training, peer support, management and leadership.

Does teamwork in mental health work?

Despite their ubiquity and acknowledged central importance to mental health service provision there has until recently been little research on CMHTs in the UK aside from controlled studies of government demonstration projects (for example, Dean *et al.*, 1993; Marks *et al.*, 1994; Merson *et al.*, 1992), service descriptions (for example, McAusland, 1985) or large-scale surveys (Onyett *et al.*, 1994, 1997; Sayce *et al.*, 1991). The large team effectiveness study referred to earlier concluded that CMHTs are effective in a range of domains, but only if certain team characteristics are in place (Borrill *et al.*, 2000).

Controlled studies of CMHTs are problematic. As they are so ubiquitous it is difficult to envisage a site where standard care would not include CMHT provision of some kind. A systematic review of controlled studies by Simmonds *et al.* (2001) found that CMHTs achieved some of the benefits of ACT but to a lesser extent. For example, the impact on reducing in-patient bed use was interpreted by the authors as less than ACT but greater than case management. As with much of the ACT literature (for example, Marshall and Lockwood, 1998), they found no evidence of gains in social functioning and clinical symptomatology. Definitional problems abound in that some of the teams covered may have been very similar to some of the teams covered in reviews of ACT. For example, they include the team described by Merson *et al.* (1992) which included many of the features of an ACT team, including home visiting and clinical co-working with colleagues within and outside the team. (This team used to be managed by the author).

The research on different approaches to intensive community treatment (such as ACT and home treatment teams) is more substantial than that on other CMHTs but the overall messages remain contested for reasons that bear both on methodological issues, and the complex relationship between social policy, research and prevailing cultural norms described in Chapters 1 and 2.

The methodological challenges

Even if we just consider the methodological challenges, the search for definitive answers soon becomes elusive. Huxley (1991) argued that, in order to be able to demonstrate the effectiveness of community services in achieving positive outcomes for users, four elements need to be achieved:

- a specific, closely defined target group or groups;
- concrete objectives specifying individual outcome goals;
- specific models of practice and skill mix which are designed to meet the user's needs in the chosen areas, and
- outcome measures which are chosen to reflect the areas in which change is expected.

Evaluations that achieve these elements are extremely rare. The CMHTs of the 1980s were criticised for failing to adequately specify their target group and their aims (Patmore and Weaver, 1991a;

Sayce *et al.*, 1991). As a result, they were rarely designed with a specific purpose in mind and their composition tended to be shaped by the current availability of staff. Poor service design in turn makes service evaluation less robust. Unless the criteria for team effectiveness are clear it is difficult to assess the extent to which objectives are achieved. It is also important to understand how objectives were achieved and how the evaluation findings might be applied to other contexts. Given the methodological shortcomings of the early CMHT research, Dowell and Ciarlo (1983) were forced to conclude that:

> currently ... the weight of evidence for the effectiveness of CMHCs derives partly from evidence for the effectiveness of psychotherapy and partly from the accumulation of studies on community mental health. The available evidence appears to warrant a conclusion of probable effectiveness for CMHC services at least to some degree. Unfortunately too little is known to be more specific (114).

Although these problems endure, the situation has improved with the development of case management, ACT and crisis resolution teams. These developments have benefited from previous clinical experience and are more focused on a particular client group with more specific team design and operations. Nonetheless, the use of outcome measures outside of demonstration projects is still not routine. Such demonstration projects are unusual in being created *de novo* in atypical funding circumstances. It is therefore difficult to generalise conclusions from these evaluations to inform the development of services in more ordinary contexts. Spindel and Nugent (1999) also expressed concern about:

- The problem of researchers evaluating their own services, including the problem of data being collected by case managers themselves.
- Over-reliance on staff accounts rather than independent assessment of user perspectives and direct observation.
- Poor definition of the service that was actually being delivered and a tendency to compare ACT with underfunded, overworked individual case management teams.
- Neglect of the effects of social inequalities arising from race, gender, poverty and previous involvement in the criminal justice system.

- Failure to take adequate account of the effects of high drop-out rates, and views on the adequacy of the service among those who dropped out.
- The short time-span (often two to three years) of many studies. Given that this is such a short time in the life of someone with severe mental health problems, results gained from such evaluations may have limited validity.

Even if Huxley's (1991) criteria were to be achieved, determining the effect of CMHT provision on outcomes for users remains problematic because of the range of other uncontrolled simultaneous events, not least the user's involvement with other services. As ever, there is tension between rigorous experimental control, and the implementation of a service that resembles everyday practice in an ordinary environment that could be modelled by others in similar circumstances.

Thornicroft *et al.* (1999) distinguished between 'efficacy' and 'effectiveness'. Efficacy describes the extent to which a specific intervention achieves its aims under ideal experimental conditions, whereas the authors define 'effectiveness' as the extent to which these aims can be achieved under ordinary clinical conditions. If CMHTs are to be seen as a robust framework for service delivery and coordination to planners and policy-makers, they will also need to demonstrate that they are cost effective (in terms of providing valuable outputs at a reasonable cost) and efficient. When considering the costs of an intervention, it is also important to take into account the *opportunity cost* of funding CMHTs. That is, the value of an alternative to CMHTs that was foregone in order to develop CMHTs. Efficiency describes 'that output at which the excess of benefits over costs, called the net benefit, is largest' (Le Grand and Robinson, 1991).

Chapters 1 and 2 highlighted basic concerns about what constitutes a valued output, and who values it. The efficiency argument concerning net benefit is a good example of this dilemma. Intensive community services require a large investment to produce a 'net benefit' for a comparatively narrowly-defined group of service users with particularly complex and challenging needs. Who decides if this is right? Is it best to direct support to people with the most severe problems, rather than to those people who would benefit from interventions most rapidly and visibly?

Dowell and Ciarlo's (1983) review of the outcome of the American CMHC movement concluded that on a service-by-service basis

CMHCs appeared to be a comparatively inefficient approach. However, they point out that this does not take account of their goal of improving the well-being of whole communities by providing a range of services. Appropriate evaluation would therefore need to take account of the net benefit encompassing user outcomes, the effects on their informal carers, service use, hospitalisation, involvement in the criminal-justice system and other indicators of community mental health. Very few studies have achieved such comprehensive evaluation although the Madison experiment (Stein and Test, 1980) and the study of the Crisis Intervention Service in New South Wales (Hoult, 1986) provide notable exceptions, and both argued strongly for the intensive community interventions described.

An innovative study by Provan and Milward (1995) also looked at the whole system of community support. They examined the 'network effectiveness' of four community mental health services. Networks were evaluated rather than specific organisations as outcomes for users will depend on the integrated and coordinated actions of a range of agencies concerned with a wide range of provision. They concluded that integration of providers was unlikely to improve outcomes unless the network was stable, adequately resourced and centrally and directly controlled.

Many of the shortcomings described above are acknowledged in the literature, though rarely completely addressed. However, some of the outputs from teamworking of a particular intensive and targeted style are robust enough to argue for further investment in such services, as we shall see below. The approach of this discussion will be to highlight the key findings on the outputs from teamworking, and particularly from reviews of the more intensive models of CMHT working (such as ACT or home treatment teams). How these outputs link to team inputs and processes will be the subject of closer scrutiny in later chapters.

Outputs from teamworking

This discussion on the merits of teamworking will conclude by looking broadly at the outputs achieved from CMHT working. The inputs and processes required to achieve them will be described in the remaining chapters.

Innovation: a key output

Innovation can be regarded as the process by which team effectiveness may be achieved; 'the intentional introduction and application within a role, group or organisation of ideas, processes, products or procedures, new to the relevant unit of adoption, designed to significantly benefit the individual, the group, organisation or wider society' (West and Farr, 1989). Watts and Bennett (1983) highlighted the importance of innovation in rehabilitation work with people with severe and long-term mental health problems. Innovative solutions to apparently intractable problems are often demanded and practitioners need to be able to think independently and urgently in crises. The most direct study of innovation in CMHTs using a validated measure concluded that external ratings of innovation and effectiveness were strongly associated with team clarity of and commitment to objectives, levels of participation within the team, the team's emphasis on quality, and practical support for innovation (Borrill *et al.*, 2000).

Changes in symptomatology, social functioning and quality of life

Marshall and Lockwood's (1998) review of randomised controlled trials concluded that significant and robust differences between ACT and standard community care could be found on accommodation status, employment and user satisfaction but not for mental state or social functioning. Other key reviews, that take less account of UK studies (Mechanic, 1996; Mueser *et al.*, 1998) make claims for gains in symptomatology, functioning and quality of life as a result of ACT that are about as modest as that for CMHCs (Dowell and Ciarlo, 1983), although more recent studies have shown improved gains. For example, a randomised controlled trial of intensive case management compared with routine case management in Sydney reported significant advantages of intensive case management in clinical functioning and engagement at 12 months (Johnston *et al.*, 1998). This intensive service saw people on average twice a week compared with less than once a week within the standard service. In the UK, the Daily Living Programme in London achieved superior outcomes in terms of symptomatology and social functioning after 20 months (Marks *et al.*, 1994). When the service was discontinued, the gains in social functioning, and reduced time in hospital, were lost 15 months later (Audini *et al.*, 1994).

Merson *et al.* (1992) conducted a randomised controlled trial of an early intensive community treatment team and a standard hospital-based service. There was greater symptomatic improvement among users seen by the team which was also less costly and preferred by users. Holloway and Carson (1998) evaluated an intensive case management service in East Lambeth that provided a mean of 45 user contacts per worker per month. Although there were no advantages in symptomatology and social functioning at 18 months in a controlled comparison with a standard service, there were significant benefits in quality of life.

Key commentators (for example, Gournay, 1999) have argued that service models such as ACT should be evaluated in terms of their roles as a platform for the delivery of care, and that the achievement of positive outcomes will be determined by the quality of that care. In other words ACT will provide the context in which good care can be provided, but unless practitioners are equipped to provide effective and relevant interventions, positive clinical and social outcomes should not be anticipated. It may also be that the linkages of the ACT to other key services such as supported employment may have a strong impact on outcome (for example, Chandler *et al.*, 1996).

Reduced use of inpatient beds and increased community tenure

Much stronger evidence is found for reduced time in hospital and increased housing stability as a result of intensive case management, particularly for people that already have substantial involvement in mental health services (Mueser *et al.*, 1998). A review by Marshall *et al.* (1998) of randomised controlled trials examining case management concluded that it increased admission rates and had no significant positive impact on other measures. However, this review included studies where the investigators described the intervention as 'case' or 'care' management. Since care management in a UK context at that time was very different from case management as widely understood in an international context, it is difficult to be confident that homogeneous and coherent service models were being described. Furthermore, the introduction of case management services is likely to have increased inception of care for many people with severe mental health problems who may previously have been underserved. In these cases, increased use of in-patient beds may have been appropriate.

There are many examples of assertive, targeted teams that reduce in-patient bed use (Burns *et al.*, 1993b; Dean *et al.*, 1993; Marks *et al.*, 1994; Marshall and Lockwood, 1998; Merson *et al.*, 1992). A home treatment team in north Birmingham was able to reduce local in-patient beds from 30 to 16 per 100,000 population (44 to 23 beds; Minghella *et al.*, 1998). The Cochrane review of crisis intervention (Joy *et al.*, 2001) reported only a limited effect on admissions but found home care to be as cost-effective as hospital care with respect to loss of people to local services, deaths and mental distress. Crisis services reduced the burden on families, and were preferred by both users and families. Overall, it is reasonable to conclude that intensive community teams that specifically aim to reduce admissions by providing an alternative, for example, by ensuring that they sit in the pathway between the community and in-patient care, are able to have a positive effect.

Cost effectiveness of intensive community treatment

ACT has been shown to be cost-effective, although often more expensive, principally because of its impact on hospital services, (Burns *et al.*, 1993b; Knapp *et al.*, 1994; Mechanic, 1996). The Daily Living Programme in London was shown to be a cost-effective alternative to in-patient admission even when taking into account the unusually high cost of admission in that locality (Knapp *et al.*, 1994).

Minghella *et al.* (1998) compared home treatment with a traditional hospital-based acute service. The increased community costs for home treatment were more than offset by savings in in-patient care. The overall costs were significantly lower for a sample of 58 pairs of users matched across the two sites at six months' follow-up. The savings achieved allowed in-patient staff to transfer to community work. The cost-effectiveness of home treatment in comparison to hospital care was also underlined by the Cochrane review of crisis services (Joy *et al.*, 2001).

Effective engagement with service users

Subsequent to discharge, intensive community teams are better able to ensure that difficult-to-serve people maintain an adequate level of service contact (Ford *et al.*, 1995; Holloway and Carson, 1998; Johnston *et al.*, 1998). Cochrane reviews of randomised controlled trials found that those receiving ACT, case management and crisis resolution services were more likely to remain in contact with services that people receiving standard community care (Joy *et al.*, 2001; Marshall and Lockwood, 1998; Marshall *et al.*, 1998).

Risk

Risk of harm to the users themselves or others is a major concern for users, staff and policy-makers. Marshall and Lockwood (1998) concluded that there is insufficient data to make firm conclusions about the advantages or disadvantages of ACT with respect to risk. Mueser *et al.* (1998) were also unable to draw firm conclusions concerning key risk factors such as impacts on substance abuse or medication compliance. However, it can be concluded that there is no evidence to suggest that working intensively in community settings as a potential alternative to hospital admission is more risky than in-patient care (Marshall and Lockwood, 1998; Joy *et al.*, 2001).

Impact on carers

On the basis of the limited number of studies that have specifically examined carer satisfaction with more intensive provision, Mueser *et al.* (1998) concluded that there was an emerging trend towards increased carer satisfaction and speculated that this was associated with a more community- rather than hospital-orientated locus of care.

User and carer satisfaction

Advocates of ACT argue that the equivocal outcome findings for ACT are due to problems of implementation, and argue for their promulgation on the grounds that it is generally cost-effective and preferred by users and carers (Holloway and Carson, 1998; Hoult *et al.*, 1983; Marks *et al.*, 1994; Merson *et al.*, 1992). The same argument could now be made for home treatment teams as an alternative to admission (Joy *et al.*, 2001).

While it is true that users value ACT, this is often because of non-specific features such as the quality of relationships with staff (McGrew *et al.*, 1996). It is important to recognise that, latterly, users have been more vocal in expressing reservations about key aspects of the model. Spindel and Nugent (1999) expressed concern about the emphasis paid to a biomedical approach both in terms of ideology and the emphasis in practice on 'medication compliance' and the home delivery of drugs. They particularly stress the social control role of ACT in the USA and Canada, particularly the control that ACT teams assume over users' access to money, and the teams' collaboration with other agencies, such as probation services, to enforce compliance. Similar concerns have been expressed about the future development of ACT in the UK (Smith *et al.*, 1999a).

As described above, Spindel and Nugent (1999) also highlight user concerns about the more extreme application of a 'team approach' whereby relationships between users and particular, individual staff members are discouraged. As evidence of the negative perceptions of ACT among many users, they underline the fact that some ACT evaluations report high rate of drop-out (for example, McGrew *et al.*, 1995) despite their supposedly positive evaluation by service users. Overall, they criticise ACT teams for failing to give adequate account or credence to user perspectives, and conclude:

> Nowhere is the experience of clients discussed, nor are the reasons why they are 'disengaged' from services or from their friends, families and communities. Being disengaged from services is seen as negative, and demonstrated proof that an individual is in need of 'rehabilitation'. If these criteria were applied to any other member of society, they would be seen as intrusive and disrespectful of individual's right to choose how they want to live (1999: 4).

Drawing conclusions from the research

Interpretation of research is not a value-free or disinterested activity. This was dramatically highlighted in November 1998 when ten papers on intensive community services were published by a well-respected research group within a single issue of a highly prestigious journal (Thornicroft *et al.*, 1999). The devotion of a single issue to one research study was unprecedented and seemed to signal that the study was a major breakthrough in our understanding of community care. The study claimed to be a valid examination of real-life clinical effectiveness of intensive provision, rather than just efficacy (as defined above). It provided a comprehensive evaluation of the effectiveness of non-experimental community services. Tyrer (1998b) introduced the study by highlighting the finding that the standard service was 'at least as good' as the intensive service in its general effects on symptoms and disability, and that the cost advantage of intensive provision shown in previous studies as a result of the reduced use of in-patient beds was not evident.

Subsequent analysis revealed that the study suffered from many of the usual and predictable flaws of such studies. Two key critiques (Marshall *et al.*, 1999; Sashidharan *et al.*, 1999) pointed out that the models of care were inadequately specified and that they did not appear to include key elements that would have predicted effectiveness, such as consistently low caseloads, or an integrated service approach where the team provides a single point of responsibility.

Some commentators asked themselves why such a flawed study was given such a high profile. At a time when the government rhetoric stressed the 'failure of community care', while at the same time was poised for a major shift in resources from psychiatric hospital to community settings, Sashidharan *et al.* (1999) interpreted the publication of the study as a move against the advance of community care as an alternative to hospital (although the authors were proponents of community care). Sashidharan *et al.* stated: 'despite the impressive history of major advances in social psychiatry in this country, the reluctance of British psychiatrists to embrace community care models of proven value, benefit and acceptability by service users and carers is becoming increasingly clear' (507). Pelosi and Jackson (2000) appear to make their point by attacking the evidence for crisis resolution teams on the faulty premise that the research evidence compares such teams with asylum care and is therefore outdated, and that crisis resolution teams ignore primary care and do not take account of the work of other teams providing long-term care to users. In fact, such crisis resolution teams are highly reliant on primary care teams and other community teams (see Minghella *et al.*, 1998). It is difficult to avoid the conclusion that there remained a body of psychiatrists who were ideologically opposed to intensive community provision while others among them were at the very forefront of innovation.

Despite the imperfections of the current research, it is possible to conclude that where teams are intensive, proactive and centred on developing good working relationships with users they can effectively engage them, keep them out of hospital and in many cases improve important aspects of their lives. However, in order to be economically viable, the intensity of provision needs to achieve a threshold where it becomes a valued alternative to in-patient care for people with severe mental health problems. Sashidharan *et al.* (1999) made the point that, from the perspective of an experienced clinician informed by the existing research, it would be mere common sense to expect more intensive and targeted community services to make a difference. The challenges lie in implementation. As they state: 'effectiveness research should now be about examining in an empirical way the particular factors which constrain a proven treatment when it is applied within ordinary clinical settings' (505). These factors will inevitably include the attitudes of powerful and influential local people, which is why we shall look at approaches to managing change in the concluding chapter.

Teams can only completely fulfil their potential when they form an effective part of a whole system of mental health care within a locality. This requires that they are clear about whom they are serving and how users will benefit from the team's provision in their pathways to, through and out of involvement with services. The next chapter looks at how team design may accommodate this local context.

CHAPTER 4

The Team in Context

For teams to be effective they require clear aims and objectives. This chapter focuses on some of the 'bigger' issues of team design that require the involvement of a range of agencies working in partnership. This strategic context has been neglected in the past, resulting in teams that are unclear about their role or how they should manage the demands that are made of them (Onyett *et al.*, 1994). This in part is because CMHTs are caught in the conflux of competing interests about who constitutes a priority. An assumption of this chapter is therefore the necessity of achieving shared values about whose needs should be served first, of finding a common language for describing clients groups, and an understanding of the best way to meet their needs supported by shared and credible tools (such as stakeholder conferences, and client group definitions) to be able to look at what is happening locally now and what ought to happen in future.

Usually more than one team will be serving clients with a range of needs within a locality. Their respective roles and users' pathways through them must be considered. This requires effective processes for local needs assessment and planning supported by effective integration across health and social care, and primary and specialist care.

This chapter emphasises effective targeting of services towards people with complex health and social care needs as the group for which intensive, coordinated teamworking is most required and most appropriate. There is therefore an emphasis on promoting access to people with severe mental health problems. How the team will address the needs of people with concurrent substance misuse and mental health problems is another early team-design decision to be considered. Since most of the research on CMHTs is drawn from urban environments, particular attention is given to lessons learnt about the implementation of intensive community teams in rural environments.

Strategic context

West *et al.* (1998) stated that: 'Perhaps the major change in emphasis in research on teams in the last 15 years has been the shift from discussion of intragroup process to the impact of organisational context on the team'. CMHTs function within a complex social environment typified by a chronic lack of resources, multiple demands from external constituents, and often overwhelming requests for assistance from those in need. Ideally, the defined and stated role of the CMHT in this context should form part of a mental health strategy drawn up by a range of key stakeholders. This in turn should be in response to the outcome of an effective process for assessing local need.

The introduction of the NSF has created a much stronger emphasis on the achievement of local implementation plans based upon partnership working at local level. This partnership working requires strong and credible involvement from health, social services, primary care, the statutory and voluntary sectors, and users and carers. The involvement of users and carers will be explored in more detail when looking at continuous quality improvement in the final chapter. This discussion will focus on the integration of health and social care, and across primary and specialist care, before then looking at how this translates into the external team management and planning that will be required to provide it with a clear strategic context.

Integration across health and social care

We saw in Chapter 2 how the integration of health and social care has proved a major challenge since the inception of the NHS. The 1990 NHS and Community Care Act, the NSF and the subsequent NHS Plan all continued to provide an impetus towards fully integrated working. The 1999 NHS Act allowed for 'new flexibilities', the removal of technical barriers to joint developments such as pooled budgets and the delegation of functions from one agency to another. This cleared the way for joint health and social care providers and the possibility of either health or local authorities becoming the lead commissioner for mental health services.

Joint working is now encompassed within broader arrangements for partnership working at strategic level (through Health Improvement Plans and joint commissioning arrangements), at managerial level (for example, through the joint management of CMHTs) and at practice level through integrated care coordination roles. Partnership working is thus multi-layered but amounts to little if it fails to result in strong inter-agency care planning and assessment where providers meet to assist service users. Without joint policies at this level, members of CMHTs are left to struggle 'like parentless children' (Foster, 1998) deciding among themselves how to integrate policies and procedures. There needs to be inter-agency ownership of decisions to commit resources to meet the wide range of needs of individual users and their carers. Without this connection between policy-makers and practitioners, effective, jointly managed and operated CMHTs may be frustrated by an absence of structures that translate needs-based information into changes that impact on service design (Poxton, 1999).

It is essential for partnerships between agencies to address the challenge of different political structures, different systems of accountability (for example, social services' accountability to local councillors), different ways of considering the needs of patients and users (for example, in terms of who is deemed a priority), different statutory responsibilities, different professional backgrounds of those charged with making it work, and different operations, customs and practices, (for example, regarding confidentiality, case closure, file destruction, complaints, and so on). A lack of identifiable resources to drive joint commissioning, and difficulties in making linkages across the layers concerned with influencing and implementing strategic level decision-making, can also be significant barriers to change (Poxton, 1999)

Examining successful examples of joint working allows some pointers towards effective partnership working to be drawn out (Hardy *et al.*, 1992; SCMH, 2000a). They could equally be applied to other attempts to provide partnership, such as that between specialist and primary care below, and partnerships involving housing departments, users, carers, service providers and voluntary organisations.

Clarity of purpose

Partnership working is not an end in itself. There should be some agreement about what types of services are appropriate to deliver. This should be underpinned by an explicit statement of the agency's collective aims and objectives that includes service values and principles, as well as agreement about joint management philosophy and principles.

It is also important to keep in mind that the agencies involved will have separate aims and objectives. Honest and candid communication is required to acknowledge that there are differing inter- and intra-agency motivations and expectations. Organisations will have the interests of their own staff in mind and it is important that the worries of staff, and their differences are acknowledged. People at practice level need to be able to articulate the pros and cons of integration from their perspective.

Clarify of purpose can sometimes be promoted by starting with small, focused developments that allow some early wins and celebrate achievement. If taking this approach, it will be important that the project is not set up to fail and that expectations are appropriate.

Commitment and shared ownership

Identifying and agreeing resources will be a first key step. There also needs to be confidence that the 'rug will not be pulled out from under the feet' of participants by ensuring a public commitment to maintaining investment or an agreed process for shared discussions about further change. The development of Joint Investment Plans may make the financial underpinning of partnership working more robust and tie it to concrete outcomes.

The commitment of resources also needs to include ensuring that enough *time* is defended for partnership working, particularly among senior managers who have to 'fire-fight' problems on a daily basis while coping with successive centrally-driven change initiatives.

Joint working often starts with a small number of champions and depends on their ability to generate a broader commitment. In establishing joint working structures it is vital to involve senior members and officers, and ensure comparability of rank across agencies. This is particularly important where their ability to represent their host organisation and make joint decisions is critical. It is also important in that those involved should be able to have the capacity, willingness and authority to explore new approaches to service delivery rather than being tied to existing practices and providers.

The style of leadership exercised within these arrangements is crucial. It is helpful for leaders, managers and champions to be perceived as credible while not being partisan with respect to their core profession, agency or background.

The breadth and depth of ownership of the work needs to be fostered through relationship building amongst constituent agencies and departments, service users, service providers and service managers, and carers. The early involvement of GPs and medics in specialist services is also often crucial. This relationship building often needs to focus on building trust by avoiding a sense of their being 'senior' and 'junior' partners in the work but rather acknowledging the equal legitimacy of everyone involved. There can sometimes be a danger of establishing 'core' groups while others have only an advisory role. It is helpful if senior people can model not being precious about who owns what resource and who is actually in charge.

Ultimately, people and their relationships are everything when it comes to successful partnership working. Having established appropriate structures, it is important to maintain a consistency of commitment through establishing stable representation and ensuring that new people to the process will support and promote the project's values and practices. In establishing structures it can be helpful to capture the personal networks of particular change champions in order to help preserve and enhance their energy for change. Where possible, joint recruitment policies and effective staff induction should help. Having the right people in the right place at the right time is critical.

A shared understanding and ownership of the work among middle managers (directly above team managers) in respective agencies appears to be particularly important. Ownership is easier to promote if building on existing good practice, and if the work is explicitly valued through allocation of attention, resources and praise. Where service delivery is the focus of joint working then explicit models of care supported by joint training will be vital. (The Tameside and Glossop Beacon service described in the NSF is a good example).

Robust and coherent management arrangements

In bringing about change, it is important to be clear about the delineation of areas of responsibility and lines of accountability, prior to inception of the work. For inter-agency working between statutory services, co-terminosity of boundaries will also be a major advantage.

At service level, it is important to agree from the outset the principles and policies for joint management including explicit and detailed agreements on resourcing (funding and financial controls), staffing (appointments and disputes/disciplinary procedures), mechanisms for conflict resolution (including those between disciplines and agencies) and servicing and administration prior to inception. These can be enshrined in a joint operational policy.

Management arrangements need to ensure relevant linkages to the organisational hierarchies of the constituent agencies with systematic briefing and reporting arrangements. Development needs to be built in by ensuring that an appropriate breadth of skills and expertise is available for effective joint working, and team building and training needs to foster this as a continuous process. For example, at service level, the 'PACT' team in Nunhead reviewed their skills mix every time someone left the service.

Organisational learning

In order to promote organisation learning across the agencies involved in partnership, the following are advocated:

- Establishing formal and systematic joint monitoring procedures; deriving performance indicators; and undertaking periodic evaluation. This needs to include inter-agency agreement on how to manage purchaser-provider relationships, and a shared understanding of how joint initiatives will be evaluated.
- Treating projects as deliberate experiments in inter-agency coordination.
- Proactively seeking feedback to the service from stakeholders, and being open to visitors and enquiries.
- Ensuring feedback to and from other projects in the locality.

- Creating and publicising early success 'on the ground'.
- Using the learning to inform training and development.

The NHS Plan promoted the development of PCTs into Care Trusts that integrate social care. Increasingly, joint working between health and social care will be enacted in partnership with primary care staff.

Integration across primary and specialist care

The development of PCTs and the 'Shifting the Balance of Power' (Department of Health, 2001c) changes have continued a policy drive towards a primary care-led NHS. The population served by a given PCT usually forms the basis around which partnership working, planning and coordinated service delivery takes place. With these developments, boundaries between primary and secondary or specialist care shift, and accepted definitions of care are eroded as more specialist work is undertaken both in primary care settings and in people's homes. What could be more 'primary' than working in someone's home?

In asking, 'What is primary health care?' we need to be aware that it is not synonymous with general practice and general practice is not synonymous with the work of general practitioners. Otherwise many important services may be overlooked. The term 'primary health care team' is used very loosely, and is often quite differently understood by professionals working in the primary and specialist care. For most GPs it means the practice staff they employ and work closely with, and sometimes the community nursing staff who are closely aligned with their practice. There is a danger that we think of the primary health care team as closely linked to general practice, when in fact community health service practitioners such as district nurses, health visitors, community physiotherapists and occupational therapists will often be working with considerable degrees of autonomy and with particular groups of people with mental health problems.

Cultural differences between specialist and primary care also need to be borne in mind when developing partnerships. In contrast to professionals working in mental health services, GPs have a history of independence, providing services through service contracts, rather than job descriptions; and subject to nationally determined requirements, rather than those of local purchasers. This will change as GPs opt to become NHS employees under the NHS Plan. However, historically GPs have been more concerned to address those issues that have the biggest impact on their day-to-day practice than implementing government policy. Their world is understandably shaped by the needs of people on their practice list. Their priority is often the large volume of people they see with common mental health problems rather than the fewer people with severe mental health problems. This can cause a conflict of priorities between primary and specialist care, for which the priority is serving people with the most complex health and social care needs. This tension is exacerbated by a lack of capacity in both primary and specialist care to meet demand for mental health services.

Primary care has been perceived as difficult to engage in partnership working (Poxton, 1999). Reasons include a desire not to surrender control of finances to a joint commissioning process following the abolition of fund-holding, lack of time, lack of information, indifference and a lack of cohesion within and between practices (Hine and Bachman, 1997).

There is some historical antipathy between GPs and psychiatrists that may stem from their very different social constructions of mental health problems. One study found that among GPs without formal links to mental health professionals, closer links were sought with all disciplines *except* psychiatry (Thomas and Corney, 1993). Another study found that 12 per cent of the GPs surveyed did not see contact with psychiatrists to be necessary for patients diagnosed with schizophrenia (Nazareth *et al.*, 1995). The introduction of structured psychiatric assessments to primary care was unpopular among GPs and had little impact on their management of patient care (Kendrick *et al.*, 1995). Diagnostic labels and clinical features may be of only secondary importance in the GP's decision to refer, leading one author to conclude that 'one should not be too 'prescriptive' when defining the types of problems general practitioners should not deal with' (Verhaak, 1993).

The proximity of the GP's view of mental distress to the lay view makes them attractive to users in comparison with psychiatrists (Rogers and Pilgrim, 1993). This needs to be borne in mind when developing protocols in primary care for the care and treatment of people with mental health problems (for example, as required by NSF standards 2 and 3). It may be that we need to be cautious about devaluing this aspect of the GP's practice when advocating initiatives aimed at improving detection and management of mental health problems using methods derived from specialist provision.

The commissioning and management context

Hackman (1990) highlighted five 'trip wires' to be avoided when establishing productive work groups. They have strong resonance for CMHTs:

1 *Describing the performing unit as a team but continuing to manage members as individuals.* When piloting a definition of CMHTs for a national survey we found that the most valid definition of CMHTs for respondents was based simply on whether management had *told* them that they were a CMHT (Onyett *et al.*, 1994). There was usually an absence of more concrete criteria such as shared aims, operational policy or the establishment of integrated management that spanned disciplines.
2 *Failure to exercise appropriate authority over the team – leaving it to clarify its own aims and operations.* For 43 per cent of the 302 CMHTs in the survey above, the team 'as a whole' was reported as having most responsibility for deciding the client group of the team. Clearly, this is the first critically important strategic decision for any CMHT, yet management or steering groups had most responsibility in only 23 per cent of teams and individual managers or planners outside the team in a mere 10 per cent.
3 *Inadequate provision of internal structures for operational management – leaving the team to 'work out the details'.* Clarifying lines of accountability for staff within CMHTs is not simple (see BPS, 2001 and Chapter 7) and requires strong external, and joint inter-agency management.
4 *Failure to provide organisational supports in the form of rewards, training, information, and the material resources required to get the job done.* Lack of resources and work overload were the major sources of pressure reported by members of CMHTs (Onyett *et al.*, 1995). This undermines practitioner's ability to be effective which in turn destroys the major source of self-worth and meaning that is derived through work (see Chapter 8). Achieving effective resourcing of the team and joint training is the job of external, senior managers in the host organisations.

5 *Assuming that team members already have all the competence they need to work well in teams.* Teamworking has enormous potential but is problematic in implementation. The ability of staff to work effectively in teams cannot be assumed. Core professional training leaves staff ill-equipped to work effectively with very distressed individuals, often in chaotic and impoverished conditions and in an environment characterised by lack of resources and poor inter-agency collaboration (SCMH, 1997).

The most obvious improvement to the conditions for CMHT management will be made by leaping the trip wires identified above. External managers have a key role in:

1 *Ensuring that joint commissioning (involving health, social services and primary care) delivers CMHTs with clear mandates, realistic objectives and adequate resources.* The role of the CMHT should not be left to its members but rather be informed by local needs assessment and local partnership working. Host organisations are responsible for ensuring that a coherent CMHT management role is operational. Experience shows that this is greatly facilitated if the role is supported by a management or steering group that brings together key people from the agencies involved (Onyett, 1998). It is also helpful to have a general line manager with devolved authority from this joint agency group who will work alongside the CMHT manager as an ally, advocate and buffer against the more unrealistic exigencies from above, and occasional hostility from collateral providers (ibid.).
2 *Achieving a management role with enough authority to ensure that all the various disciplines within the team work to an agreed operational policy.* The NSF requires that CMHTs integrate health and social services staff within a single management structure. Senior, external managers need to be able to equip key staff in CMHTs with the clout needed to do their job effectively. As the CMHT will need to have an inter-agency role, this authority will correspondingly need to be drawn from more than one agency. Joint NHSE/SSI (1999) guidance describes how the care coordination role should be implemented. It is this core role that will need to be managed within teams, while separate lines of accountability may exist for the management of the more specific competence that is accrued through

professional and post-qualification training, and personal life experience.

3 *Providing the CMHT manager with enough time and resources to ensure that systems for monitoring allocation, caseloads, and clinical review processes are in place.* The NSF highlighted the importance of clinically useful information systems. It is also important to develop explicit systems for conflict-resolution between disciplines, their line management and operational managers within the teams (see Chapter 7).

4 *Recognising the nature of the work and it's demands, and providing appropriate time, training and resources to ensure staff are able to retain a sense of competence, achievement and professional identity.* Chapter 8 will explore the importance of achieving a sense of self-efficacy and identification with both their discipline, their team, and ideally, their service agency as a whole.

5 *Involving service users in a variety of formats, and providing them with material and personal support to promote their maximum impact on the shape and relevance of the service.* While implementing this will be a key responsibility of managers within the team, it is the job of external managers and steering or management groups to ensure that it happens.

The need to prioritise client groups

The issue of equity is a major criterion against which service systems can be evaluated. Rogers and Pilgrim (1996) highlight three common definitions of equity: (1) a minimum standard of care for all those in need, (2) equal treatment for equal need, and (3) equality of access. They point out that the operationalisation of this concept is influenced by who determines and defines need. For example, people with severe and long-term mental health problems are particularly liable to lose contact with services largely as a result of inadequate and poorly coordinated aftercare (see Sheppard, 1996). However, in many cases their 'need' to stay in contact with services is premised on an imperative to prevent harm or inconvenience to others rather than the experienced need for care or treatment on the part of the individual concerned.

The definitions of equity described above may also be in conflict with each other. In a context of limited resources, it may not be possible to provide a minimum standard of care for *all* those demanding support from mental health services, while also providing equality of access to those people who are most difficult to serve effectively. This has formed the rationale for 'targeting' services on people with severe and long-term mental health problems. This rationale is, however, contested on the grounds that it merely provides a justification for rationing resources and requires that people accept a label indicating dependence in order to achieve access to services. Morris and Davidson (1992) questioned whether it is useful to divide people with severe and long-term mental health problems from other groups at all and lamented the fact that this was antithetical to the achievement of a 'comprehensive' service which has been central to the CMHC movement.

> To characterise the 10 per cent of the population likely to suffer a mental health problem as either 'the long term ill' or 'the worried well', is no less crude or destructive for its professional popularity. It does nothing to advance knowledge of incidence or outcome, to promote the dignity or rights of sufferers or to reflect the breadth and complexity of disorder and psychological damage experienced, yet this absurd characterisation is regularly cited as an appropriate axis on which current priorities should be re-balanced, and, as such, seems to dominate the discourse in relation to planning community mental health services (Moms and Davidson, 1992: 297).

Nonetheless the authors do permit the necessity of prioritisation: 'the mission of comprehensiveness... in which the CMHC is seen as responsive to all the individuals from whom it attracts contact, is unsustainable in the new environment' (297–8).

Challis and Davies (1986) make an important distinction between two different forms of service accessibility. *Horizontal target efficiency* describes the degree to which a service connects with all potential users in a locality. The aim is that everybody who could benefit from the service has access to it. *Vertical target efficiency* describes the extent to which the service engages *only* those people that it was set up to serve. It requires unambiguous specification of the client group and gate-keeping to screen out people whose needs would be better met elsewhere. The NSF aims to improve both types of efficiency. For example, the introduction of NHS Direct whereby people can phone up for advice at any time will improve horizontal target efficiency while vertical target efficiency is required to prioritise people on 'enhanced' CPA as the first group to be provided with access to specialist mental health services round the clock.

Target efficiency is likely to be influenced by the context of the service. For example, a service that is part of a planned re-provision programme for people leaving a long-stay hospital will find it much easier to achieve horizontal target efficiency than a street agency serving homeless people with severe mental health problems. The large-scale 'Care in the Community' evaluation of reprovision asserted that 'no one was "dumped" in the community, each had a case manager or keyworker, and each had a planned and supported place to live' (Knapp *et al.*, 1992: 303). Similarly, a service that operates with a single point of entry where gate-keeping and screening can be carried out will find it easier to achieve vertical target efficiency.

CMHCs were strongly criticised for their failure to target resources effectively. At the end of 1987, CMHCs defined their target group extremely broadly (Sayce *et al.*, 1991). Similarly, Dowell and Ciarlo's (1983) authoritative review of American CMHCs found they improved equality of access, but people with severe and long-term mental health problems continued to be comparatively neglected. Brown (1985) found that some CMHCs had caseloads of which at least 70 per cent were people with severe and long-term mental health problems. However, even where high case-load dedication to people with severe and long-term mental health problems is achieved and sustained, staff time may not be concentrated on working with this group. McAusland and Wibbautt (1988) reported an analysis of staff activity over a two-week period and found that, while nearly a quarter of open cases concerned people with long-term severe disabilities, only 3.3 per cent of staff time was spent on individual work with these people. This compared with 23 per cent of staff time dedicated to individual work with other client groups. There was also no evidence that this difference was compensated for through group work with people with more severe and complex mental health problems.

Unless premeditated steps are taken to focus provision on meeting the needs of people with the most complex health and social care needs, history shows that their needs are likely to be neglected. This is likely to result in a reactive rather than proactive service where users' involvement in services is instigated by crises or the sort of social transgressions that require the involvement of the criminal justice system. There are therefore solid grounds, on the basis of basic human values about meeting the needs of society's most vulnerable members, for focusing resources on those with the most complex health and social care needs.

The extent to which the needs of people with severe and long-term mental health problems are afforded priority by mental health services is influenced by a range of factors to do with the context in which teams operate and their own organisation and process. These are considered later in this and subsequent chapters. These aspects of organisational design and process also need to be informed by the social context in which difficulties accessing services occur and the enduring effects of social inequalities on the ways in which people access services. This can only be examined by first undertaking a comprehensive and on-going local needs assessment.

Local needs assessment

This is about asking:

'*What do services achieve for people?*' One way to address this question is to organise stakeholder conferences that employ a comprehensive framework for evaluation such as Developing Individual Services in the Community (Smith, 1998). The use of such a framework serves to establish some key values and a shared language about what mental health services should be achieving for people (for example, with respect to finance, occupation and accommodation). It therefore supports the complex negotiation between users, service providers and purchasers concerning what constitutes legitimate need as discussed in Chapter 1. It also specifically focuses on building on existing strengths within the service rather than assuming that new services need to be created to fulfil specific functions.

'*How many people use the services, what do they get, how often, and what does it cost?*' This will require joint approaches to examining the range of existing services and their activity (locality profiling), and examining what they cost (resource mapping).

'*How does the service respond to what we know about local levels and types of need?*' This requires continuous evaluation by users and carers, for example through a process such as user-led evaluation (for example, Rose *et al.*, 1998), in combination with population-based needs assessment (for example, using deprivation indicators as proxies for mental health service need), and routine and aggregated individual assessment of needs and service outcomes. Local needs assessment also needs to be mindful of the ways in which social inequalities impact on the ways in which people become involved in services. This is explored in detail later.

Exploring the allocation of resources

The configuration of local services with respect to client groups and teams will be unique to local circumstances. A starting point will be to candidly explore where and how people are currently being served. This requires a systematic and transparent approach as how people are currently served may not reflect their needs and preferences. For example, there may be people who are being served by mainstream CMHTs who have very similar needs to people being served through the rehabilitation service but have difficulty accessing the skilled resources located in the more specialist service.

The framework described in Box 1 below provides one approach to exploring this by providing a crude language as the starting point for mapping out the different ways in which people present to services. Such an analysis will only ever provide a broad overview and sense of direction. Over the longer term, services should be shaped through quality assurance processes such as user and carer consultations and evaluations, and the ongoing local needs assessment processes described above. However, developing services to previously underserved populations may require that this process is punctuated by one-off evaluations of the current focus of resources, and dedicated case-finding exercises to identify those people with severe and long-term mental health problems who are currently not being served.

In order to examine the current focus of resources, practitioners within the mental health services could be asked to review their caseloads and allocate users according to the definitions supplied below. By focusing on what practitioners are doing already, and with whom, the service development process can specifically build on current strengths, and particularly the strong relationships between users and staff that are already there.

The outcome of this analysis may mean that users who present less of a priority to specialist mental health services, perhaps because of the minimal risk they present to themselves or others, become less well served as a result of increasing the quality of care to those presenting with higher levels of risk. At least, if this conclusion is reached through a transparent analysis of current resource use as described here, the authorities involved will have gone some way to achieving the 'methodology agreed between all the partners for ordering priorities' (90) described in the NSF. Local stakeholders may then be more aligned and ready to engage in joint problem solving and resource procurement to achieve the quality of care of people who present as lower priorities. It is also important that difficult issues concerning the respective allocation of resources is pursued by the whole health and social care community, rather than hiving off the development of primary care provision (for example, as described in standards 2 and 3 of the NSF) and the associated resources to primary care organisations. Such an approach would handicap the pursuit of equity, and risk failing to address the needs of those with the most complex health and social care needs, as has so often been the case in the past. It would also fail to adequately address the important role of primary care in both screening for the needs of people with severe and enduring problems, and continuing to take a shared role in their care and treatment.

Matching client groups to team configurations

How do we begin to define a group of people with 'severe and enduring mental illness' that should be our first priority for service development? Many authorities have used the definitions in the 'Keys to Engagement' report (SCMH, 1998a). This explicitly uses a definition of severe mental illness that emphasises the disruption of socially valued roles. It defines severe mental illness as 'a mental disorder (i.e. psychotic disorders including schizophrenia, manic depression or severe depression or severe neurotic conditions and personality disorders) of such intensity that it disables people, preventing them from functioning adequately as determined on the basis of their culture and background'. However, the people within this group that require ACT are defined far more narrowly. Specifically the client group requires:

- *Long-term provision* over at least 12 months but often many years. This is what differentiates ACT from other 'outreach' approaches that provide home-based care such as crisis services or home treatment.
- *Intensive provision*, with a need for input at least on a weekly basis.
- *Efforts to achieve effective engagement* with the team and other services.

This most challenging group would be expected to include people identified within 'enhanced' CPA, and Section 117 aftercare. The 'Keys to Engagement' report assumed that black and minority ethnic groups would be over-represented in the group, and that it would be important to consider issues of homelessness, dual diagnosis of severe mental illness and substance misuse, problems of homelessness and substance misuse combined, and dual diagnosis combined with a history of offending. Following the demands of the NSF, the service may also need to consider assertive 'in reach' to people within prison who may require this intensity of provision. ACT may also be the service required to ensure their effective engagement with mental health services on release from prison.

Box 1 incorporates this priority group within a broader framework of client groups and outlines some initial thoughts regarding usual and desirable service responses. The first three categories have been developed from Shepherd (1999). The latter two categories have been added to allow a more comprehensive analysis within a locality.

Implicit in the service responses described in Box 1 is a continuum of intensity of teamworking. Effective teamworking is most needed where the nature of work with users actually requires cooperation and communication between workers in order to achieve optimal provision (Tannenbaum *et al.*, 1996). In other words, that there is some inter-dependence between team members to get the job done. This is most evident in ACT teams focusing on people with severe and complex health and social care needs. Teague *et al.* (1998) recommend that at least 90 per cent of users on the team's caseload should have contact with more than one team member over a week, and that the service should meet four or five times a week to plan and review services for each user.

Group A would need to be served by a team that had many of the features of ACT teams. Thornicroft *et al.* (1999) argued that

Box 1 *Client groups and service responses*

Client group	Service response
A New long-term users who place a high level of demand on services.	Effective and well-coordinated multi-agency programmes are needed to get users out of the 'revolving door' of hospital admissions, and other chaotic service contacts. Shepherd (1999) stressed the need for the 'right kinds of interagency links (for example, with housing, day provisions, etc), and the right kind of attitudes and 'philosophy' to provide consistent long term support'. People in this group are more likely to have other specific treatment needs (for example, regarding substance misuse, reduction of self-harm, anger management). They are a highly visible group who will be known to staff on acute wards, social workers, GPs, police, probation, and so on. As well as diagnoses of severe mental illness, people in this category may also have been assessed as having a personality disorder. Although heavy users of services, people in this group may often have lower levels of enduring disability than people in group B below. Group A most closely fits the definitions from 'Keys to Engagement' described above. This report placed the numbers of people requiring intensive service provision, for example, through ACT at around 45 per 100,000 population but with considerable variation (14–200) depending on the nature of the locality (Sainsbury Centre for Mental Health, 1998a).

Box 1 (*Continued*)

B New long-term users with high levels of disability but low levels of demand. They usually have low motivation to continue with programmes of care and treatment.	Considerable input is needed to maintain community living for this group; otherwise they fall out of follow-up care and live a very marginalized existence with poor quality of life. They are likely to live in a variety of sheltered and supported housing. Some may live in their own homes cared for by families and/or support staff. This group is most easy to overlook in a busy 'acute' or primary care orientated service. Without input from a specialist team, they are likely to deteriorate, particularly socially, and lose contact with services. Some lose contact with specialist services completely and are seen in primary care if at all. The numbers falling into this group are very difficult to estimate. Wing (1992) put it at around 100–300 per 100,000 population. The survey by Lelliot, Wing and Clifford (1994) estimated that an average of 6 beds (range 1–21) per 100,000 population were occupied by people who had been in hospital continuously for more than six months but less than three years.
C Long-stay patients who have been resettled into the community as part of a programme of hospital closure.	The basic needs of this group are likely to be met by the residential setting in which they have been placed. These settings will normally be operated by non-statutory, private or 'not for profit' organisations. There is nonetheless a need for regular contact with statutory services, not least because of the highly variable quality of care in such settings (Shepherd *et al.*, 1996).

D New users with severe mental health problems (for example, psychosis) who do not have major problems with effective engagement.	This category was advocated by psychiatrists who felt that a significant proportion of the people that they saw as out-patients had severe mental health problems (for example, a diagnosis of psychosis) yet could be assessed, treated and discharged without an expectation that they would need long-term involvement with specialist mental health services. The main distinction between this group and the group described below was their psychotic diagnosis and the increased likelihood that they would be seen mainly by a psychiatrist.
E People with severe health care or social care needs whose difficulties can be resolved through contact with one discipline or agency within specialist mental health services.	These people require input from practitioners with considerable training and expertise in health or social care provision, who will need to communicate effectively with each other in order to work most efficiently. This may *not* require a dedicated team approach, meeting frequently to allocate and review cases. Such care could be provided on a more open multidisciplinary, multi-agency basis with practitioners operating within a defined network. It may be advantageous to have a regular weekly or fortnightly forum for peer consultation on particularly difficult cases, but routine review of all cases is unlikely to be necessary. Peer consultation meetings would be in addition to the practitioner's own consultation or supervision from a nominated person. One format for such a service would be a psychological therapies and counselling service operating predominantly in primary care settings. Examples of referrals might include people diagnosed with

Box 1 (*Continued*)

	agoraphobia, panic disorder, moderate depression, people with sexual dysfunctions, and *some* people diagnosed with borderline personality disorders, or eating disorders.
F People with less severe health or social care needs which do not require specialist mental health services.	Increasingly people presenting with minor to moderate mental health problems are having their needs met within primary care settings or the independent sector, for example, by GPs, counsellors, practice nurses, health visitors, or community workers. Examples of the kinds of mental health issues addressed might include minor degrees of anxiety, depression or emotional disturbance related to life stressors, personality problems in the absence of other mental health or social care needs, substance misuse problems in the absence of mental health service needs, or referrals for counselling, anger management, assertiveness, social skills or anxiety management training.

a well-functioning CMHT may offer most of the advantages of more intensive community treatment while also offering more long-term support, increased flexibility and a simpler service structure. However, experience of previous teams suggests that incorporating assertive outreach as a function of existing CMHTs can give rise to problems in maintaining the level of coordination, skill development, and cross-support needed (for example, Burns and Guest, 1999), although in some rural catchments developing a single team to meet the needs of this group may not be feasible. The team itself and its caseload should not become too large, otherwise people have difficulty getting to know all the users being seen by the team and the intensity of the provision drops. Practitioners should not have caseloads above 12 and the whole team of around seven to eight members should not have more than 60–100 cases. If the numbers within a locality are low enough, then incorporating users fitting the profile B above into the work of the team could be advantageous as the style of work is similar, with team members needing to be active in working with other agencies to ensure that the needs of the users are met and outcomes monitored.

Although members of the C category may share a similar history to some of the people described above in terms of institutional care, their stable functioning and secure accommodation means that they could be incorporated within larger caseloads, albeit with mechanisms to ensure regular and routine review. They are unlikely to require the same service response as people who are less easy to involve effectively in services. Achieving effective working relationships may nonetheless be a challenge and practitioners will need to be able to work flexibly and over long periods. This may be an area where the greater deployment of community support workers has a very great deal to offer (Murray *et al.*, 1997), either as part of CMHTs or more specialised community rehabilitation teams.

Practitioners working with groups D, E or F will usually be used to a more linear style of work with users whereby people's needs are formulated, addressed and then resolved. In contrast, work with people in groups A to C is more iterative with constant assessment, re-assessment (or review) and concurrent adjustment of provision to ensure the best configuration of treatment, care and support.

Crisis resolution or home treatment staff are most likely to be involved with users in categories A, B, or E, and will need to be able to link effectively to the parts of the service that are more routinely involved in their care.

Pulling it all together

How teams within a locality work together as a whole system is critically important. This is best explored by looking at current user pathways to and through services and configuring services to keep the number of discontinuities and duplicated or unhelpful events to a minimum. At the same time, we need to implement service models with enough fidelity to models known to work to ensure users get an effective service.

The influential North Birmingham service configuration has generic CMHTs with specialist functions supplemented by a crisis resolution and an ACT team. Primary care liaison teams for people with more common mental health problems and opportunities for supported employment also have a key role to play in providing a comprehensive service. Thornicroft *et al.* (1999) highlight the advantage for the crisis team of having another team to refer to that can provide intensive intervention over a longer period. However, they also highlight the possible complexity of the local service configuration from the perspective of users, carers and referrers and the danger of frequent transfers between one service and another. It is important however to bear in mind that helping users through such complexity by providing continuous human relationships was the original imperative behind case management in the USA (see Chapter 2; Onyett, 1998). Staff have a key role in supporting effective linkages between teams for service users and attempting to minimise disruption.

Another approach is to have a generic CMHTs that includes an augmented crisis or ACT function. This approach may be particularly common in rural areas where geographical dispersion of users does not support the creation of separate teams (see below).

Thornicroft *et al.* (1999) argue that recent evidence would tend to support the merits of focusing more on particular evidence-based interventions to achieve improved clinical and social outcomes, rather than any given service configuration. They particularly highlight the beneficial effects of early intervention, family work, medication compliance, cognitive behaviour therapy and vocational rehabilitation. Thus another option is to operate separate specialist teams providing specialist forms of treatment to subgroups of users. Where there may not be enough staff to form teams, or the creation of such teams creates unnecessary complexity, it can be advantageous to locate skilled staff with existing teams. They will require good access to colleagues that are working with similar clients within a similar model of care, which may require the formation of specific networks of support.

Promoting effective access to the team

So having defined in broad terms the client group and the nature of the service response, how is effective access to be achieved? Promoting effective access requires first that we are clear about who we are trying to promote access for and the social inequality issues that might impair effective access. As we saw above, we will need to reach out to identify and engage as many of our target client group as possible while also gate-keeping so that the service remains focused upon this group. This discussion will assume that the team will want to focus on people with complex health and social care needs (primarily groups A to C above).

Social inequality and access

Williams and Watson (1988) described social inequality thus: 'Social inequality exists when an ascribed characteristic such as sex, race, ethnicity, class, and disability determines access to socially valued resources. These resources include access to money, status and power, especially the power to define societal rules, rights and privileges' (292). A historical and critical perspective illustrates how psychiatry tends to label the experiences and behaviour of oppressed people as psychiatrically disturbed or distressed, and exacerbates the effects of social inequalities (for example, Busfield 1996; Rogers and Pilgrim, 1996; Thomas *et al.*, 1996). Williams (1996) argued that mental health workers need to acknowledge the implications of the research on inequalities and mental health, and refuse to provide care based on causal models that ignore the effects of abuse, discrimination and disadvantage. The NSF, with it's explicit emphasis on reducing inequalities, means that there has never been a better time for mental health workers to work alongside users in highlighting and addressing the structural inequalities that are a major cause of psychological distress and disturbance.

The mechanisms for how social inequalities for a range of groups impact on access are beyond the scope of this book (see instead Rogers and Pilgrim, 1996; Williams, 1996). However some key implications are drawn out below.

Minority ethnic groups

African-Caribbean mental health service users are more likely than other ethnic groups to be diagnosed as psychotic (Strakowski *et al.*, 1993), admitted to hospital with the involvement of the police, and detained under the Mental Health Act (Thomas *et al.*, 1993). Goater *et al.* (1999) found, in the fifth year of a five-year prospective study of ethnicity and outcome of psychosis, that black people were more likely than other ethnic groups to be detained, brought to hospital by the police and given emergency injections.

The higher incidence of diagnoses of psychosis among black service users and the tendency to use physical (as opposed to verbal) and coercive interventions has been attributed to the personal and social pressures of belonging to a minority group in Britain (King *et al.*, 1994) combined with the Euro-centric underpinnings of British psychiatry (Francis *et al.*, 1989). Studies using very specific diagnostic criteria support the view that higher rates of diagnosed schizophrenia represent misdiagnosis rather than the actual incidence of the disorder (Mahy *et al.*, 1999; Strakowski *et al.*, 1993).

The implications are that people from ethnic minorities, and in particular African-Caribbeans, have less involvement with primary care, contact helping agencies later in the course of a breakdown in mental health, and are more likely to be involved in emergency services (Gunn and Fahy, 1990; Harrison *et al.*, 1989). They thus tend to experience more adverse contacts with mental health services and do not get the early, proactive therapeutic support that is likely to stop emotional distress escalating.

The introduction of ACT could exacerbate a cycle of fear and mistrust that exists between black communities and mental health services unless it is carefully and sensitively implemented. The negative experiences of mental health services described above can be predicted from racist assumptions and perceptions of black service users as being disproportionately violent. This perpetuates a cycle of distrust and avoidance of services leading to more coercive provision which further feeds a legitimate desire to avoid service involvement. If ACT is perceived as a way of overcoming this through coercive pursuit and surveillance then the cycle is likely to be perpetuated, particularly if it is seen as a vehicle for the early introduction of drug therapies without consideration of more acceptable alternatives.

Innovative services that have attempted to address this problem, such as Frantz Fanon Centre in Birmingham, again stress the importance of achieving a relationship with users that results in a more accurate assessment of their needs and their own perspectives on the current situation (Fuller, 2000). In order to achieve this, practitioners themselves need to understand the impact of racism, and its effect on an individual's mental health and their basic survival in society. It is essential for this to be acknowledged and incorporated into their work with the user, and particularly their relationship building and assessment. Assessment needs to take fuller account of who is defining 'risk' and how. The process of relationship building is also supported by a policy of self-referral and the requirement for individuals to consent to the referral if their referral comes from elsewhere.

Approaches to prioritisation by teams

A variety of approaches have been developed by CMHTs for prioritising referrals, though often they suffer from having failed to invest effort in agreeing the process with primary care. Harrison (2000) described a process whereby a CMHT in Manchester wrote to all local GPs explaining the need to prioritise people with severe mental illness, explaining the type of referrals that would be appropriate and inviting further discussion. This was followed by visits by the team psychiatrist to GP practices where each practice was given feedback on their referral patterns in the previous year. The psychiatrist and another team member presented data on referral patterns plus statistics on levels of need in the area at the local GP postgraduate meeting. This provided an opportunity to explore what could constitute an appropriate referral and alternative sources of support for cases that fell outside of the team's priority group. The CMHT adopted a link-worker model where each team member attached themselves to a practice and visited at least monthly as a point of communication and to provide feedback on users registered as being on the CPA. This was also an opportunity to discuss particular users of the service. Refused referrals were accompanied by a letter from the consultant making alternative suggestions for management and offering further discussion if necessary. CMHT staff reported that with their more focused caseloads they were more able to concentrate on providing care for people with severe mental health problems. This was confirmed by GP ratings of the service for people with severe mental illness, and their satisfaction with the service. However, for many, this was accompanied by a perceived deterioration in the service for users with less severe needs.

Job (1999) described an initiative in Newbury that involved a more elaborate framework for deciding priorities. A GP survey had identified dissatisfaction with the length of the waiting list, which prompted the need to become more explicit about prioritisation. The team reviewed systems for prioritisation and felt that most were too narrow and would exclude too many people from the service. They developed a six-factor weighting tool based on level of distress, disruption of functioning, level of motivation, risk of harm to self or others, and the involvement of other agencies. These were assessed at interview or using standard measures. Another factor was introduced to give priority to people who had been on the waiting list for a long time. The process of prioritisation became more explicit and transparent and the team felt more in control of the high demand that it experienced. No referrals were left indefinitely at the bottom of waiting lists. Disadvantages, however, included the extra administrative load and a concern among some clinicians about the lack of flexibility of their caseloads, as individuals are allocated in priority order to the most appropriate member of the team.

The Newbury team screened all new referrals on receipt so that inappropriate referrals could be redirected to more appropriate sources of help at the earliest stage. The Early Intervention Service in Paddington also found that screening at an early stage on the basis of very clear parameters (for example, age, catchment area) was a key task that could be undertaken by someone in an administrative role (Onyett, 1998). This service devised a registration form and encouraged referrers to refer by phone to the administrator who could confirm this first level of eligibility and collect the kind of information that would be most helpful in effectively planning the initial contact with the person referred (for example, choice of assessor, location, involvement of other agencies). This service was very positively evaluated both by users and referrers (Onyett *et al.*, 1990).

Accepted sources of referral

Open access, and accepting referrals from all sources was a feature of the comprehensive CMHC model. As this model has become discredited, limiting access to the team by only accepting referrals from particular sources has been adopted by some services as a strategy to promote gate-keeping. There is little evidence to support this strategy. Onyett *et al.* (1994) found no significant association between the team's caseload composition and accepted sources of referrals among English CMHTs. Open referral networks were most frequent, although if referral was restricted it was often to exclude self-referrals. The next most frequent restriction was to allow referrals via or approved by GPs only. A review by Hagan (1990) found that limiting access by only allowing GP referrals did not achieve more referrals of people with severe and long-term mental health problems. Similarly, Marriott *et al.* (1993) studied 590 referrals to an inner-London CMHT over a two-year period and found that only 21 per cent of those referred by GPs had 'severe' mental disorders. Of the 31 per cent of referrals with severe mental disorder, significantly more were referred from non-medical sources. Social services, social work departments and self-referrals constituted the main non-medical sources of referrals. In common with Patmore and Weaver (1991a), the study concluded that the medical sources did not refer fewer inappropriate referrals.

Restricting referrals seems to be based upon the faulty assumption that other agencies, such as the voluntary sector or housing agencies, are involved with people with substantially less severe mental health problems. In many cases, the opposite may be true. Those people who are most difficult to involve effectively in mainstream mental health services may have actively opted to rely on more diverse and non-stigmatising sources of support in the community.

The Compass Project in London specifically accepted self-referrals in order to be more accessible to the two-thirds of their target population who were not registered with GPs. It is notable that the guidance on the implementation of care coordination stated that: 'Systems of self-referral for assessment should be introduced where they do not already exist' (NHSE/SSI, 1999: 8).

The need for a local focus

It can be concluded from the above that it is possible to maintain a focus on people with the most severe mental health problems by accepting referrals from a wide range of sources but then 'gate-keeping' to ensure that only the team's defined client group are taken on for assessment and on-going work. Aside from the substantial literature on ACT and case management underlining the importance of an 'assertive' style of provision that overcomes many of the practical barriers to access, there is little else that can be concluded from research into the implications of other aspects of team operational policy for users' access to services. Hagan (1990) concluded from her review of the topic that it was impossible to reach firm conclusions because of the enormous variability both in intent and practice between teams, and the other major influences on the ways in which people access services. It is also clear that issues of access will be determined by the local context. This means being clear about the target population and finding out where and how they would find the most accessible and acceptable first contact with mental health services. A team that has active outreach as the core to its philosophy will be well placed to work alongside these points of contact in order to promote effective and equitable access.

The issue of co-morbidity

Concurrent misuse of alcohol or drugs may be an issue for all the client groups described earlier but by definition it will particularly be a feature of people served by ACT. The very high prevalence of co-morbidity is increasingly recognised and has a strong impact on the use of other services. For example, a survey in a south London catchment found that 36 per cent of users diagnosed with psychosis also misused drugs or alcohol. Their admission rates were almost doubled in comparison with users diagnosed as psychotic in the absence of substance misuse (Menezes *et al.*, 1996). A similar prevalence rate was found among people with first-episode psychosis in Nottingham (Cantwell *et al.*, 1999). This study also found evidence of an increase in substance-related psychotic disorders over time.

The increase in substance-related psychotic disorders described above, and the presence of co-morbidity at the first break of psychosis (Cantwell *et al.*, 1999) has lead to a strong imperative to provide integrated treatment that avoids cross referrals between agencies (Drake and Noordsy, 1994; Lehman and Dixon, 1995; Weaver *et al.*, 1999). There is a need for active, early intervention to impact on the user's future psychiatric career, and avoidance of sterile debate about whether mental disorder or substance misuse is the 'primary' problem for intervention. Gournay *et al.* (1997), in reviewing integrated models, observed that the outcome is significantly better among co-morbid substance misusers who are engaged before they become alcohol or drug dependent. Improved integration may also serve to ensure that dependent and non-dependent users are differentiated at assessment. Many of the key principles of substance misuse work, such as a focus on motivation and the need to match level of engagement with the mode of provision supplied (Rollnick and Miller, 1995) have invaluable application within mainstream mental health services, particularly as they increasingly focus on the younger, new long-term population with higher expectations of community integration and self-determination.

The development of such integrated provision is now advocated as Government policy (Department of Health, 2002c) and presents a significant challenge, given the UK tradition of separate services for substance misusers. It also clearly has significant training implications, not least for the psychiatrists who are likely to have a key role in determining care pathways and service responses (Day *et al.*, 1999). However, if ACT is to be developed in a comprehensive fashion that avoids the traditional border disputes that characterise work with this client group there may not be a better opportunity to address the issue.

Implementation in urban areas

Onyett *et al.* (1994) found that urban teams had a significantly higher proportion of people with severe and long-term mental health problems on the team's caseload (63 per cent), compared with both mixed/suburban (54 per cent) and rural teams (47 per cent). This reflects both the lower prevalence of severe mental health problems in rural environments and the associated pressure for services to be less specialised in developing their response. Urban environments often have particular problems because of transient populations, social deprivation and poor inter-agency working. In this context, primary care services may make excessive use of accident and emergency departments, direct referrals to the police or compulsory admissions in crisis. This can further disadvantage already disadvantaged groups. Also, while the majority of the population are registered with GPs, many are not, particularly in areas with mobile or transient populations. Some primary health care teams have developed novel forms of promoting access to people who are homeless, or living in insecure accommodation, who may find it difficult to register with a GP. An important principle is often to locate mental health service provision alongside services that particular client groups would access for other reasons. A good example of this is the early intervention service in Plymouth, which is run within the Youth Enquiry Service, a street-level organisation looking after the needs of young people within the Plymouth area.

The development of intensive community services such as ACT has arisen largely to address problems of achieving effective access for people who are difficult to involve effectively in mental health services. Most of the research on these services has been done in urban environments and so should be more easily applicable. Rural environments have been comparatively neglected by the research community and so are given special attention below.

Implementation in rural areas

Rural environments vary considerable and not all the issues identified here will apply. They are drawn from the literature (for example, McDonel *et al.*, 1997; Onyett *et al.*, 1994, 1997; Sherlock, 1994) and my own consultancy work.

Problems accessing services

A number of factors contribute to problems of access in rural communities. There is a reported heightened fear of lack of confidentiality and gossip made worse by a culture of stoicism and conservative values. This varies widely and there are, for example, a significant number of people pursuing 'alternative' life-styles in rural communities. Overall, however, the research suggests that heightened stigma and fear of exposure creates delays in seeking help, particularly among men who are at risk of depression (Sherlock, 1994).

Difficulties with transport among dispersed rural communities create problems accessing services and discontinuity of care. For example, rural teams are more likely to transfer all responsibility for planning and providing care to in-patient staff when people are admitted (Onyett *et al.*, 1994). Transport difficulties are exacerbated by the increased poverty and unemployment often found in rural communities. One implication is that teams as a whole tend to be less specialised with more services provided on site.

Rural teams are less likely to offer access out of hours or at weekends, or crisis services (Onyett *et al.*, 1994). Rural teams need to build on the most accessible, least stigmatising first point of contact for individuals, whether it is a statutory or non-statutory provider. In many cases this will be primary care. Close collaboration between GPs and mental health services has been shown to improve early detection and treatment of psychotic episodes in rural environments and improved outcomes for service users (Falloon *et al.*, 1990). The use of case registers and protocols may be particularly helpful in ensuring that people with long-term mental health problems are not neglected on GP practice lists.

Pressure to be generalists leading to reduced teamworking

Rural teams tend to have greater shortages of qualified staff but a lower turnover (Onyett *et al.*, 1994). Although this may be an advantage with respect to continuity of care, smaller teams combined with a lack of other local services creates a pressure for rural staff to be generalists dealing with a wide range of clinical problems. This can result in less collaboration and teamworking. The CMHT survey (*ibid*) found that compared to urban and mixed/suburban teams, rural staff were less likely to pool referrals, each discipline was more likely to keep separate records, and teams were less likely to have team managers or coordinators. Obscure team roles, poor targeting, lack of specialised staff or services, weak operational management and under-developed user involvement were problems of implementation that were amplified in rural settings. Similarly, McDonel *et al.* (1997), looking at the implementation of ACT in a rural environments in the USA, found that there were no team meetings for organising and prioritising work, and no clear planning to reduce the problems of travel time. Staff interpreted teamworking as an imperative to visit in pairs rather than through independent but coordinated visits.

Issues involved in implementing ACT

Implementing assertive outreach as a function of rural CMHTs, rather than as the role of separate teams, is attractive where there are unlikely to be sufficient people with severe and long-term mental health problems who could be served within a small enough catchment to make a single dedicated team operational. McDonel *et al.* (1997) found that with poor integration of ACT staff with the local CMHT, ACT staff lacked organisational support. They also had inadequate contact with other disciplines such as psychiatrists and psychologists. This meant that the ACT service was unable to integrate efforts aimed at addressing health, social care and training and development needs. The clinical aspects of their work became most neglected. However, if the ACT function is to be built into existing teams it is important that those teams are effective, otherwise team membership is likely to be an impairment for ACT workers. McDonel *et al.* (1997) found that the non-ACT staff had negative attitudes toward users' recovery which, given their higher status, created difficulties for the ACT service. This was exacerbated by the supervisors of ACT staff lacking the training and expertise to support work with people with severe and enduring mental health problems. As a result, the authors noted high staff turnover, which runs counter to the better retention usually observed in rural catchments.

Care coordinators incorporating a proportion of ACT users on their caseload may provide better integration and cover. This is likely to be effective where those care coordinators already have caseloads dedicated to people with severe and long-term mental health problems. Where they are operating more generically, there is a danger that those people with severe mental health problems will be neglected unless there is strong multidisciplinary review, peer support and management. If the ACT workers are not the care coordinators, they will need to establish strong links with them at both individual and agency level in order to ensure that the ACT staff are able to operate with adequate autonomy and authority.

It will also be helpful if the ACT workers can achieve a positive identification for themselves as a sub-team for the purposes of team support, carrying a team ideology concerning ACT work, and effective management.

A tendency towards reducing intensity in practice

McDonel *et al.* (1997) observed that the rural ACT team tended to have fewer visits taking place, and less often in users' homes. The CMHT survey also revealed that rural teams saw users least often (Onyett *et al.*, 1994). As with the implementation of ACT in other contexts, there needs to be special measures to ensure adequate intensity of service. This will include effective caseload management, and support from managers, peers and mentors/supervisors.

Poor staff morale

Onyett *et al.* (1997) found that rural team members had the lowest job satisfaction and highest burnout. There was particular dissatisfaction with the design of the organisation and work relationships, and particularly low team-role clarity and identification with the team. Aside from the reduced teamworking above, which in itself impairs morale (Borrill *et al.*, 2000), the literature also reveals reduced access to opportunities for continuing professional development and a risk of professional isolation. Some rural environments will suffer from the lack of a local university. This may lead to slower dissemination and acceptance of new approaches to care and treatment among staff which will be made worse where reduced staff numbers create poor access to clinical supervision. It is particularly important that managers understand the ACT model and support maintained intensity. McDonel *et al.* (1997) found that managers were actively encouraging staff to stop home visiting in order to save money.

There is clearly a particularly high imperative to support rural staff through team-based training, ideally spanning intensive community services and other CMHTs so that a mutual appreciation and understanding of each other's roles is achieved. In order to maintain fidelity to intensive community treatments, the leadership and management of teams requires committed long-term support.

Despite these challenges, there are examples of successful intensive community treatment in rural environments. Santos *et al.* (1993) described an ACT team that achieved a 79 per cent decrease in hospital bed days, 64 per cent decrease in the number of admissions per year, 75 per cent decrease in the average length of stay and a 52 per cent decrease in the estimated costs of care. Lachance and Santos (1995) identified those elements of ACT that must be retained in order to achieve effective outcomes as 24-hour availability (albeit by phone after hours, with increased training for A&E staff, families and carers); small, stable caseloads; ongoing and continuous services; home visiting; and *in vivo* rehabilitation services. Some corroboration of this was offered by McDonel *et al.* (1997) comparing the rural implementation of ACT to controls. They found at 24 months that ACT users had fewer symptoms, increased quality of life, increased level of functioning, and increased user satisfaction. However, these differences were not apparent within the first year and these benefits were only achieved when specific problems of implementation were addressed. These problems included the poor integration with the CMHT, poor management and supervision, and lack of training.

Conclusion

Teams will not be effective unless those developing the team are clear about their client group and their needs, and how the team can work most effectively with other local agencies. Different contexts and different client groups provide particular challenges. When equipped with a good understanding of the local context, those responsible for team design and development are better able to tackle the issues that face all teams aiming to serve people with complex needs. The next chapter looks at those team-wide issues before going on to explore individual practice within teams in Chapter 6.

CHAPTER 5

Designing Teams to Respond to Complex Needs

This chapter continues the work of Chapter 4 in exploring features of teams that are effective in working with people with complex health and social care needs. Having identified broad issues about how to respond to need, and how to access the service, it looks at the importance of the range of services offered, where the team is based, team composition, the demands of teamworking on staff, and the team's history.

The range of services offered

If a key role of CMHTs is to provide or coordinate access to a range of services through care coordination, then clearly there is a need to consider the range of services available.

Studies of CMHTs have found psychotherapy and counselling to be the most ubiquitous services offered by the team (for example, Onyett *et al.*, 1994, 1995; Patmore and Weaver, 1991a; Sayce *et al.*, 1991). This has been framed as part of the team's failure to serve people with severe and long-term mental health problems, implying that psychotherapy and counselling is inappropriate for people with the most severe health and social care needs. This is an unfortunate inference, particularly given advances in psychological interventions for people diagnosed as psychotic (BPS, 2000). Users are not drawing this conclusion themselves. Increased access to counselling and psychotherapy feature highly among the services sought (Rogers *et al.*, 1993; Shepherd *et al.*, 1994).

Sayce *et al.* (1991), in their survey of CMHCs, were critical of the small number of CMHCs undertaking activities of particular relevance to people with severe and long-term mental health problems such as support for carers, occupational therapy and practical assistance (see Table 1). While it is notable that psychotherapy and counselling remained the most ubiquitous activities in the CMHT survey (Onyett *et al.*, 1994), many more teams were providing these services. Teams providing user access to team members after hours and at weekends, work opportunities, practical 'hands-on' help with day-to-day problems, and assessment of activities of daily living (for example, using money, help with personal hygiene) had a significantly higher percentage of people with severe and long-term mental health problems on their caseloads. Such services closely mirror the priorities identified by users in Chapter 1.

Access to asylum care

Even the most intensive community services encounter users who require a level of support that cannot be provided in the community. The positive impact of intensive services is to reduce reliance on in-patient provision, not to remove the need for it completely. The aim is to be able to use such provision flexibly according to need, and to ensure that the planning of care, and the communications that surround it, continue while the person is admitted.

Evaluations of intensive community treatment have stressed the importance of the CMHT controlling access to in-patient care (Marks *et al.*, 1994). This usually requires sectorisation where beds are linked to a locality served by a community team.

Teams in the CMHT survey were asked to indicate how the team accessed hospital beds. All teams used hospital beds, and most (73 per cent) had direct access to hospital beds via a team member. These teams had significantly more full-time equivalent (FTE) input from psychiatrists and other doctors compared with teams that required referral elsewhere to gain admission. This highlights the importance of achieving adequate psychiatric input to the team in order to ensure flexible access to beds, although a new mental health act may extend admission rights to other team members.

Continuity of care between the in-patient environment and the community is critically important. The care coordination process should ensure that the care planning and implementation process

Table 1 *Comparison of services offered in 1987 and 1993*

1987 survey	*% of CMHCs*	*1993 survey*	*% of CMHTs*
Individual group or family psychotherapy	74	Therapy or counselling for individuals	97
Counselling	73		
Assessment	53	Multidisciplinary assessment – two or more disciplines at the same time	81
		Formal assessments under the 1983 Mental Health Act	79
Social support/skills groups	49	Day care or other occupation	46
Medical treatment	46	Drug treatments (other than depot clinics)	75
		Depot clinics	56
Rehabilitation	31	Services particularly for people with severe and long-term mental health problems	89
Non-specific group work	29	Group therapy	73
Crisis intervention	19	Immediate response to crisis in the situation in which the crisis is happening	71
		Client access to team members after working hours and at weekends	23
Support for carers	17	Support/education for carers	91
		Therapy or counselling for families	68
Occupational therapy	16	Assessment of activities of daily living (for example, using money, personal hygiene, and so on)	89
		Training in activities of daily living	78
Practical assistance	8	Practical 'hands-on' help with day-to-day problems (for example, shopping, transport).	70

continues into the in-patient environment and informs what happens there. Existing supportive relationships should be maintained. It is particularly important that supportive contacts are provided in the week following discharge when people have been found to be particularly vulnerable. Users of intensive community treatment highlight how important it is for the same people to maintain relationships with them through the good times and the bad (Morgan, 1996).

Respondents in the CMHT survey were asked to indicate: 'What usually happens following admission for in-patient care?' with respect to the transfer of responsibilities for planning and providing care. The largest proportion of teams (42 per cent) reported that, although the team continued to provide care on admission, responsibility for planning care was transferred to in-patient staff. The remainder were divided between those teams where responsibility for planning care was retained but most care was provided by in-patient staff (28 per cent) and those where responsibility for both planning and providing care was transferred to in-patient staff (27 per cent). A mere seven teams (2 per cent) reported retaining the major responsibility for planning and providing care during in-patient stays. Although a crude indicator, this data gave some indication of the level and nature of in-reach from community teams into in-patient services.

There were significantly more social workers in teams that retained responsibility for planning care when users were admitted to in-patient care. A causative link is speculative, but it may reflect their particular responsibilities for discharge planning under section 117 of the Mental Health Act (1983). Good practice would suggest that this planning should commence from the point of admission (Department of Health, 1994b) and teams that fully integrate health and social care are clearly better placed to do this.

There remains considerable scope for the further development of 'in-reach' by community staff into in-patient care, thereby promoting the maintenance of relationships and effective communication at admission and discharge. This may take the form of teams whose members work in both in-patient and community settings.

Increasingly, crisis resolution teams will be locating themselves in the pathway from the community to in-patient care with an active role in preventing admissions wherever possible. The evidence would suggest that this should reduce admissions (Joy *et al.*, 2001) but will also have the impact of making the use of in-patient care more targeted towards highly distressed and disturbed individuals who require very high input and quality of care. The quality of this care to-date has not been good and is a national priority for development (SCMH, 1998b). User-led, non-medical alternatives have considerable potential to increase the breadth of options available for asylum care, for example the Nile Centre in Hackney, Highbury Grove in Islington, and Anam Cara in Birmingham.

The team base

The CMHT survey revealed that in the early 1990s most teams were based in community mental health *centres* (CMHCs). Aside from primary care-based teams, CMHCs had the lowest proportions of people with severe and long-term mental health problems. The 'other' located (mainly office-based) teams in Table 2 below were the most focused on people with severe and long-term mental health. Their more successful targeting argues for a team-base where service

Table 2 *Team base location*

Team base location	*Teams in each location (Numbers and as a proportion of the whole sample)*		*Mean proportion of caseload dedicated to people with severe and long-term mental health problems*	
	N	*%*	*mean %*	*sd %*
Community mental health centre	134	44.4	53.0	21.6
In-patient unit or hospital site	43	14.2	64.0	27.3
Day centre or day hospital	28	9.3	57.0	22.4
Community resource centre	25	8.3	59.4	21.7
Primary care	9	3.0	38.0	28.8
Residential	7	2.3	60.9	32.7
Other	26	8.6	66.4	29.1
Not based together	29	9.6	62.9	25.0

users are not seen for clinical work and help is provided in ordinary environments such as the person's home or primary care settings (for example, Burns *et al.*, 1993b; Marks *et al.*, 1994; Merson *et al.*, 1992). As services become more focused on working with users in ordinary environments, their choice of base is likely to be determined by the availability of infrastructure for administration (for example, information technology) and the ease with which it promotes effective communication among key team members (for example, by having health and social care staff located in the same facility) or other key staff such as GPs, housing workers or benefits advisers. It is also likely to promote effective targeting if the team is based in a facility where the identified client group would naturally congregate (for example, the Plymouth early intervention service based with the Youth Enquiry Service, or locating mental health services for homeless people in facilities where they attend for other reasons).

The CMHT in relation to the primary health care team

The primary care-based teams in Table 2 had the smallest proportion of people with severe and long-term mental health problems on their caseloads. One primary care-based team reported a 'conflict for staff between the demands of anxious and unhappy people with overwhelming social and domestic difficulties on the one hand, and the formally ill but often less demanding patients on the other' (Jackson *et al.*, 1993: 377). This same team also found that the team's availability resulted in GPs doing less counselling and had no effect on the GP's ability to detect or manage mental illness (Warner *et al.*, 1993). However, more recent initiatives have shown that it is possible to develop strong joint working with primary care while continuing to focus on priority groups (see Box 2).

Tomson (2000) encapsulated the issue of working with primary care as being concerned with care, communication and capacity. The functions that need to be delivered in primary care include:

- *Developing therapeutic interventions for individuals with a whole range of mental health needs.* This can be delivered by specialists working in primary care setting or members of the primary health care

Box 2 *St. Hilary Brow Group Practice – An example of a primary-care based service that prioritised people with severe mental health problems*

This practice recognised that people with serious mental health problems were not receiving adequate care in the community, resulting in high admission and re-admission rates, and high bed-occupancy rates. There was a lack of an effective needs assessment and no information on people with severe and long-term mental health problems within the practice. By establishing a register of people with severe mental illness (see Kingsland *et al.*, 1999), and basing specialist mental health staff in the practice, they achieved earlier intervention, earlier discharge and better management which eventually eliminated out-patient referrals, radically lowered in-patient admissions, re-admissions, and lengths of stay. They also prescribed less anxiolytic drugs, which freed up resources for developing talking treatments.

Notable features of this initiative are the use of a widely available database to establish the register (Microsoft Access) and the deployment of staff with very specific roles. The community mental health nurse (working one day a week) focused on working with people diagnosed with schizophrenia. The clinical psychologist (working a half day a fortnight) focused on those people with very complex problems that were not responding to help, such as people diagnosed with personality disorders. The occupational therapist (working half a day a week) worked with large numbers of people with anxiety problems through time-limited group sessions. The practice's three counsellors also had their own specialisation. One focused on relationship problems, one on cognitive therapy and another on bereavement. A psychiatrist visits the practice acting in a consultative role. The fact that the service was not 'medically dominated' was cited as important. The service was coordinated by a senior nurse employed by the local trust, who also had a lead role in physical health screening.

team who have received specialist training. Barr (2000) particularly advocates the development of the practice nurse role. Tomson (2000) provides details of the qualities that should be sought among new staff introduced to primary care work. In contrast to earlier judgements, there is also increasing optimism about the therapeutic impact of well-trained counsellors (Mellor-Clarke, 2000).

- *Assessment and triage.* Triage involves specialists working with GPs to ensure that users are directed to the worker with the appropriate skills and experience. For example, in North Birmingham, a consultant psychiatrist and a community mental health nurse (CMHN) based in a GP surgery act as a focus for advice, consultation, assessment, treatment, and production of information and models of best practice. With no extra investment of resources and demand on GP time, this approach aims to promote accessibility to a model of care that is explicitly more socially orientated rather than medical. Its proponents argue that it blurs traditional primary-secondary care distinctions and paves the way for all mental health service provision to be based in general practice, or that it is even more 'primary' in that it promotes direct access to mental health assessments without having to go through the GP.
- *Teamworking and communication,* both with other primary care team members and other agencies.
- *Facilitating systems to support effective care,* such as the creation and implementation of protocols, developing and maintaining self-help resources, and ensuring information systems support registers and audit.
- *Care planning, coordination and review.*
- *Supervision, teaching and professional development.*
- *Mental health promotion and prevention.*

Detailed discussion of these areas is beyond the scope of this book. The National Primary Care Research and Development Centre has provided guidance on good practice in these areas (Gask *et al.*, 2000).

Team size

The median size of teams in the CMHT survey was 9.6 (mean = 11.4, sd = 6.3) in full-time equivalents (FTEs) and 13 (mean = 15, sd = 7.4) in people. There is no available research on the optimal team size for CMHTs, although Borrill *et al.* (2000) noted in their study of CMHTs that effective communication is less likely in teams larger than 12 members. They also noted that innovations carried out by relatively large teams were rated more favourably by independent observers, perhaps because they had a larger pool of ideas to draw upon.

For ACT, Stein and Santos (1998) advocated the deployment of ten core staff serving around 100 users. Similarly, Burns and Guest (1999) advocated teams of people with caseloads of up to 12 people each, but that the whole team should not work with more than between 60 and 100 people. They found that a team size of 13 was too large for ACT in an urban environment because too much time was absorbed in team communication, and all team members were unable to get to know all users. The ideal for ACT is therefore to achieve small focused teams of between 5 to 9 people. Teams smaller than five hands-on workers will find it harder for care coordinators to double-up as co-workers, and are likely to be less able to cope with staff absences (Patmore and Weaver, 1991a). Small focused teams will need to rely heavily on good links with other services to achieve the breadth of services required by service users. See Department of Health (2001a) for guidance on team size for other service configurations.

Team composition

People with long-term difficulties are only likely to show improvements in health or social functioning when they have access to relevant therapeutic input and practical assistance (for example, Brooker *et al.*, 1994; Ford *et al.*, 1995). Workforce planning in mental health increasingly emphasises the knowledge, skills, experience and attitudes needed within a team for effective working, rather than a particular combination of traditional disciplines. Weaver and Patmore (1990) described a logical argument used by a team that was successful in serving people with severe and long-term mental health problems. This was that (a) the project existed to serve people with complex and long-term needs, (b) such people therefore require a comprehensive and coordinated service, and (c) a comprehensive service requires multiple inputs from skilled specialists. Watts and Bennett (1983) also highlight the advantages of a team that encompasses a cross-section of ages, sexes, ethnic backgrounds, social classes and educational attainment in order to inform their work with a similarly diverse client group. The importance of teams that comprise a range of skills has also been highlighted by outcome studies. Muijen *et al.* (1994) found comparatively poor outcomes from a uni-disciplinary CMHN team even when they were providing intensive support. Disappointing outcome evaluations of the CPA have also stressed the need for multidisciplinary input (Franklin *et al.*, 1987; Marshall *et al.*, 1995; Tyrer *et al.*, 1995).

Changing the skill mix in teams presents a challenge. Table 3 compares the full-time equivalent input of each of the disciplines across the surveys undertaken in 1987 (Sayce *et al.*, 1991), 1993 (the CMHT survey – Onyett *et al.*, 1994) and 1995 (Huxley, 1996). It reveals remarkable continuity in the input provided by nurses and social workers as the core of CMHTs. It is important when interpreting the 1987 data to note that the authors did not differentiate CMHNs from other nursing staff, and also conflated consultant psychiatrists

Table 3 *Mean full-time equivalents of disciplines in 1987, 1993 and 1995*

Discipline	*Survey*		
	1987	*1993*	*1995*
Community mental health nurses	3.6*	3.55	3.50
Social workers	1.5	1.53	1.20
Administrative staff (including receptionists)	1.3	1.32	1.10
Nurses (other than CMHNs)	*	1.01	0.50
Occupational therapists	0.9	0.75	0.90
Generic mental health workers	0.2	0.65	0.69
Consultant psychiatrists	1.2*	0.62	0.75
Doctors (other than consultants)	*	0.59	0.51
Clinical psychologists	0.9	0.50	0.47
Others	0.7	0.36	0.18
Volunteer staff	*	0.07	0.04

Note: * When interpreting the 1987 data, it is important to note that the authors did not differentiate CMHNs from other nursing staff, and also conflated consultant psychiatrists and other doctors within the category 'psychiatrists'.

and other doctors within the category 'psychiatrists'. If the consultant and other doctor categories of the 1993 data are summed they approximate to the FTE staffing levels for psychiatrists found by Sayce *et al.* (1991) in 1987. The only discernible trends in the CMHT workforce are therefore an increase in the numbers of generic mental health workers or community support staff over time and a decline in the input of clinical psychologists.

Patmore and Weaver (1991a, b) applauded the deployment of non-professionally affiliated staff, directly managed by professionally qualified staff. This provided high levels of contact and considerable support with activities of daily living such as housework, shopping and leisure activities. These activities also usually occurred in ordinary environments. Deploying staff without professional backgrounds may help to bridge cultural gaps between providers and community members, and free up professional time for other needed services (Murray *et al.*, 1997). With adequate supervision, non-professionally affiliated staff have been found to deliver services at least as effectively as professionals (Christensen and Jacobson, 1994; Faust and Zlotnick, 1995), although professional input may be required to achieve lasting benefit from more sophisticated psychological interventions such as group cognitive-behaviour therapy (Bright *et al.*, 1999). Murray *et al.* (1997) found that compared with professional staff, community support workers were more likely to be active in those areas of provision that users rated as most important. This included emotional support, assistance with housing, informal day-care, household tasks, and finance. Users often felt that, as a result, these workers had been instrumental in keeping them out of hospital. Community support workers were also rated by users as being significantly more available, more understanding of their needs, and more honest and open when compared with professional staff. The community support workers spent more time than professional staff in direct contact with service users.

In the USA, there is a long-standing and positively evaluated tradition of case management services employing current or ex-service users in case management roles (Nikkel *et al.*, 1992; Sherman and Porter, 1991; Williams *et al.*, 1994). Randomised trials find them to be as effective as case managers as non-service users, (Solomon, and Draine, 1995b). In the UK, Perkins *et al.* (1997) reported positive outcomes associated with employing users as CMHT staff, including their taking less time off sick that non-users. The Government's

Post-NSF Workforce Action Team (Department of Health, 2001d) advocated the greater deployment of 'Support, Time and Recovery' workers, giving recognition to the enormous role to be played by staff who do not have professional qualifications.

Going beyond individual disciplines and their associated skills, it may also be important to achieve an appropriate mix of personalities within the team. Belbin's (1981) work with over 200 senior management teams is perhaps the most influential work on the effects of personality on group effectiveness. He showed that successful and unsuccessful teams contain people with different resources and organise themselves in different ways. Effective teams were shown to require a diversity of roles within teams (for example, 'shaper', 'plant', 'completer-finisher', 'resource investigator', and 'teamworker'). He argued that problems arise with groups that do not have the appropriate mix of resources. For example, Belbin (1981) described 'Apollo' teams comprising clever and creative people. Although they were sometimes very effective their average level of performance was very poor. The members were intelligent individuals who were competitive and were not motivated to work as a team. Arguably, this group perhaps comes closest to the typical composition of a CMHT.

In critiquing Belbin's work, Hosking and Morley (1991) highlighted that a focus on personal characteristics fails to take into account the fact that organising is an interpersonal activity, and individual action is constrained, guided, regulated and supported by the context in which it occurs. Understanding organising requires models that examine what behaviours and attitudes are required in which situations to address particular tasks. Such comprehensive theoretical models have still to be developed for CMHTs, and are best pursued through looking at very specific types of teams and the tasks that they have to achieve. At this stage, it is important to consider that in terms of team composition, form will need to follow function. For example, if easy access to hospital beds is important then the increased input from psychiatrists is likely to be important. The overriding imperative to achieve good quality relationships with users argues for effective values-based training, a workforce that reflects the cultural diversity of local residents, and the importance of professionally non-affiliated staff and service users as employees. The staff attitudes, knowledge, skills and experience that make a good care coordinator will be further explored in Chapter 6.

The fragmentation within teams

The CMHT survey found that teams with lower levels of part-time working had significantly larger proportions of people with severe and long-term mental health problems on their caseloads. The mean FTE commitment across disciplines was around four days per week. Only nurses, social workers, occupational therapists and generic mental health workers or support workers offered this average level of time commitment to teams. For most other disciplines their input was more fragmented. Consultant psychiatrists, clinical psychologists and non-consultant doctors offered only a very part-time input to CMHTs. For example, teams had an average of one consultant per team but this represented only 0.62 FTE.

A more positive picture of team fragmentation emerges from Borrill *et al.*'s (2000) sample of 1443 staff in 113 CMHTs for their study of the effectiveness of health care teams. They found that 78 per cent of their sample were full-time workers, and 12 per cent of CMHTs sampled were comprised solely of full-time workers. Part-time practitioners tended to be psychiatrists, psychologists and occupational therapists. A sub-sample of 33 teams revealed an association between low part-time working and external ratings of effectiveness.

There is a need for committed whole-time working within CMHTs if they are to provide effective relationships over long periods with people with severe and long-term mental health problems. This again argues for comparatively small teams of five to nine staff (or up to a dozen staff if the team is not providing intensive community treatment) where those staff have a high full-time commitment to the team.

There may be a number of barriers to achieving this, not least the ambivalence among some professionals towards CMHTs, including the more recent service models. CMHTs have always invoked anxiety in the professional journals about loss of autonomy, unqualified role blurring, isolation from professional peers, diminution of clinical skill, and a devaluing of one's unique contribution as a trained professional. Psychologists and psychiatrists have been particularly vocal concerning the implications of multidisciplinary team working and stronger operational management (for example, Anciano and Kirkpatrick, 1990; Galvin and McCarthy, 1994; Leong, 1982; Paxton, 1995).

It is important for team membership to be socially valued by potential recruits, which in turn requires that teams are adequately resourced and supported by good quality training, leadership and management. It also essential however, that the cultural demands of teamworking are understood.

The cultural demands of teamworking among team members

Lang (1982) pointed out that: 'The concept of community mental health calls for an unlearning of traditional patterns of professional interaction and of traditional conceptions of the nature of psychiatric disorders. Mental health workers are asked to break free of the historically grounded frameworks which have shaped their ideas, their respective professional identities, and the habits of their individual and collective work' (160). This breaking free has still to occur. This may be partly attributable to the continued absence of a prevailing ideology of care, tensions between care and control, ambivalence about teamworking, and problems inherent in the ways in which mental health practitioners are trained.

The demands of collective working and group membership and the ways in which this is influenced by existing views of oneself as a professional practitioner are central to the sense of self-worth that staff derive from team membership. As Hayes (1993) points out, 'in-groups and out-groups are endemic in organisational life'. The concentration of practitioners into teams places them in a special dilemma. They become members of at least two groups: their discipline and the team.

Foster (1998) suggested that some staff uprooted from the host cultures of their employing organisations, and in some cases moved from hospital to community care, adopt a fight or flight response to defend against the anxiety of working with disturbed people in community settings. The in-group-out-group identifications described below provide a rich vein of conflict that provide plenty of fighting opportunities. She describes two typical modes of flight. The first involves reverting to old tried-and-tested methods of working, keeping your head down and getting on with working with users in the way one has always done. The other is to avoid struggling with difference by behaving as if everybody in the team was the same. This results in 'staff functioning at the lowest common denominator of sameness' (Foster, 1998: 137). This sacrifices expertise for cosiness and denies the user the benefits of the differences and choices inherent in properly functioning multidisciplinary teams.

Resolving team and professional identity

Social identification is a construct that examines the experience of belonging to groups, and the tensions this creates. Identification bears directly on an individual's self-concept. It involves the adoption of the norms, values and behaviours of groups, and the prestige associated with the group will directly affect the individual's self-esteem. This perhaps explains much of the passion that is engendered when discussing the impact of group membership for practitioners. (You need only note the titles of papers by Anciano and Kirkpatrick, 1990; Paxton, 1995).

Turner (1982) viewed self-concept as comprising personal identity and social identity. The former is represented in personal or idiosyncratic references (for example, 'I am a moody person'). Social identity is achieved through defining oneself as a member of a group (for example, 'I am a clinical psychologist', 'I am a member of the Early Intervention Service', 'I am a feminist'). The respective strength of personal and social identification may vary with the situation. For example, as part of a football crowd, loss of personal identity may accompany an increase in social identity with concomitant changes in behaviour.

Social identity theory (Tajfel and Turner, 1979) suggests that people derive a sense of social identity through group membership and inter-group comparisons. Group membership also influences social processes such as stereotyping – the tendency to see members of other groups as tending towards uniformity (for example, 'Psychiatrists have difficulty with intense interpersonal relationships', 'All social workers are woolly liberals'); and the tendency to see oneself as relatively interchangeable with others in the same group (for example, 'We see diagnosis as important in this team'). West and Hennessy (1999) found that strong identification with work groups was related to high levels of in-group favouritism among the staff of an NHS community trust.

Social identity theory generates specific predictions relevant to CMHTs. Multidisciplinary teams are social groups including members of other social groups. For example, a psychiatrist is both a member of the medical profession and a member of the team. The early social psychological literature would predict that clear superordinate goals would promote more positive feelings between these two groups (for example, Sherif, 1966). It could therefore be predicted, for example, that there would be less role conflict for practitioners within teams where the team goals were clear. However, social identity theory also illuminates why this does not always work in practice, and bears upon the conflicts over professional and operational management described later. Where clear group goals threaten identification with another more socially valued group, the predicted positive feelings towards the group may not result. Experimental studies that ask college students to engage in cooperative tasks for real rewards lend support to this prediction. Studies by Brown and Wade (1987) and Deschamps and Brown (1983) brought groups together in order to achieve superordinate goals while varying the similarity of the group's tasks in achieving those goals. They observed that positive feelings towards other groups were related to the distinctiveness of the task that the in-group was being asked to perform. Where the tasks of different groups were similar or not clearly defined, hostility towards those groups was greater. Relating this to CMHTs, it would be predicted that superordinate goals may not produce greater team identification, or positive feelings towards other disciplines if the individual's own role in achieving those goals is ambiguous or undifferentiated from the roles of others. This will constitute a threat to their distinct professional identity within the team and, in this context, professional identification may compete with team identification producing severe role conflict.

Concern over role blurring in teams can also be considered as a fear that the distinctiveness of a socially-valued professional group will be undermined, and with it a major and valued part of the team member's self concept. This appears to describe the situation in many mental health teams where clear team goals are identified with strong operational management, which can conflict with an autonomous practitioner role and the professional identity that goes with it.

So how would we get identification with the team and identification with one's discipline or profession to coexist? Social identity theory would predict that this occurs where the practitioner has a clear and valued role in achieving team goals. Deschamps and Brown (1983: 194) concluded that 'policies aimed at integrating rival groups should endeavour to preserve or even enhance the social identities of their members by allowing each group some recognisable part in any joint activity'. The social psychology of groups would therefore suggest that the best outcomes will result when practitioners are able to identify both with the team and their own profession. This is more likely to occur when they are clear about the aims of the team *and* their own personal role as a practitioner. There is therefore a need for clarity regarding each professional group's respective contribution towards the achievement of team objectives. If true, this would suggest that it might not be helpful to break down professional identity in the interests of a less distinctive generic mental health worker role unless that role offered reduced role ambiguity. This was exactly the conclusion reached by a major review of the future role and training of mental health staff (SCMH, 1997). While there was a need to develop shared training to address ideological issues, there was also a need to celebrate the differences between disciplines and the varied contributions that they brought to the team.

It is important, however, to note that the achievement of a clear role within a team need not necessarily be linked to a clear role for your discipline. For example, in the description of the St. Hilary Brow Group Practice above, each *individual* with the team had a very clear role that went beyond their identification as a member of a particular discipline (for example, counsellor).

Delineating a team to identify with

Social identification also requires that a team can be recognised and differentiated from other groups, and that there are cues for team membership. It may therefore be influenced by the clarity of team boundaries, and the salience of team features such as operational policies, the employment of team managers, and opportunities for the team to meet as a unit.

Social identification will also be influenced by the social constructions of what team membership means, as created by its members or its constituent groups. For some, team membership may be linked to the idea that everybody in the team must have equal status and perform essentially the same job (as exemplified in radical interpretations of the 'team approach' described earlier). If this were the case, it would be easy to see why higher status practitioners may experience greater role conflict and disenchantment with the prospect of teamworking. Similarly, team identification may be influenced by existing beliefs about the nature of teams. If practitioners labour under the misapprehension that effective teams never disagree or always reach some agreement at the end of the decision-making process, then their disaffection with the reality of teamworking may be all the greater.

Team identification in relation to leadership, management and change processes

Albert and Whetten (1985) distinguished between 'ideographic' organisations where staff identify specifically with the sub-unit in which they work and 'holographic' organisations where staff share a common identity across the sub-units. More cooperation and less conflict would be predicted in the latter, while ideographic organisations require inter-group comparisons to be made in order for team members to identify positive differences in their own group. A good example is the splitting and demonising that can go on between community and in-patient staff in mental health. Most organisations, including the community trust studied by West and Hennessy (1999) are ideographic in nature, and so conflict can be predicted.

Hayes (1993) illustrates some of the processes employed by individuals to enhance their positive identification with certain in-groups. These include redefining the importance of their group (for example, 'We may not count for much but they could not run the place without us'), distancing oneself from the devalued group (for example, 'Yes I am a psychiatrist but I don't espouse the medical model') or actually ceasing membership (for example, when a nurse reconstrues her or himself as a particular type of therapist). Hayes particularly emphasises the tendency to redefine the importance of the group by disparaging superiors. This provides the seedbed for counter-cultures. Since the immediate work group is the main source of socialisation for newcomers the denigration of management can become self-perpetuating. As management is denigrated, so too is the team because of its inevitable dependence on management for resources and strategic leadership. Thus devalued, the need to denigrate management may become heightened and a vicious circle is created. This may partly explain the concern of teams to preserve their autonomy, and the enduringly negative view of managers among many practitioners (for example, Newnes, 1996; Smail, 1989).

Social identification with the team compared with identification with one's own profession may be powerfully influenced by different configurations for team management and operation (Ovretveit, 1993, 1997). For example, joint accountability models wherein the practitioner is accountable to professional line managers for profession-specific concerns, and operational managers for operational concerns may, if the forms of management are adequately differentiated, promote role clarity and the co-existence of professional and team identification. This has not been researched to-date, but this dual accountability model appears to have become more prevalent as a model for team management in the light of field experience. Hayes (1993) notes that good operational and management practices, 'team building' and effective leadership can all be construed as mechanisms for promoting a positive social identity among the work-group.

Change itself may exacerbate conflicts between team and other identifications. As Lang (1982: 165) pointed out: 'The very efforts to develop democratic[1] forms and new treatment orientations ultimately engender pressures for reversion or retreat to more traditional psychiatric orientations'. This may explain some of the energy in the debate within British psychiatry on the merits and demerits of intensive community treatments (for example, Marshall *et al.*, 1999; Pelosi and Jackson, 2000; Sashidharan *et al.*, 1999; Smyth and Hoult, 2000; Thornicroft *et al.*, 1999).

Working with identification issues

So what are the implications for team design and the way in which the team works arising from this discussion of cultural challenge and the importance of social identification? In summary, teams should pay particular attention to:

- The clarity of team aims, and how the roles of team members explicitly address those aims.

- The need to celebrate differences between the roles of team members rather than expecting everybody to do the same thing.
- The importance of a reflective space in which the key issues of teamworking, what it feels like to be a team, and how one's other identifications complement or conflict with team membership can be explored.
- Remaining aware that the team forms part of a system and strong team identification may be fed by and reinforce the denigration of out-groups such as management or other agencies. Maintaining the team's awareness of this tendency may be important, as its level of dependency on other agencies and management is such that denigration is likely to harm team performance in the long run and ultimately becomes self-defeating and denigrating. It also serves to avoid responsibility for change. As Hutchison (personal communication, 2001) has observed through her training work, when a team adopts the posture of saying: 'You don't have to convince us, it's the managers that are the problem' one can be confident that change will be very difficult to achieve.
- The importance of elements that maintain the team's identity such as away days where values and practices are reviewed, an appropriate name for the team that promotes a positive sense of belonging, a 'living' operational policy rather than one that sits on a shelf, and the configuration of management roles that promotes team cohesion and avoids role conflict.

Team history

The way in which a team is established may influence its structure and organisation in a variety of ways. It is, for example, important to consider which services were previously aiming to achieve the functions of the new CMHT, and how the planned and actual role of the CMHT was shaped by the operation of other local services and the demands of key stakeholders such as users, carers and GPs. Patmore and Weaver (1990) caution against CMHT 'blueprints' delivered by planners with little regard to local circumstances and the existing strengths of developed services. An urge toward adopting a fresh start rather than risking contamination by the existing services and their shortcomings was highlighted as problematic in a qualitative evaluation of a Government-funded demonstration project (Charman and Clifford, 1989). Patmore and Weaver (1990: 1512) argued that: '*Fresh starts cannot change the system*'.

There are many anecdotal accounts of new CMHTs encountering considerable hostility at early stages in their development (for example, Onyett, 1998; Witheridge and Dincin, 1985) but it is questionable whether some demonstration projects would ever have been established had they not been created *de novo*. Indeed Ridgely *et al.* (1996) suggested that development from within existing CMHCs was a major factor in failure to implement case management with sufficient fidelity in a major US demonstration project.

Often antagonism arises from peers who are concerned about the effect of service innovation on their working practice, and a fear that the new arrival will devalue the work of existing services. Innovative programmes are often vulnerable to the local political and resource context (Mechanic, 1996) and have difficulty surviving intact beyond the term of their central funding, even when they have demonstrated very positive outcomes (for example, Marks *et al.*, 1994). This argues for a sophisticated and sensitive approach to undertaking local service developments that specifically and explicitly build on current achievements while being guided by users' experiences and the need to address shortcomings in current provision.

Patmore and Weaver (1991a) reported that team composition was shaped by the way the team was formed, and this in turn influenced the extent to which it remained targeted. For example, one team that was successful in targeting people with severe and long-term mental health problems incorporated local CMHNs, their caseloads and depot clinics. Where this did not occur, rivalry between the CMHC and the community mental health nursing service became a barrier to serving people with severe and long-term mental health problems. Clearly, the value of incorporating CMHN caseloads into the team as a means to promoting more effective targeting crucially depends on whether those staff are already working with people with severe and long-term mental health problems. In the case of CMHNs, this is sometimes not the case (Mental Health Nursing Review Team, 1994). Huxley (1996) pointed out that one consequence of including existing users being served by CMHNs within the team's caseload is that it forces the team to be selective about new cases, thereby establishing the practice of targeting from the outset.

Conclusion

In general it can be concluded from this and the previous chapter that teamworking is more likely to be successful where the team (a) has a clear role in a strategic context, particularly regarding who its clients are and the outcomes that it aims to support them in achieving, and (b) is specifically designed to achieve those outcomes.

We saw at the beginning of this book that CMHT aims are diverse and promote the interests of different stakeholders. These tensions are a recurring theme of this book and need to be addressed through effective partnership working at a variety of levels.

Positive relationships between CMHT staff and service users are likely to maximise the possibility that they will remain working together on challenging problems. Such relationships are, in turn, likely to be promoted by the CMHT's allocation of resources to the provision of relevant and sought-after services such as out-of-hours and weekend access, work opportunities, practical assistance with everyday problems, and support with activities of daily living. Teams are increasingly providing such services. Purchasers and senior managers must ensure that an appropriate range of skills is available within or via CMHTs in order that relevant services are available to service users.

Effective relationships between users and staff also require a solid core of full-time commitment to the team, small caseloads and teams that are small enough for at least three team members to get to know each user of the service. As we shall see, however, it does not matter how many people you have working with you if they do not have the right attitudes, knowledge, skills and experience to form effective relationships with users.

Note

1 In fact democracy is unlikely to be helpful in a team context. This is returned to in Chapter 7.

CHAPTER 6

Individual Practice in Teams

Organisational changes count for nothing unless they make a difference in terms of what the service user experiences face-to-face and day-to-day. This chapter focuses on the vehicle for the delivery of interventions with service users: the care coordinating role within CMHTs. It examines those aspects of the role that are generic and required of anyone working in a team serving people with complex health and social care needs. It does not include the evidence-based psychological and pharmacological interventions that are required to achieve specific outcomes for service users, but does explore issues concerning how they are integrated into the care coordinator role.

A recurring theme concerning the effective delivery of both psychological and biological interventions is the importance of achieving effective working relationships with users. This chapter therefore focuses on key aspects of that relationship, and particularly how power is exercised.

The care coordinator role

The CPA guidance on 'Effective care coordination in mental health services' (NHSE/SS1, 1999) described practice within multidisciplinary teams that integrates the work of a range of practitioners and agencies while providing care that is tailored to the needs of individual users. It stressed that care coordination is a 'framework of care regardless of setting' and that the care coordinator should have the authority to coordinate the delivery of the care plan across agencies. The role therefore goes beyond the role of a keyworker within any one provider agency. The care coordinator needs to work with families and other natural supports, as well as liaising with other agencies such as employers, housing providers, primary care, in-patient facilities, education providers, leisure services, the Benefits Agency and criminal justice agencies. The role should also include 'in-reach' into in-patient settings and prisons. Indeed, the multi-agency nature of the work is such that the guidance states that: 'No one service or agency is central [to the system of relevant agencies involved]. Service users themselves provide the focal point for care planning and delivery' (3). The effective care coordinator is therefore much more than a clinician. They are also active in helping users achieve or maintain citizenship and social inclusion. A summary of the role is given below in Box 3.

Box 3 *The care coordination role in summary*

- Using clinical and personal skills to work collaboratively with users and maintain close and regular contact with them. This should include the involvement of the user's relevant networks as part of the working team for that client.
- Carrying out core assessments, including assessments of risk.
- Ensuring that other team members, or other specialists, contribute to a more comprehensive assessment as required.
- Leading care planning, including planning for the most appropriate action to be taken by all parties in crisis, and contingency planning for situations where, at short notice, the care coordinator is not available or other parts of the care plan cannot be implemented.
- Acting as a consistent point of contact for users, carers and others involved.
- Ensuring that the user is registered with a GP and working in close contact with the primary health care team and other involved professionals.
- Maintaining awareness of relevant resources, and providing information or referrals as appropriate.
- Achieving appropriate input from other statutory and independent providers. This may include the use of a devolved (preferably pooled joint health and social services) budget.
- Monitoring the outcome of provision and feeding this back to team reviews. This will require regular and long-term contact with the client.

- Collecting and maintaining information from everyone involved for continued monitoring and review.
- Presenting this information coherently at clinical review meetings and to the parties involved within the agreed bounds of confidentiality.
- Ensuring that the views of people involved within and beyond the team are represented at clinical review meetings, particularly those of users and the people close to them.
- Ensuring continuity of care by assertively collaborating with staff of other agencies (for example, in-patient staff), ensuring that information is transferred, and that users are introduced to new care coordinators when such transitions take place. This should happen long before the care coordinator ceases their involvement.

Studies of the implementation of care coordination (for example, Ward *et al.*, 1999) underline the consensus among practitioners on the need to embed the role within a team process. Multidisciplinary teams are needed to support the care coordination process in that implementation requires:

- A single point of access for health and social care assessments.
- A unified health and social care assessment process, including common and agreed risk assessment and management processes as part of a single operational policy.
- Effective coordination of the input of each agency in the system providing health and social care.
- Access through a single process to the support and resources of health and social care.
- Shared information systems.
- Joint training across health and social care staff. This training should be team based.

What makes a good care coordinator?

In recruiting to a well-established and successful case management service in California, Williams *et al.* (1994) stressed the merits of focusing on attitudes and interpersonal abilities rather than educational level. They emphasised the importance of optimism about the potential for service users to change. People who were patronising towards users, had difficulty working with a user-driven philosophy of care, and were reluctant to help with necessary, but less glamorous activities, or to be available for occasional weekends or evenings were specifically avoided.

The SCMH (2000b) identified the 'capabilities' that mental health practitioners should have in working to implement the NSF. This analysis was based upon the systematic collection and analysis of expert opinion, and, for CMHTs, it particularly highlighted the importance of responding flexibly to changing user need, developing effective partnerships with users and carers, care planning coordination and review, positive risk-taking, applying knowledge of relevant legislation, and effectively and faithfully implementing treatment strategies.

Other capabilities are likely to bear on the practitioners skills in being able to work effectively with people with challenging difficulties such as 'difficult to treat' psychosis. For this client group, Kuipers (1996) stressed the importance of people who were able to listen to users, give importance to their views of their predicament, establish collaborative relationships, empathise with their distress, and normalise 'even the most bizarre personal experiences' (47). Staff need to be prepared to be persistent, recognising that it may take up to six months to developing a therapeutic alliance. They also need to be able to focus on at least one aspect of the user, which can be viewed positively and focused on, regardless of disturbed or challenging behaviour. It is also important that staff are able to make use of the team, for example, by allowing time for ventilation of staff anger and frustration while acknowledging and rewarding successful behaviour.

Towards an integrative ideology

Norman and Peck (1999) study of CMHTs found that an adherence to uni-professional cultures was bolstered by the absence of an alternative strong and shared philosophy of community mental health services. Since then there has been a remarkable convergence from a range of stakeholder on the 'recovery' approach as an integrative ideology for mental health services (Carling and Allott, 2000). It appears to have the strength of not coming from any one identifiable source but rather representing the fruition of thinking and research of a variety of people on a number of fronts. It bears a striking resemblance to the 'strengths' approach to case management (Rapp and Wintersteen, 1989) that underpinned the training, evaluation and publishing output of key agencies in the UK mental health field such as the Sainsbury Centre for Mental Health. The strengths model is founded on six general principles that are well reflected in the care coordination guidance:

1 *Focus on individual strengths rather than pathology.* The guidance stresses that: 'Recognising, reinforcing and promoting service user strengths at an individual, family and social level should be an explicit aspect of the care plan' (24).
2 *Interventions are based on the principle of user self-determination.* The guidance refers to the need for 'positive risk taking' (21) and the need for users to be fully informed about the CPA process and have copies of the care plan.
3 *Assertive outreach is the preferred mode of intervention.*
4 *People with long-term and severe mental health problems can continue to learn, grow and change and can be assisted to do so.* The guidance states that: 'Care plans should focus on users' strengths and seek to promote their recovery', and that: 'Care plans should recognise the diverse needs of service users, reflecting their cultural and ethnic background as well as their gender and sexuality, and should include action and outcomes in all the aspects of an individual's life where support is required, for example, psychological, physical and social functioning' (24).
5 *Resource acquisition goes beyond traditional mental health services and actively mobilises resources for the entire community.* The community is defined as a resource and not as an obstacle. The guidance stresses the need for the integration of the inputs of a range of agencies, including those that should be accessible to anyone in a local community. This should be reflected in care planning and reviews.
6 *The care coordinator–user relationship is primary and essential.* The guidance stresses that the care plan should include 'who the user is most responsive to' and that the care coordinator 'can understand and respond to the specific needs of the service user that may relate to their cultural or ethnic background' (22).

The guidance goes on to stress the importance of involving carers in line with the subsequent NSF requirement that carers have their own assessment of their caring, physical and mental health needs, and their own written care plan for implementation.

The recovery approach goes beyond the strengths model in that it places a greater emphasis on individuals finding personal meaning in the experience of carrying a diagnosis, and on their developing an 'other than disabled' identity (Carling and Allott, 2000). Recovery is not about cure. It is about recovering valued roles. Recovery is the active, ongoing individual process through which an individual is enabled to assume responsibility for his or her life. It is about developing specific strategies to deal with symptoms and dealing with the secondary impacts of the disability, including stigma and discrimination.

The centrality of effective relationships between users and staff

Nearly a generation ago Intagliata (1982: 660) stated that the, 'most influential aspect of the case management process is the quality of personal commitment that the case managers develop towards their clients'. What is significant is the way in which this key ideological strand has endured and is now supported by a body of research evidence and clinical experience.

If we want users to work effectively with staff then clearly their satisfaction with services is a very significant outcome. British research on case management has stressed the importance of effective relationships, particularly when case management has been evaluated from a service-user perspective (Beeforth *et al.*, 1994). In the USA McGrew *et al.* (1996) found that users who were asked about the features of ACT they liked best most frequently highlighted the helping relationship. Users highlighting such non-specific aspects of the service reported most satisfaction.

There has been a resurgence in interest in the therapeutic alliance between users and staff as a medium for achieving other positive outcomes. Indeed, one GP argued that compassion, 'fellow feeling that is likely to be expressed', improves the outcome of a variety of health interventions, and advocated for a return to more personal doctoring in primary care (Taylor, 1997). In mental health, working alliances have been shown to be slow and hard to achieve, but reap the benefits of increased adherence to medication regimes, the need for less medication and better outcomes in terms of symptomatology, quality of life and satisfaction with mental health treatment, (Frank, and Gunderson, 1990; Gehrs and Goering, 1994; Solomon *et al.*, 1995). The tendency to over-prescribe antipsychotics to black service users is reduced when efforts to engage users more effectively in treatment were rated more highly (Segal *et al.*, 1996). Effective collaborations may thus serve to attenuate some of the more oppressive aspects of mental health service provision.

Long-standing working alliances are also required to achieve a shared understanding of the subjective *meaning* of phenomena experienced by service users diagnosed as psychotic. Such appreciations are critical to understanding the experience of psychosis from the perspective of service users, and the success of innovative psychological approaches to coping with hallucinations and delusions described below. For example, Links *et al.* (1994) suggested that negative symptoms of schizophrenia, such as apathy and social withdrawal, may represent a psychological reaction to the experience of acute psychosis, rather than just independent symptoms of a disorder. Clearly, they may also represent a reaction to the poverty and chronic employment that so often accompanies long-term mental distress (Warner, 1985). This is unlikely to be appreciated by individual practitioners unless they are supported in taking a holistic view of the user's needs and circumstances.

Effective relationships have also been highlighted as a means of preventing homicides and suicides by service users, (Morgan, 1997; see below). Dvoskin and Steadman (1994) also showed that intensive case management can reduce violence where case managers have low caseloads, 24-hour availability, and the skills that allow them to work with medical, social and legal systems.

Often the success of assertive approaches in producing better outcomes has been attributed to improvements in the users adherence to prescribed medication regimes. However, in practice, the most promising approaches to improving adherence to medication regimes place great emphasis on examining the user's own conceptualisation of their difficulties and their beliefs about the merits and demerits of taking medication (Kemp *et al.*, 1998; Smith *et al.*, 1999b). These approaches stress the user's role as an active agent in their own treatment, and employ techniques such as motivational interviewing (Rollnick and Miller, 1995) to help users resolve their ambivalence about a given course of action in the context of a balanced power-relationship between user and staff.

The centrality of effective relationships between users and staff also becomes clear when taking a long-term view of the development of multidisciplinary practice within teams. Mueser *et al.*'s (1998) review of 75 case management studies described an evolution of models over time. Case management emerged as a means of connecting users to required services as they left declining long-stay psychiatric hospitals and had to navigate complex service systems in the community. The limitations of this brokerage role became evident when experience showed that case managers needed to use a high level of clinical skill in order to engage people in care, assess their needs and then intervene effectively. Leonard Stein, the originator of ACT in the USA argued that brokerage was effective only insofar as there were resources to deploy and agencies with an interest in collaborating (Stein, 1992). As this is usually absent, mental health workers had to be able to act as direct providers. Clinical models of case management emerged, such as the 'strengths' approach described above. These 'clinical' approaches were shaped by experience of implementation, and stressed relationship building, working more holistically with service users, and promotion of users' self-determination.

The challenge of giving people what they want

The principles that individuals are responsible for all decisions affecting their treatment, recovery and quality of life (except where legal powers are invoked) is central to the recovery approach (Carling and Allott, 2000). Working to agendas users set themselves, respecting the importance of those factors that users themselves deem important in describing their situation, and providing a choice of options for making things better are likely to promote more effective involvement in services and thus positive outcomes. Effective working alliances are promoted by providing contact as soon as possible after the need for support has been identified (Axelrod and Wetzler, 1989) and proactively offering practical support and assistance that is valued by users (Repper *et al.*, 1994).

Self-determination

Perkins and Repper (1998) reviewed a number of the most dominant ideologies of care operating within mental health services and conclude that ultimately they need to be judged against the extent to which they promote relationships in which 'the person is facilitated in living the life they wish to lead and achieving their own goals... (24) Client choice and self-determination are at the heart of effective relationships (29)'.

The principle of self-determination should not be confused with the 1980s' culture of individualism (see Chapter 2), or the human potential movement of the 1970s. It is not assumed that anyone can be what they want to be if only they take responsibility for themselves and their lives. This too easily equates with blaming those experiencing enduring social inequalities for their own disadvantages. Self-determination is concerned with maximising the power of users and carers in decision-making concerning their lives, ensuring that they are able to exercise choice wherever possible, and developing a collaborative approach to the core tasks of working together.

Issues of care and control in practice

Self-determination involves users making choices, which in turn requires the power to make decisions that workers consider to be wrong. Perkins and Repper (1998) assert that workers must be prepared to allow users to make such decisions, intervening only where the worker's 'duty of care' to avoid harm to others or the user themselves is invoked.

Hutchison (2000) states: 'Power does not lend itself to be handed out like so much lost property. The aim must be to create environments and situations where users can take power back for themselves by being involved in realistic and meaningful ways', (32). She notes that even where services have made efforts to involve users, their involvement in the planning and delivery of *their own* care and treatment can be very variable. It requires staff to share power in a more immediate and local sense. They may resist change by deeming users incapable or uninterested in contributing to their own care planning. Alternatively, their views may be discounted as being unrealistic or a product of their mental health problem.

Traditionally, within long-standing professionalised work cultures, the professionals 'know best' what is good for users, assess and interpret their reality, and provide the solutions.

To really understand the complex ways in which good-hearted people are socialised into becoming overly controlling, it is helpful to explore some of the excellent ethnographic studies that have undertaken, such as Handy's (1988) qualitative study of psychiatric nursing. The nurses in this study had a strong self-image as professional people who cared about and for users. However, direct observation revealed that their daily activities centred on social control and on the maintenance of ward routines rather than helping users understand, alter, or come to terms with the personal circumstances of their lives. This conflict was partly resolved by conceptualising users as either 'bad' or 'mad'. She states:

> The first group was regarded as abusers of the system who were not only undeserving of help but also prevented other patients from receiving the help they deserved. The second group tended to be conceptualised as lacking control as a result of their illness, which enabled control-orientated activities such as the administration of tranquillising medication to disruptive patients to be re-interpreted as therapeutic activities. This interpretation neatly integrated the social control and treatment concerns of staff in a manner which helped maintain the psychiatric ideology of uncoercive care but often had the unintended consequence of heightening patient's hostility toward the nurses and increasing the necessity for further control-orientated activities.

She goes on to describe how new entrants to this system become socialised into it.

> ...the interview data revealed that many of the younger nurses were aware of, and troubled by discrepancies between their daily routines and therapeutic ideals. This awareness sometimes led to piecemeal attempts to develop more therapeutically-orientated relationships with individual patients. Unfortunately, such innovations often failed because of both the nurses' inexperience and the control-oriented structure of the hospital environment. The repeated failure of their attempts to help often triggered feelings of intense insecurity in staff and frequently led to defensive reactions in which they blamed patients for being unmotivated to change. One solution to these feelings of rejection and incompetence was to adopt a more instrumental and routine-orientated attitude toward work. This strategy was encouraged by more experienced

> staff, partly because it facilitated the smooth maintenance of ward routines, and partly because they saw it as a way of helping younger staff avoid the disappointments of close patient contact. The potential for change which was inherent in the younger nurses' dissatisfaction with their working conditions thus became channelled into the maintenance of existing patterns and facilitated the re-creation of the very system many nurses found unsatisfactory and stress producing (Handy, 1988: 355–6).

The social value attached to the 'smooth maintenance' of routines and administration has increased as organisations become increasingly concerned with minimising risk. Often staff with a talent in this regard are highly valued by managers because they make them feel that greater safety is being achieved by ensuring that things are 'done by the book'. Such individuals often get promoted, for example, to ward or team manager level, and thus become role models for other staff. The need for alternative role models that demonstrate positive risk-taking and an ability to form effective relationships with users becomes crucial.

Honesty in, and about the relationship

Although the relationship between the practitioner and user is of paramount importance, the relationship between them is not 'normal' in the way that one might have a relationship with a friend, relative, or colleague. Professional staff always have power over users and it is important to acknowledge this. Good and professional practice is about recognising this power and avoiding its abuse by making the relationship as collaborative as possible. This involves mental health workers fully appreciating the context they find themselves in as workers and particularly the contradictory imperatives of care and control that operate upon them. This could be achieved through direct education about their responsibilities, group work aimed at consciousness raising, and studying ethnographic research that examines these issues and their implications for the socialisation and practices of staff.

On the basis of this understanding, staff are in a good position to realistically communicate their role to those users where issues of social control may arise. In this way, users are in a better position to exercise choice about how to handle the relationship. In practice, I have found it is rare for users to reject the relationship on the grounds that they may have control taken away from them if they present an actual risk to themselves or others. Instead, it may provide a sense of containment, and only serves to confirm what was known by them already. It also provides the opportunity for collaborative planning concerning crisis and relapse so that the individual has exercised maximum control over those situations where and when they may not be as in control of their lives as they would like to be.

Another domain in which staff may need to be proactive in informing users about the limits inherent in their role concerns confidentiality. While there is a duty of confidentiality on all staff, there is also a responsibility to seek and to relay relevant information to others on a need-to-know basis. Service users should know with whom information about them will or might be shared, what is being recorded and how, and their rights of access to the information. Users should consent to these arrangements, and their wishes should be respected unless where there is a significant risk to their well-being or another party arising from failure to disclose.

Information, choice and advocacy

The same rigour concerning honesty over the choices that are available to users should be applied to all other aspects of the user's care and treatment, for example, regarding medication and its side effects, psychosocial interventions, and options for housing, work and leisure. Good information, effective support and advocacy are necessary to make user participation meaningful. Users should be informed of their rights, the different options available to them for treatment, care and social support and the costs and benefits of these options. The information should be written down but also imparted verbally, face-to-face. It should be presented in a way that is appropriate to the culture and language of the user.

Hutchison (2000) criticised psychiatrist's reluctance to impart too much information about the short-and long-term effects of medication, and argued forcefully that the provision of information should not be contingent upon professional perceptions of how it will be interpreted and used. She asserted that self-determination is a basic human right and information is necessary for that choice to be exercised.

Sometimes extra help is required in the form of advocacy to ensure that users' interests are safeguarded. This may be because of an unsupportive treatment environment, difficulties experienced by users in communicating their views and preferences, or particular circumstances. Advocacy is a process by which the voices of users are heard, their views respected and their interests defended. It may take different forms but all have the aim of working towards self-advocacy.

- *Legal advocacy* concerns representation by legally qualified advocates, usually solicitors,
- *Citizen advocacy* is a long-term, one-to-one partnership between user and advocate,
- *Formal advocacy* refers to services run by voluntary organisations, usually employing paid advocates, and
- *Peer advocacy* involves support from advocates who themselves have experience of using mental health services.

None of these forms of advocacy are mutually exclusive and all share the key criterion that they must be independent of the organisations providing services to users. Although the practitioner should be working on behalf of users, ultimately they lack the independence from service systems necessary for advocacy work, particularly if they hold budgetary or resource rationing responsibilities. However, practitioners have a role in helping the user identify an advocate to act on their behalf.

Promoting self-management

The principle behind self-management is that users are the experts on their own distress (Faulkner, 2000). It does not imply that users can manage without help but rather that they can become more aware of changes in themselves, and when they need to get support. Provider staff can help users in this by acknowledging the value of strategies that they have already developed, as well as helping them develop new ones. Organisations such as the Hearing Voices Network, the National Self-Harm Network and the Manic Depression Fellowship have described self-management techniques. Faulkner (2000) describes the stages developed by the latter organisation as:

Recognition: the development of awareness about triggers and early warning signs, in order to develop the ability to forward plan.

Action: making a personal action plan describing the steps to be taken to improve or maintain mental health and the circumstances in which they will be taken.

Maintenance: the routine of attending to aspects of lifestyle that support and maintain mental health (for example, exercise, getting enough sleep).

Crisis management: the planning in advance for crisis using 'advance directives' to specify the action to be taken by others, the options that should be offered, and those that should be avoided.

Motivational interviewing: working from where users are

The foregoing discussion has stressed a clinical style that is user-centred in that it seeks to base interventions on the values, views and perspectives of the user and takes their aspirations seriously. This spirit underpins motivational interviewing (Rollnick and Miller, 1995). Motivational interviewing is best understood as an interpersonal style, rather than a set of techniques (see Box 4). It seeks to explore and resolve ambivalence about change by actively drawing out those core values that are likely to underpin those choices that the user will act upon. It is directive in that it seeks to draw out those values, while avoiding the direct confrontation or persuasion. This only serves to increase resistance to change. Rollnick *et al.* (1999) advocate a 'quiet and curious' interpersonal style where users persuade *themselves* of the need to change.

Motivational interview focuses on users' readiness to change, how important change is to them, and the confidence they have that they would be able to bring about change. It helps users to articulate the costs and benefits of changing and not changing, and respects those valuations while providing new information. Motivational interviewing requires reflective practitioners who are able to actively listen to users while also maintaining an awareness of what is happening within the therapeutic relationship.

Motivational interviewing was originally developed in the substance misuse field where research has supported its implementation

Box 4 *Principles of good practice in motivational interviewing (from Rollnick et al., 1999)*

Value base

- Respect for the autonomy of users and their choices is paramount.
- Users should decide what behaviour, if any, to focus on.

Skills

- A confrontational interviewing style is not productive.
- Information exchange is a critical skill.
- Readiness to change should be continually monitored.
- The importance of, and readiness to change should be assessed and responded to.

Practitioner role

- Providing structure, direction and support.
- Providing information sought by the user.
- Eliciting and respecting the user's views and aspirations.
- Negotiating change sensitively.

User role

- Being an active decision maker.

as an effective and efficient therapeutic style (Noonan and Moyers, 1997). In that engagement in care is a key issue for people with severe mental health problems, motivational interviewing offers considerable promise. However, Perkins and Repper (1999) highlight the tension between a directive role for therapists and the need to authentically maintain the user's role as the expert in how to manage their own lives. It therefore requires trained and supported practitioners operating within a therapeutic environment that affords relationship building the time that it requires, and a team ideology of care that is supportive of its essential principles. Although not focused on mental health service users, Rollnick *et al.* (1999) provide excellent practical guidelines to practitioners who wish to explore the approach in more detail.

Understanding the user's perspective requires more than just an effective interpersonal style, however. The practitioner will also need to reflect on how their own beliefs and assumptions influence their behaviour. This behaviour will include the issues the practitioner pursues and the areas that they feel should be the focus of clinical work. Argyris's (1990) 'Ladder of Inference' (see Figure 4) describes how the attachment of particular meanings, based upon our culture

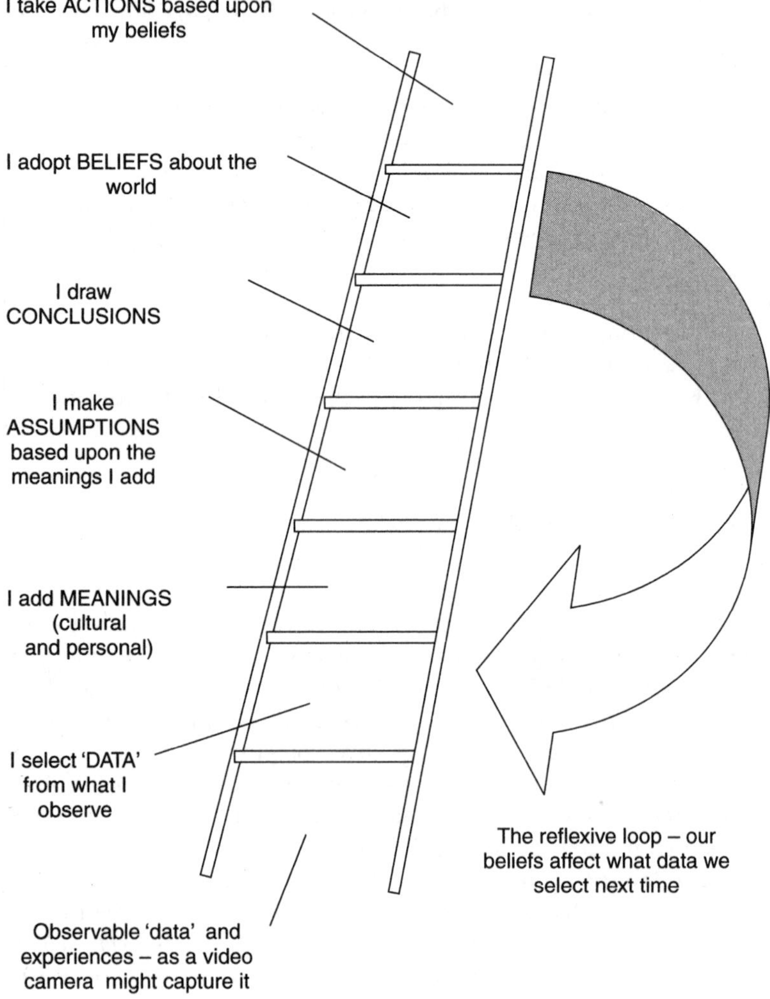

Figure 4 *The Ladder of Inference*

and personal values, leads to certain beliefs which in turn feedback to influence the ways in which we select and add meaning to experience. This issue is particularly important when the user and the practitioner share little of each other's culture or experience.

Effective care planning and assessment

Morgan and Akbar-Khan (2000) define care planning as 'a continuous process of developing and reviewing actions, stated as achievable tasks, allocated responsibilities and agreed timescales. In this way it is a practical function in the here and now, both enabling agreement of goals for the future, and the monitoring of past achievements and progress' (77). Figure 5 describes the process as a cycle of activity starting with engagement, and then continuous relationship building and assessment. Once interventions are underway a continuous process of monitoring of the outcomes of intervention begins which is punctuated by reviews at which changes to the care plan are made with the involvement of the user and other key people. The interventions include generic tasks that are core to care coordination and likely to be required by most people, and others that are more specific, and require more specialised training in evidence-based psychosocial and biological interventions. The guidelines below draw from a range of sources but particularly the work of the Frantz Fanon Centre (see Fuller, 2000) in Birmingham, which particularly aims to serve the black community.

Engagement and relationship building

The initial phase of contact with users where the practitioner focuses on developing an understanding of their perspective is pivotal. The aim is to create the best context for establishing a relationship built on trust, respect and mutual understanding.

In planning initial contact, it is important to make the best use of the information available to proactively create a situation that will be most conducive to effective communication and understanding. This may suggest the need to involve others known and trusted by the individual (for example, their GP or advocate), involving interpreters

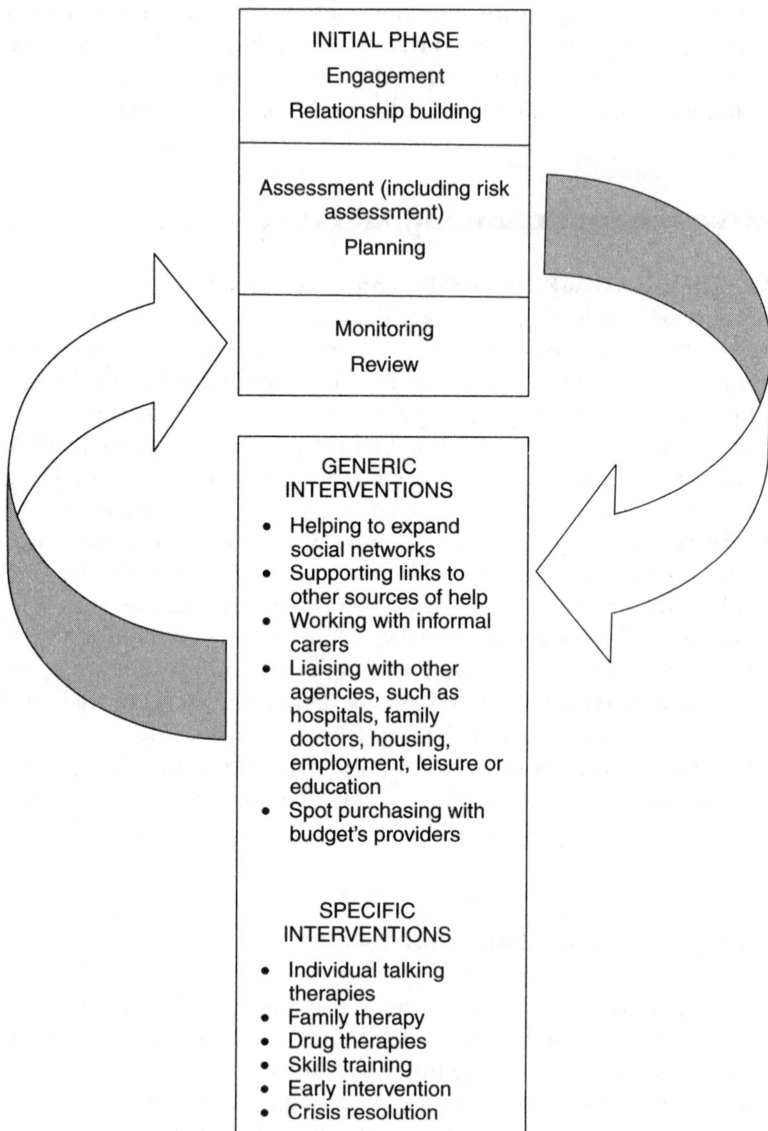

Figure 5 *The on-going cycle of work with users and their networks*

where necessary, and choosing a worker intelligently on the basis of their history and cultural background. It may be necessary to explore concerns or misinformation arising from the referral or information supplied. For example, if the user has avoided mental health services or is described as presenting a risk, the practitioner should explore the nature of this risk, who is at risk from whom, and the sense that the individual concerned makes of their history (including the material written down in referral letters and notes). This needs to take place within a context that ensures the safety of all involved.

Several contacts may be required for the user to be able to make sense of where the practitioner fits in to their world and how they might be able to be of benefit to them. This may mean the practitioner proactively demonstrating their commitment to support by providing practical assistance in advance of a formal assessment. For example, a relationship may be established by simply supplying groceries to someone who is having difficulty leaving their home.

Persistence is necessary but it is also important to respect the user's right to refuse help. There are existing powers to instigate a formal assessment under the Mental Health Act where users are judged to be a risk to themselves or others, but where this does not apply the team can only work to make the service as relevant as possible to the user. The team should act as a resource for creative thinking in this regard. Where there is a failure to engage there may be another way that could be tried, for example, by trying a different approach from a different member of the team, or simply leaving information about how the team might be able to help.

In building a relationship with the individual it is important to observe the need for honesty, which includes being clear about what you can and cannot do for them. It is important to leave users with as much power to control the process of engagement as possible while also allowing them to rely on you where necessary. As in any new human relationship the imperative is to listen, communicate effectively, provide relevant information, and work to understand the other person's world as they experience it.

Assessment

The assessment phase begins when the practitioner starts to explore the user's needs and expectations. These may be different from the objectives of the referral as received from the referrer. Procedures for assessment should be:

- *Valid – for example, compiling a true picture of the user's situation.* This requires that the practitioner is aware of how their own values and interpretations add meanings to what they experience, and the extent to which this can create misunderstanding about the user's experience and their behaviour (see Figure 4 on the ladder of inference above). The validity of the assessment will also be enhanced if it takes place in the user's own environment, or somewhere else where they can be most relaxed. Where they agree, assessment can usefully involve other people that are important to and trusted by the user.
- *Efficient – for example, avoiding duplication with other services.* Care coordinators are not qualified to assess every area of need and certain domains may have already been assessed or require more specialist skills (for example, with respect to mental state or activities of daily living).
- *Reliable – so that the results would be similar whoever did the assessment.* Having a clear structure to the assessment, while not constraining the natural flow of information, should ensure that the relevant domains are covered (see below).

Fuller (2000) advocates a holistic assessment that addresses a broad range of physical, emotional, social and spiritual needs. The following list of domains to be explored is adapted from her framework for working with black service users at the Frantz Fanon Centre.

- *Life events.* It will be important to explore key events and the individual's reactions to them. These may have triggered the referral. Understanding them from the user's perspective will be critical. Working with users in the context in which a crisis has occurred will help with this, and allow other key people can be involved. This will also help to promote understanding of the environment that the individual will be coping with in future.
- *Personal relationships.* It is important not to be presumptive about what constitutes an important relationship for the individual. Disengagement from other family members does not mean that there will not be other key people who should be involved or who are an ongoing source of support or stress for the individual.

- *Social and economic circumstances.* The assessment should consider those material aspects of life that everybody needs to ensure survival in communities. This includes access to enough money, decent and secure accommodation, meaningful activity and freedom from the anxiety of debt, abuse or exploitation.
- *The impact of social inequalities.* Fuller advocates that these be considered in relation to social and economic circumstances. For example, racism will impact on access to employment, housing, education and a range of other supports. She alerts us to the dangers of labelling behaviours that are not understood as having a 'cultural framework' if the individual is not of the host culture. In this way, culture is spuriously cited as an obstacle to engagement or the achievement of valued outcomes when in fact the user's difference is actually being exaggerated. Such assumptions lead to oversimplified generalisation to other people of the same 'culture' (see Figure 4). This also leads to the simplistic assumption that a practitioner from the same ethnic group will be able to work most effectively with the individual. The fact of sharing the same ethnic group does not remove the obligation to have an understanding of the individual's unique situation.
- *Spiritual and emotional life.* Fuller refers to spirituality as 'the breath of life itself, the soul and spirit of the individual that incorporates their beliefs and framework of reference for living'. Such spirituality may or may not have a religious foundation. Exploring how it influences the way the user construes their world and their experiences will be critically important. It may be an important part of how the individual copes with life. The practitioner should respect the individual's spirituality without analysing it and judging it in comparison with their own beliefs and values. The aim is to achieve understanding.
- *Mental health.* In undertaking a comprehensive assessment it will also be important to assess the user's mental state, the phenomena they are experiencing as part of their mental distress, the attributions they make about them, and the ways of coping they may be adopting.
- *Physical factors.* The physical health of people with mental health problems can often be neglected. For example, among black users, Fuller cites the example of Sickle Cell Anaemia and Systemic Lupus Erythamatus as diseases that are likely to have a significant impact on mental health. There is also a danger that symptoms

may be attributed to mental distress when there is an organic cause. Other key indicators of poor health such as impaired cardiac function need to be borne in mind when considering treatment options.

Managing clinical risk

In a clinical context, risk pertains to harm to others, self-harm, suicide and severe self-neglect. It is important to put it in context. Morgan (2000a) points out that there is a greater chance of winning the National Lottery than being killed by someone with a mental illness, and that there is no evidence to suggest that risk of harm from users is increasing (Taylor and Gunn, 1999). This would be persuasive were it not for the fact that unfortunately people do not in general think and act rationally on the basis of such probabilities. The lottery slogan: 'It could be you!' exploits the same reasoning bias as that exploited by the popular media when they sensationalise homicides by people diagnosed with a mental illness.

It is important to recognise that every novel act requires some level of risk. Without risk there is no change, no development and no learning. As Morgan (2000a: 97) states: 'Positive risk taking needs to be clearly defined, and encouraged as a routine aspect of creative, engaged working relationships. It will support risk-prevention strategies, not create more incidents'.

It is necessary to balance the positive aspects of risk against the potential for harm to self and others. This requires that we better understand risk and remain focused on the key areas of concern rather than those dictated by the popular media. The reality is that suicide among people with mental distress constitutes a much higher risk that homicide, and that service users are more likely to be the victims rather than the perpetrators of violence and exploitation (Pilgrim and Rogers, 1996). The individual's experience of, and concerns about, risk to themselves must be a key element of assessment and subsequent intervention. This includes physical, sexual or financial exploitation or abuse. It may also include social exclusion, bullying and attacks on personal self-worth, and a failure to address basic human rights such as fair access to housing and employment. The perpetrators may be neighbours, the public at large, families or indeed mental health workers.

When assessing risk it is important to recognise that incidents are rare, requiring us to make predictions on limited experience. Although, diagnosed mental illnesses *are* significant factors when assessing the potential for risk, prediction is an uncertain activity that we achieve successfully in only a minority of cases. For example, Munro and Rumgay (2000) reviewed public inquiries between 1988 and 1997 and found that only 27.5 per cent of homicides were judged to have been predictable.

It is therefore important that practitioners, their employers, and as far as possible, society as a whole recognises that risk cannot be eliminated, and that the level of coercion and control required to address the unpredictability of human behaviour would be impossible to implement, and socially and morally unacceptable; not least because of the implications of the number of false positive attributions of dangerousness that will arise because of the inadequate assessment tools that we have available (Morgan, 2000a).

Nonetheless, we can improve our understanding of the historical and contextual circumstances in which a person is more likely to be at risk to themselves or others. This will be informed by an awareness of the factors that are associated with risk drawn from large-scale studies of risk behaviour (for example, Steadman *et al.*, 1994). Box 5 describes the risk indicators taken from Morgan's (2000b) clinical risk assessment tool. However, risk assessment is no substitute for effective relationship building. As Morgan (1997) notes: 'Risk factors are somewhat like weather prediction: better at providing an overall picture than a guarantee that we can be sure of what will happen in any specific situation' (214). In light of this, he concludes: 'Perhaps our most appropriate approach should be to refine and evaluate our basic clinical skills. Suicide rates might well then look after themselves' (216).

The Confidential Inquiry into Homicides and Suicides by Mentally Ill People (1996), was also clear about the central importance of relationships:

> Although it was evident that regular contact had been made with most patients prior to the death, we were concerned that the time for *one-to-one contact*, where skills in developing a *therapeutic relationship* and opportunity for listening to the patient might be used were very limited... Audit programmes should address the *extent* and *quality* of direct staff: patient contact. (66; my italics).

Box 5 *Morgan's risk indicators*

Suicide risk indicators

- Previous attempts on their life
- Previous use of violent methods
- Misuse of drugs and/or alcohol
- Major psychiatric diagnoses
- Expressing suicidal ideas
- Considered/planned intent
- Believe no control over their life
- Expressing high levels of distress
- Helplessness or hopelessness
- Family history of suicide
- Separated/widowed/divorced
- Unemployed/retired
- Recent significant life events
- Major physical illness/disability

Aggression or violence risk indicators

- Previous incidents of violence
- Previous use of weapons
- Misuse of drugs and/or alcohol
- Male gender, under 35 years of age
- Known personal trigger factors
- Expressing intent to harm others
- Previous dangerous impulsive acts
- Paranoid delusions about others
- Violent command hallucinations
- Signs of anger and frustration
- Sexually inappropriate behaviour
- Preoccupation with violent fantasy
- Admissions to secure settings
- Denial of previous dangerous acts

Neglect risk indicators

- Failing to drink properly
- Failing to eat properly
- Difficulty managing physical health

Indicators of other risks

- Self injury (for example, cutting, burning)
- Other self harm (for example, eating disorders)

- Living in inadequate accommodation
- Lacking basic amenities (water/heat/light)
- Pressure of eviction/ repossession
- Lack of positive social contacts
- Unable to shop for self
- Insufficient/inappropriate clothing
- Difficulty managing hygiene
- Experiencing financial difficulty
- Experiencing significant debts
- Difficulty communicating needs
- Denies problems perceived by others
- Stated abuse by others (for example, physical, sexual)
- Abuse of others
- Harassment by others (for example, racial, physical)
- Exploitation by others (for example, financial)
- Exploitation of others
- Culturally isolated situation
- Risks to child(ren)
- Non-violent sexual offence (for example, exposure)
- Arson or other damage to property

In a societal and work context that is risk-averse, there follows the negative implications of a blame-culture emerging. This, in turn, gives rise to concerns about scape-goating and defensive practice in which practitioners cover their backs before considering the real needs of service users. Defensive practice can also encompass building emotional defences. Any effective human relationship requires emotional investment. Where staff feel personally vulnerable and blamed when tragic events occur, such as a suicide, it can give rise to a culture in which staff defend themselves emotionally from developing strong attachments to users. As a clinician, I have experienced a dynamic in which staff encounter an implicit lack of permission to express their distress when someone they have been working with commits suicide or has a major relapse. Often this lack of permission is experienced as a concern not to 'break ranks' when there is blame to be attached. Emotional detachment may be positively connoted as a manifestation of professionalism. Indeed, there may be a team ideology that suggests that such events are simply part of the job and thus should not be lamented. Thus, staff have little opportunity to do the emotional work associated with such events and may therefore learn to defend themselves from the pain of seeing people die or in acute distress by ensuring that they do not get too emotionally involved in the first place. Tragically, this very detachment may contribute to users feeling themselves to be unheard or misunderstood, which in itself creates risk. Consequently, there is a danger of creating a vicious circle, which may partly explain why some environments seem to experience more adverse incidents than others.

Hence, there is a balance to be struck within organisations and teams between the need to avoid complacency about risk, while developing a realistic perspective on the mental health practitioner's power to stop people killing or harming themselves. The environment also needs to give permission for people to express concern about tragic events when they occur, and learn from them. This means that people should not feel that they will be personally blamed. It is usually the case that adverse incidents are due to failures of communication and coordination within care systems rather than because of the behaviour of any one individual (Sheppard, 1996). Effective communication and coordination are key tasks of care coordination, but it requires effective management and teamworking to support their execution.

Achieving a working formulation

On the basis of a comprehensive assessment, the practitioner will need to sketch out a working formulation of what is happening in the user's world, and how different elements of their experience interconnect. Functional analysis (Owens and Ashcroft, 1982) is an approach to achieving a dynamic and evolving picture of the user's experience. It requires a clear description of the user's main concerns or problems which are then analysed in terms of the various events and variables that surround them in terms of (a) whether they serve to increase or decrease the probability of the event, and (b) whether they occur before or after it. It is, therefore, similar to a behavioural analysis in which events are classified in an A-B-C configuration in which B is the behaviour in question, A is its antecedents (for example, what happened before, where it happened, who with?) and C its consequences (for example, what happens as a result, how do others respond?). The difference between functional analysis and a behavioural analysis is that the former does not aim to represent an objective reality but rather serves as a problem-solving tool to inform the perspectives of the user and the practitioner, and to guide interventions. It attempts to find a common language and shared formulation of the situation that will inform future work. It is also more permissive about the events in question, which may be behaviours, feelings or thoughts. The aim is to look for circularity in the way that events are connected as the focus for intervention. The development of a working understanding of what is going on can also inform the exploration of the user's readiness to change, the importance of the change and their confidence in achieving it. I have often found it helpful with users to actually draw out on pieces of flipchart how different events may be connecting with each other. This is likely to be most effective where the individual is encouraged to challenge the salience of the events in the formulation and how they connect. The picture of their situation will evolve, informed by experience of how attempts to bring about change influence events captured within the formulation. Onyett (1998) provides a worked example of a full functional analysis. Such formulations of cyclical processes form the basis of many of the psychological approaches described later.

Planning, monitoring and review

In planning care, it is important that the care coordinator is clear about those decisions that fall within the discretion that they can exercise in their working relationship with the user and those that require the involvement of the rest of the team and others involved (see Chapter 7). The care planning process will need to be punctuated by regular reviews that involve a wider network of individuals and the information that they bring to the decision-making process.

Running alongside the care planning process is a process of continuous monitoring on the part of the care coordinator. Along with changes in the user's social or mental health status, the care coordinator will be continually evaluating the outcome of their own and other's interventions with the user, and the actions that the individual initiates themselves. Close monitoring maintains continuity of input and support for the user, allows on-going assessment of emerging strengths and needs, and early implementation of efforts to correct discrepancies between assessed need and provision.

Maintaining and expanding social networks

Someone to talk to, and social support emerge as dominant themes when users are asked about how to cope with emotional distress (Faulkner, 2000). It is easier to maintain social networks than to rebuild them. This underlines the need to work with people in context, and complement their existing supports. It is also important to minimise the disruptive effects of service involvement by intervening early to prevent crisis, and joint working with agencies already involved. Teams have an important role in supporting self-help groups, and links to other forms of support from people who may have relevant experience in common with the user. However, it is important to stress that not all individuals will seek to expand their social network. Some may need respite from the intensity of emotional relationships that they are already involved in. It is important that people remain in control of their relationships and the pace at which they develop.

Linking

Linking is the task of helping service users connect with valued sources of support. It is the care coordination task that most resembles advocacy and may involve negotiating with other agencies for help or resources. This includes agencies concerned with material support such as welfare benefits and housing. Wherever possible, it should focus on services used by the general public rather than specialist mental health agencies. The topic is more thoroughly addressed in Onyett (1998) but the key points are summarised here.

- *Maximise user autonomy.* The aim is to work alongside and support the user, not foster their dependency by connecting them up to sources of help that they have little investment in maintaining. Taking a long-term view, a slow pace and employing the principles of motivational interviewing should promote effective engagement.
- *Establish contacts.* The care coordinator will require good local intelligence on sources of support. What do they do? What do they feel are their particular strong points? Who are they most able to help? Are they bound to specific exclusion criteria? They also need to be aware of the expectations of other services so that they can help the user and the service understand each other and to ensure that the user is not set up to fail.
- *Be personal.* Linking is often about overcoming bureaucracy. This requires that the care coordinator make the process as personal as possible. When making contact with an agency it is important to identify named individuals who appear to be able to make things happen. When advocating for the user, it is important to convey a holistic picture of a person with rights. The user is not 'a schizophrenic needing a home' but an individual with a particular and unique set of needs deriving from specific aspects of their circumstances. The need for honesty also extends to work with other agencies. While it is important to present the user in a positive way, it is also important not to distort the facts in order to get a result as this will erode any trust that has been established between the team and the agency in question.
- *Assume an intention to help.* Assume that the other worker will attempt to assist the user if possible, even if this may not accord with experience. This avoids a combative stance, and draws the other worker into a collaborative, problem-solving approach to overcoming obstacles.
- *Assertion not machismo!* Lamb (1980: 764) points out that, 'Too often . . . , the advocacy role becomes like a war – a licence to ventilate hostility'. The care coordinator needs to overcome any fear of the telephone, and clearly communicate the desired outcome to the person they have identified as being able to help. However, when obstacles are encountered it is tempting to assume a more aggressive stance. Where the other party is denying a resource to which the user has a clear right this may be appropriate. However, it is often better to acknowledge that an alternative

solution may be needed, and that adopting an aggressive stance without the legitimate authority to achieve the desired outcome is unlikely to benefit the user or the reputation of the team.

- *Reinforce the link.* It is easy to forget to acknowledge the help that others have provided. We are all susceptible to having our behaviour shaped by other people and any achievements by others should be explicitly responded to and reinforced. This may increase the likelihood of them performing similar miracles in future, and creates a more positive environment for joint working.
- *Learn from set-backs.* Users' needs will be constantly changing and every failed attempt to link to a resource provides new learning and should inform future work. The user may not have been adequately prepared with respect to their own readiness, their skills or their confidence. It may be that the opportunity offered required skills that were not predicted, or the scale of change itself may simply have been too large and stressful. Perhaps the experience suggests that the goal may not have been as important to the user as the care coordinator assumed, and further space to explore this is needed.

Care coordinators need to tread a fine line between realistic goal setting, and supporting users in achieving their stated aspirations. This means being creatively positive and positively creative! If the aim in linking is to fulfil a stated need, then there may be alternative methods when one course proves fruitless. The aim is to inculcate a sense of achievement and maintain a sense of hope from which to build. The team should be used as a pool of experience to draw on and as a support for creative problem solving.

Working with informal carers

Carers are well placed to provide encouragement and support to users, offer practical assistance and help achieve links to valued support. Working alongside them and explicitly valuing them as a resource of care and support means that the care coordinator can enlist their help in monitoring the outcomes of service provision and alerting services and the user themselves to early indications of impending problems. Exposing families to your work can reduce unhelpful fantasies, feelings of exclusion, misinformation and misunderstanding. The care coordinator may have a role in helping families set boundaries on their involvement in the user's life, both for their own sakes and to promote autonomy and new learning for the user.

All the principles of working effectively with users apply equally to carers. It is important to be clear about your role, and what you can and cannot do in their interests. It cannot be assumed that the interests and concerns of users will be the same as that of their carers. If conflicts of interest arise, it is important that practitioners are clear that they are primarily serving the interests of the identified user. It is important not to be drawn into supporting the families against users. Complaints about the user should be considered as shared problems to be solved where they represent an issue for the user themselves. Where conflict does arise, it is important to respect the position of the family, avoid blame, and support carers in seeking help for themselves.

Involvement during in-patient stays

Admission should not be seen as a failure of community care but rather a necessary part of the care planning process. This can help to overcome a problematic split between hospital and community services that sometimes arises. This is likely to be ameliorated in a sectorised service where community teams have flexible access to identified beds.

The disruption of supportive social networks at admission and the increased risk of suicide in the week following discharge underlines the need for continuity of clinical contact and care planning, and for this reason the care coordinator should stay involved with users and in-patient staff during their hospital stay. The level of involvement should, as a minimum, allow participation in care planning reviews and discharge planning. The care coordinator should be in a position to be able to visit the user within a week of their discharge from hospital.

Liaising with other agencies

It may be advantageous to strategically deploy team members in liaison roles with specific agencies. By maintaining a human link, the team as a whole can maintain good local working intelligence about the network of care and support that is available to users. These links will be informed by analysis of referral networks, or a recognition that some parts of the local service system have been neglected. Links into primary care for the sake of effective communications, maintaining appropriate referrals and promoting continuity of care will be particularly important.

Brokerage – some guidelines

Although it has been shown to be a poor substitute for effective clinical work based on strong relationships, service brokerage is likely to be an increasing feature of teamworking as budgets are increasingly pooled at team level to promote flexible care planning. Onyett (1998) suggested the following key guidelines for brokerage using a budget:

- Assessment should not be restricted to those areas of need that the resources available through brokerage aim to satisfy.
- The existence of services that can be bought directly should not prejudice the up-take of other resources that may be of more value to the individual.
- There should be no implicit or explicit incentives for care coordinators to deploy specialised services rather than helping users to integrate with communities through the use of ordinary facilities.
- Users should be kept fully and continuously up-to-date with the range of options that can be bought directly, and their respective costs and benefits in both financial and personal terms.
- Decisions on the total allocation of resources to users should not be made by someone who is responsible for either identifying potential users of the service or assessing need.
- All the requirements of continuous monitoring, feedback and independent advocacy continue to apply.

Episodic closure

Team involvement with users should be aimed at achieving the maximum maintenance or recovery of valued roles on the part of users. It is therefore likely that, at times, the user's involvement with a given team will be finished. It is important that closure does not occur for arbitrary administrative reasons such as the number of sessions expended. Need should continue to be the basis on which care and treatment is provided. It will also be critical to keep the door open to future involvement for users, and others involved, by indicating exactly who and how to contact if future problems are encountered. There should be specific and recorded contingency plans concerning the possibility of future problems communicated to all involved. A closing summary should be available that will inform future work with the user. It should be communicated to relevant people (for example, the GP) on a need-to-know basis and underline that the team is no longer formally monitoring the user. It should include details of who to alert, and how, if further help is needed.

Care coordination as a vehicle for effective evidence-based interventions

Teamworking that supports collaborative relationships between service users and team members provides the necessary, but not sufficient conditions for effective mental health service provision for people with severe mental distress. CMHTs merely provide the required platform for the provision of effective interventions (Gournay, 1999; Marshall and Lockwood, 1998).

It is notable that the emphasis on effective relationships has been a long-standing theme of meta-analyses of the effectiveness of psychotherapies (Orlinsky and Howard, 1986). It is only comparatively recently that the evidence base for the effectiveness of psychological interventions for people experiencing psychotic phenomena, such as hallucinations and unusual beliefs, has emerged. Here, again, the importance of relationships is underlined. As the BPS (2000) affirmed in their review of advances in understanding and responding to psychotic experiences:

> All psychological interventions should be based on a trusting, collaborative working relationship between the professional and the client. It is possible that this is often the main 'active ingredient'. It is certainly vital, and it is important that service users should be able to find a therapist or worker with whom they feel comfortable (45).

The greater legitimisation of the user's constructions of reality and a stronger emphasis on their role as active agents in their own recovery are also important underlying themes underpinning developments in both psychosocial and biological interventions. In introducing a special section in the *Journal of Mental Health* on key advances in psychosocial approaches to psychosis, Birchwood (1998: 111) made the point that 'what unites [these approaches] is a firm focus upon the person with psychosis as an active agent, searching for meaning and control over psychosis and the survival of the self'.

Psychosocial interventions

Some of the key developments in evidence-based interventions that should be incorporated within the skill base of teams serving people with severe mental health problems include early intervention in the first episode of psychotic experience (Drake *et al.*, 2000; Garety and Jolley, 2000) and in relapse (Birchwood *et al.*, 1998), cognitive behaviour therapy (Haddock *et al.*, 1998; Shergill *et al.*, 1998), family interventions (Pharoah *et al.*, 2000), individual psychoeducational interventions providing users with support, information and management strategies drawing upon familial, social, biological and pharmacological perspectives (Pekkala and Merinda, 2000), and vocational skills training (Crowther *et al.*, 2001). Other approaches such as cognitive rehabilitation techniques aimed at improving information processing abilities, psychodynamic therapies, social skills and life skills programmes may also be important although the evidence for their effectiveness is more contested (BPS, 2000; NHS Centre for Reviews and Dissemination, 2000).

Medication

Medication, for example, in the form of antipsychotic drugs (Pratt, 1998) and mood stabilisers (Gitlin *et al.*, 1995) have a crucial role to play. Pratt (1998) provides some useful advice on best practice in administration, including the important role of pharmacists within the service.

'Compliance therapy', based upon the motivational interviewing techniques described above has been associated with increased adherence to medication regimes and improved global functioning (Kemp *et al.*, 1998). However, the approach has been criticised for failing to maintain enough fidelity to the basic tenet of motivational interviewing that the user is the expert, nor enough recognition that some people do not benefit from medication (Perkins and Repper, 1999). The BPS (2000) suggested that it is not always irrational for people to refuse their medication and made the following points from their review of the 'compliance' literature:

- People's views about their experiences are complex and cannot be dismissed as lack of insight. Some may choose to construe their experiences in psychological or social terms rather than embrace a medical model. This perspective has become more commonplace with self-help organisations such as the Hearing Voices Network stressing that unusual experiences exist on a continuum with 'normality', and that in many cases they are valued by service users.
- The strategies that people use to manage these experiences, and the use of medication are also complex. Many people are not globally compliant or noncompliant but vary their use of medication according to circumstances.
- For some people, the balance between the advantages and disadvantages of taking medication is a fine one. Rogers *et al.* (1998) found that some people found side effects to be more aversive than their psychotic experiences.
- People may refuse drugs for a variety of reasons, of which side effects may be just one. Some people simply find them ineffective. It is wrong to routinely assume that refusal to take medication is a feature of the mental health problems experienced.
- Rates and reasons given for non-adherence to medication regimes in the mental health field are similar to that in physical health.

The BPS (2000) stressed the need for (1) good information for users on treatments, including their side effects, (2) regular monitoring of people's attitudes, side effects and responses to treatment, and (3) a collaborative relationship in which users are encouraged to ask questions about their treatment. Ultimately, decisions to refuse medication should be respected except when the level of distress requires formal treatment under the Mental Health Act because of the level of risk involved. Refusal should not mean that other supports are removed or that other forms of help should not be offered.

Conclusion

This chapter started by stressing how the team merely serves to support effective individual practice with service users. The breadth of tasks that the role of team member encompasses is large and challenging. They need to be undertaken by people who have the right attitudes, knowledge and skills, and the resources necessary to remain effective in their work. Underpinning this practice, and the work of the team as a whole is a bedrock of clear aims and values. Much of the rest of this book is dedicated to how these aims and values are lived out in practice through effective leadership, continuous quality improvement and effective team processes.

CHAPTER 7

The Leadership and Management of Team Processes

The presence of a clear team leader is associated with team effectiveness (Borrill *et al.*, 2000). The leadership and management of CMHTs embodies a number of challenges concerned with (a) professional autonomy alongside accountability to management, (b) integrating health/social, primary/specialist, statutory/voluntary care, (c) achieving effective user and carer participation in service development and planning, (d) working with traditional medical leadership roles, (e) an increasingly diverse skill mix and background among team members, and (f) demands for evidence-based practice in a context of poorly developed systems and technologies for audit and evaluation (Onyett *et al.*, 1997). In this context, it is, perhaps, not surprising that an association specifically for the support and development of the CMHT manager role has been established (see *www.mental-health-link.org.uk*). In order to understand the role of team leaders and managers, this chapter defines terms concerning power, authority, responsibility, accountability, management and leadership. It considers what the team management role needs to achieve for the team and the system in which it operates, describes the delineation of responsibilities and lines of accountability, and explores the team processes to be managed.

Leadership and management

In Chapter 1, we construed CMHTs as 'complex decision-making teams' (West *et al.*, 1998) that had to survive and flourish in uncertain, unpredictable environments working with evolving models of care and practices in a context of limited resources. Change is inevitable and constant. Our understanding of leadership and management, therefore needs to encompass both how to ensure that day-to-day operations deliver the required functions, and how to innovate and evolve to achieve excellence in a changing environment.

These two emphases are drawn out in the distinction between management, (or 'transactional' leadership; Bass, 1997) and 'transformational' leadership (ibid.). Management emphasises organising and planning the use of resources, dealing with problems as they emerge and monitoring the progress of activities directed at achieving predictable outcomes and specified objectives. Transformational leadership goes beyond management and involves challenging the status quo to create new visions and scenarios, initiating new approaches and stimulating the creative and emotional drive in individuals to innovate and deliver excellence. Transformational leadership is associated with the commitment, effort, performance, innovation, harmony and job satisfaction of those being lead; the financial performance of the organisation; and performance in the public sector (Bass, 1997). *Complex organisations therefore require both management and leadership, and often, but not exclusively, it is the managers who need to demonstrate effective leadership.* The dimensions of transformational leadership are shown in Box 6.

Box 6 *Transformational leadership (adapted from Bass, 1997; my italics)*

Charismatic	Provides highly esteemed *role models*, whom followers strive to emulate, who align others around a *vision*, common purpose and mission
Inspirational	Provides *meaning* and *optimism* about the mission and its attainability
Intellectually stimulating	Encourages followers to question basic assumptions and to consider problems from new and unique perspectives
Individually considerate	Works with those being lead, diagnosing their needs; transcends their self-interests, enhances their expectations and *develops their potential*

While there are likely to be some universal features of leadership that transcend culture and context it is important to bear in mind that the most influential work on leadership has been undertaken in the USA. In a UK context, Alimo-Metcalfe (1999) undertook a study of over 250 local government and NHS organisations, which yielded usable responses from around 1100 NHS managers and 1500 local government managers. This revealed a more complex picture than the four-factor model above. Added to the model were new factors concerned with:

- openness to new ideas;
- honesty/tolerance regarding mistakes;
- being a visionary promoter of organisational achievements;
- entrepreneurial risk-taking;
- political skills;
- tenacity to achieve organisational goals; and
- integrity.

In services for people with severe and long-term mental health problems, Gowdy and Rapp (1989) conducted a qualitative study of eight community-based programmes in Kansas that were known to be effective. Interviews with programme managers, staff members, and service users, along with on-site observation, identified four principles that appeared to be central to the programme's successes. These took the form of values and principles that the managers communicated to staff, service users and the wider community and provide insights into how leadership was achieved in this context.

The '*Clients are people*' principle focused on manager's ability to inculcate a sense of service users as '*people with a future versus patients with an insurmountable past*' (1989: 34). Staff were encouraged to look behind diagnosis to see the unique qualities and strengths of users. Support was provided without undermining a view of the user as a whole person with views and capabilities. Staff were less 'experts' providing solutions and more supporters encouraging users to solve problems themselves.

The '*Learning for a living*' principle was so-named to contrast these managers with those that 'work for a living'. Successful managers sought out input and feedback on the performance of the programme and were open to visitors and observers. Managers were not concerned with the amount of information available but with the selection of sources that most meaningfully reflected the programme's ability to improve people's lives. They also used an open and enquiring structure for supervision that examined practice in detail. Thus, global attributions of success or failure were avoided in favour of close examination of what was done and how it worked. These managers also saw education, both of staff and the community, as a core part of their role, and were highly involved in the day-to-day operation of the service, observing very closely, and promoting innovation and creativity.

The '*Making something from nothing*' principle described the way in which successful managers improved the programme with few resources alongside a continual stream of demands from users, staff and other stakeholders. This principle links closely with the final principle labelled '*Focus on client outcomes*'. Specific outcomes sought by service users were at the centre of the programme's mission and activity. These outcomes were usually defined as everyday features of ordinary life (for example, loving relationships, a decent place to live and meaningful activity) rather than as 'psychobabble' (for example, 'improved ego strength', 'acceptance of family dysfunction'). The focus on outcomes was also promoted through the use of systematic goal setting, specific interventions, monitoring using a variety of sources of information, feedback and positive reinforcement.

As with the transformational managers described above, these managers constantly modelled good practice. They tended to focus less on traditional features of management such as attending meetings, preparing reports and proposals and instead spent most of their time helping users or staff to achieve their goals. The authors conclude with a quote from a manager that captures the essence of this approach:

> My favourite thing to say is, 'You help people figure out what it is they want; you figure out how to help them get it; then you figure out how to get them to keep it.' Mixed in with all that practical stuff is some kind of friendship, being a vehicle for them to broaden their support network . . . I think that's critical (Gowdy and Rapp, 1989: 49).

This echoes the centrality of effective, collaborative relationships highlighted earlier, and the need for transformational managers to be 'individually considerate' (see Box 6).

Gowdy and Rapp's (1989) study can be usefully contrasted with Drolen's (1990) more broadly defined study of 69 mental health centre directors in 27 states. Drolen found that while centre directors were familiar with prescriptions for organisational innovation and entrepreneurship, in practice they concentrated more on control and efficiency rather than developing and supporting a structure and atmosphere conducive to creative thinking and innovation. The structure of work units, work assignments, and lack of participation in decision-making all militated against innovation. This style of leadership comprised more centralised decision-making and formalised procedures. Its emphasis on bureaucracy and paperwork is very reminiscent of concerns about the implementation of the CPA (for example, North and Ritchie, 1993). Creating enough space for transformational rather than transactional management in this context is an enduring challenge.

Power and authority

'Power' and 'authority' are emotive words. They are about 'doing unto others' in a manner that may be well motivated and benign, but also may not. As words, they also invoke their inverse: powerlessness and helplessness. In mental health services they are difficult concepts even to discuss, perhaps because they feature in almost every human transaction we have. We form parts of complex webs of relationships in which we both exercise and experience the effects of power and authority all the time. Defining them clearly will provide us with important tools for analysing team processes.

Roberts (1998a) describes power as an attribute of the person and delineates various sources:

- *Personal power* comes from knowledge, experience, skills or personality.
- *Instrumental power* comes from what one owns or controls, such as money or other resources.
- *Projected power* is that which is attributed to the person by others.
- *Official power* is derived from the person's defined work role (as manifest in their job title), and what this leads others to expect of them.

Authority on the other hand is more linked to a particular role rather than the person. Obholzer (1994) defines it as 'the right to make an ultimate decision, and in an organisation it refers to the right to make decisions which are binding on others' (39). He describes three sources of authority:

Authority from 'above'

This is the formal authority that is derived from one's role in the system and is exercised on its behalf. This may be contested in organisations involving a range of stakeholders who may hold different opinions on where authority does or should come from, to whom it should be delegated and to what extent. Some multi-agency CMHTs and local implementation teams provide examples.

Authority from 'below'

Obholzer (1994) argues that those who voluntarily join an organisation sanction it 'by definition'. This is a benign view of how people join organisations, partly because it is questionable how often anyone does anything completely voluntarily (for example, people need to earn money and the range of employing mental health services locally are inevitably limited). Often there are reservations and ambivalences from the outset. Take for example the anxieties expressed by clinical psychologists as they join CMHTs (Anciano and Kirkpatrick, 1990; Searle, 1991).

Problems arise where formal authority is assumed by an individual in the absence of authority from below; for example, where a CMHT manager is appointed in a context where the other team members feel they have not been properly involved in the selection process. Perceived competence and status in the eyes of other team members will be critical to a team leader's ability to lead in practice.

Authority from within

Obholzer (1994) also highlights the importance of being able to find confirmation of one's own authority from within. He describes this as being dependent upon relationships with figures in one's inner world, which in turn depends upon past relationships, particularly authority figures such as parents.

An example of this is illustrated as follows:

> A skilled and experienced CMHN was appointed as team manager for a stable and well-established CMHT. He was well regarded and respected by his peers for his strong human values, evident clinical skills and long service in the patch. Team members were involved in designing the selection process and job description and were pleased that the job went to a familiar, tried and tested candidate. The interview panel included both health and social services senior managers who were unanimous in their agreement that he should take on the role and were pleased with the appointment. However, soon after taking up the job the new manager became increasingly unable to function. He felt he was not up to the job, that his former colleagues had seen through him, and would denigrate him for his lack of performance. There was no evidence that this was in fact happening. This was a pattern that had endured with respect to his father since childhood. His father was a successful businessman who was disappointed that his son had not chosen to follow him into the private sector. As a result, he had never felt able to understand or reward his son for his achievements, and always seemed to be looking for ways to undermine him and denigrate his efforts.

Obholzer also describes how the opposite dynamic can exist whereby inner figures play into an inflated internal picture of the self as an authority figure, leading to authoritarian attitudes and behaviour.

The relationship of power to authority is critical and clearly congruence between personal power and the authority to be exercised in a role is desirable. Where someone has authority but no power, one can predict weak and demoralised management. Where there is power but no authority, an authoritarian regime is likely to emerge where others feel oppressed.

Obholzer (1994) observed that how a role is described by an organisation may be illuminating. Where someone is described as a 'Director' or 'Manager' then it is likely that the role has some authority and the post-holder will be expected to exercise power. Where someone is referred to as a 'coordinator', as was common among CMHTs, there may be insufficient authority because key powerful stakeholders (for example, psychiatrists, or senior managers in the host organisations) are unprepared to allow the individual to exercise the official and instrumental power required to get the job done.

Unlike in other simpler hierarchical organisations, mental health services comprise people with more diverse leadership and management roles. Leadership may reside with more than one person and vary with the domain of activity that is being led. In any one CMHT, one can observe situations where an individual clearly has a lot of personal and projected power, but the official and instrumental power resides with another team member. The personally powerful individual may therefore exercise more authority from within and below, while the official leader has only authority from above to draw upon. In that authority is related to roles, some team members may be seen as particularly authoritative, and thus the best person to lead in particular domains (for example, clinical leadership) while another is seen as having better skills (and thus more authority) when it comes to running the team day-to-day.

This power relationship within a given team, and the ways in which authority can be exercised, is therefore complex when just considering staff. Add to the equation the power relationships with and between users and carers, relationships with line managers of staff within in the team, relationships between the host organisations, and the relationship between the entire project and its local community. At this point you have something that feels like running through a swamp. However, it is not helpful to deny this complexity when trying to understand the swamp. The aim here is to equip you, the reader, with a language and some clear models that will allow you to pull yourself up out of the swamp every now and then to get a clearer sense of where you are before diving back in. This is also termed achieving a 'reflective space' and is returned to below.

At this point it is important to stress that the exercise of power and authority in a team:

- *is* influenced by processes of negotiation and the ways in which meaning (or social value) is attached to a particular vision and way of working. Hence, Hosking and Morley (1991: 240) construed leadership as 'a more or less skilful process of organising, achieved through negotiation, to achieve acceptable influence over the description and handling of issues within and between groups'.

- *is* based upon personal values, knowledge, skills and experience. It requires that people not only talk about the vision being sought but actually model ways of achieving it that are based upon principles drawn from basic human values about how services should be. It is no surprise that books, such as the best-selling *Seven Habits of Highly Effective People* (Covey, 1992), are both business management texts and 'self-help' books concerned with the importance of personal growth and development, and the essential character of managers as moral individuals.
- *is not* something that can easily be captured in an organisational chart, a job description or an operational policy. It is nonetheless very important that people's responsibilities and lines of accountability are clearly mapped out in order to better inform where gaps might exist in the required power and authority to exercise the role, or whether the role as defined is inappropriately drawn or allocated.

Responsibility and accountability

Like power and authority, the terms 'responsibility' and 'accountability' are often used inter-changeably. *Responsibility* can be defined as a set of tasks or functions that an employer, professional body, court of law or some other recognised body can legitimately demand (Onyett, 1995). *Accountability* describes the relationship between the practitioner and the organisation in question. Accountability describes the mechanism by which failure to exercise responsibility may produce sanctions such as warnings, disciplining, suspension, criminal prosecution, or deregistration from professional status.

Problems arise when there is responsibility without commensurate power or authority to discharge that responsibility. The management of risk provides an example. Employers may legitimately expect practitioners to take responsibility for assessing users' level of risk and plan accordingly. However, this can be accompanied by a sense that the practitioner will be held accountable if the user subsequently harms themselves or others. The state of the art of risk assessment and management does not allow us to be confident that even the best practice will eliminate the possibility of an adverse event (see Chapter 6). There is a danger that some responsibilities are not legitimate in that the practitioner does not have the power to control the environment to a required level, and therefore holding them to account for it is unreasonable. It is therefore important that when employers define responsibilities, for example, in job descriptions, they ensure that the individual responsible will have the power to discharge the responsibility.

However, it is not only employers that can define responsibilities inappropriately. Overstating one's own responsibility can be a mechanism for appropriating power. Although increasingly unusual, some senior medical members of teams assert the notion of ultimate clinical responsibility whereby they would be 'ultimately responsible' for the work of the team as a whole should adverse events occur (for example, Isaacs and Bebbington, 1991). This assertion has no foundation. The Nodder Report concluded that there is 'no basis in law for the commonly expressed idea that a consultant may be held responsible for negligence on the part of others simply because he is the "responsible medical officer"; or that, though personally blameless, he may be held accountable after the style of a military commander. A multidisciplinary team has no "commander" in this sense' (DHSS, 1980). A generation later, a review by the BPS (2001) reported that:

> It has been recognised that health professionals work in teams, in which they have different responsibilities. It has been rejected that each team member is expected to deliver the same high standards of care, as this would mean the student would be expected to display the same level of skill as the consultant. By the same token, the English courts have also rejected the approach known as the 'captain of the ship' doctrine, which implies that the professionals in charge of teams are responsible for the negligence of their team members, even though they are personally blameless... Professionals working in teams are in the eyes of the law, likely to be held responsible for their own mistakes (BPS, 2001: Section 1.4, 1.5).

In practice where loss or injury was caused by the breach of duty of more than one person, the amount recoverable from individuals through law will be in proportion to the extent of that person's responsibility for the harm in question. Responsibility in teams is therefore *shared* among individuals, rather than collective or wholly carried by someone in a leadership role.

The assertion of ultimate clinical responsibility also unhelpfully served to conflate issues of *clinical* leadership, mentoring, support and supervision with *operational* management responsibilities concerned with running the team day-to-day. This may in itself have contributed to role ambiguity among practitioners and managers and has provided a rich vein of conflict within teams (for example, Jabitsky, 1988). With regard to rehabilitation services, Watts and Bennett (1983) stressed that the task of coordinating the input of the different disciplines within a CMHT in the care and treatment of individual users should not be part of a team leader role. Such hierarchical control produces inflexible working and no single individual will have sufficient information and expertise to control the work of the team effectively. This responsibility needs to be devolved to someone exercising a care coordinator role.

Many psychiatrists would now eschew the notion of ultimate clinical responsibility because of a clearer appreciation that to take this position would be to risk being held accountable for the actions of other clinicians in the team which the consultant does not have the power to control. Nonetheless, the relationship between psychiatrists and people in team leadership and management roles can be problematic. As stated above, Borrill *et al.* (2000) found that having a clear, single team leader was associated with the external ratings of team effectiveness. Having a single team leader was in turn associated with the absence of psychiatrists from the team.

It may be advantageous for leadership roles in the team to be shared in some circumstances, as long as the respective roles are clearly delineated and there are high levels of mutual respect and understanding between the manager and the psychiatrist.

Practitioner responsibilities

Professional practitioners within teams are accountable for different responsibilities to different authorities.

- *Employee responsibilities* are defined by a contract of employment, which usually includes a job description describing responsibilities in detail.
- *Professional responsibilities* are defined by a duty of care to users, professional codes of conduct, and in some cases state registration requirements. For staff in training, or recently qualified, this

includes formal accountability to a professional line manager in a clinical supervisory role.
- *Legal responsibility* forms part of professional responsibility and describes an obligation to recognise and observe the limits of your training and competence and satisfy yourself that anyone else to whom you refer is also appropriately qualified and competent. Certain members of the team will also have additional legal responsibilities. It is indisputable that where psychiatrists are identified as the Responsible Medical Officer for people held under the provisions of the Mental Health Act they have powers that exceed those of other members of the team.

The aim is to ensure that none of the responsibilities conflict. For example, an employer should not demand that a practitioner assumes responsibilities that they are not qualified or competent to exercise. Similarly, practitioners should not seek to control the work of another where they have no formal accountability for their work.

It is also important that responsibilities and lines of accountability are in line with the practitioner's own personal values and the values embodied in their role as a professional practitioner. As we have seen above, practitioners are accountable to employers, their professional bodies and society as a whole through the legal system. However, they are also accountable to people that use their service. They may find themselves in conflict between what they perceive as expected of them from powerful authorities around them and what they perceive to be in the best interests of their users. As Barker and Baldwin (1991: 195) observed: 'Each worker has a responsibility to determine where his or her ultimate responsibility rests. Within these constraints, many workers will decide that they are, ultimately, responsible to themselves, and will operate according to a personal ethical code'.

The responsibilities of employing authorities

It is important for practitioners to be aware that employing authorities also have a direct duty of care towards users, visitors and their own employees. They need to ensure that those they employ are suitably qualified, competent and supported to carry out their roles.

Employers also have a duty to ensure a safe system of care for both users and employees. They must provide proper facilities and equipment and ensure that staff are able to exercise their professional responsibilities (BPS, 2001). They are also responsible for the development and monitoring of realistic operational policies.

Employers also carry liability for the acts of their employees when acting in the normal course of their employment. However, this does not protect the individual practitioner from personal litigation. They remain personally responsible for their own acts, even though claims are usually made against the employer.

Configuring accountability relationships within and beyond the team

The allocation of responsibilities to team members, the lines of accountability that accompany them, and the input of different disciplines to the team in combination define different types of team configuration. The following configurations appear to be most typical, and are adapted from the work of Ovretveit (1986, 1993, 1997) and my own work on teams.

The profession-managed network

Professional line managers expect their subordinates to conform to certain agreed practices and policies regarding other professions, but the practitioners concerned do not comprise a team with a team policy. This approach may be well suited to working with common mental health problems in primary care settings where high levels of coordination of clinical work are not required, but people may still want to meet for reasons of peer support and consultation. There is no formal leader.

The managed team

One member of the team is responsible for specified management functions but does not oversee the clinical decision-making of other team members. They do have delegated authority to expect compliance with operational policy. The clarity and robustness of this authority is often central to whether the role is successful or not. Where it is weak, the manager is merely coordinating the staff with little authority to determine their role in the team. In this weaker version, staff continue to see their professional line managers as the most important managers shaping their work. Where the delegation of authority is greater, staff may choose to retain a reporting relationship to their line managers, who will be involved in ensuring their continuing professional development, but their primary allegiance is to the team. This is perhaps the most common form of team management, and the one advocated here.

The fully managed team

All management functions are assumed by one person within the team, including receipt and allocation of referrals, termination of case-work, and operational practice. Involvement of professional line managers is far less than in the other models.

The difference between this model and a managed team as described above is best demonstrated by examining allocation. In a managed team, the manager would be responsible for ensuring a case was allocated following assessment. In a fully managed team, the team manager would also determine *to whom* the case was allocated. Another example would be where caseload monitoring was being used to evaluate the clinical work of practitioners, rather than as an aid to the workload management of the team as a whole. It is much more difficult to see how this model can be applied to professional staff because of the professional and legal responsibilities described above. In a qualitative study of CMHTs, Onyett and Henderson (1996) could find no support for full team management (or 'totalising team management' as it was defined in the report). Even existing team managers did not welcome these extra powers and would themselves resist being allocated work by another profession. One consultant predicted that the introduction of such arrangements would automatically exclude medical staff from multidisciplinary teams which would be '*really retrogressive*' to service development. Another participant gave examples of where moves to the introduction of totalising team management had resulted in social workers and clinical psychologists leaving the team, or becoming team 'contributors' rather than members. In many ways totalising team management represents a renaissance in the notion of 'ultimate clinical responsibility' traditionally favoured by medical staff, but now exercised by other staff.

Ovretveit (1993) provides more detail about different team types, including situations where team managers have different relationships to different members of the team because of their different status and roles as core or associate members. However, in essence, the aim is merely to be sure that the responsibilities that need to be exercised by staff are the right ones given the needs of the client group and that, for each individual member of the team, there is clarity about who they are accountable to for that responsibility. The imperative is to ensure that all the relationships that bear upon the work of individual practitioners makes sense when drawn together in an operational policy, and strike the right balance between ensuring appropriately autonomous practice and the need for good monitoring of performance for continuous quality improvement.

Tasks that shape practitioner behaviour

In order to be clear about what needs to be achieved when establishing frameworks for responsibility and accountability, Onyett and Ford (1996) advocated that the following three tasks that shape the practice of team members be borne in mind.

1 *Clinical supervision* operates in the context of a formal accountability relationship between a line manager and a more junior team member who has yet to achieve the status of an independent practitioner accountable for their own clinical decision-making. The word 'supervision' is often used too loosely in a context where clarity is critical. It is commonly used to describe a relationship that is more akin to peer consultation or mentoring. In social services, the term is used more precisely and in accordance with the dictionary definition, which stresses 'inspection' and 'control' (*Chambers 20th Century Dictionary*, 1983). Here, the term 'supervision' describes an accountability relationship that requires the supervisee to act in accordance with direction given by their supervisor. By this definition, supervision of clinical

decision-making and actions can only operate within a relationship where the supervisor has the training required to adopt the role in question. It is not possible for a supervisor to supervise work for which they are not trained, as there is therefore no way in which they could be held accountable for that work (BPS, 2001). Clinical supervision most commonly occurs where a professional is supervising the actions of a more junior or aspiring member of their own profession who has yet to achieve independent practitioner status, for example, someone in professional training. This narrower definition should not to detract from the central importance of that process that is commonly referred to as 'supervision'. But it is a misnomer and this important process is more accurately described as 'mentoring' or 'peer consultation' where it spans disciplines.

Each independent practitioner is personally accountable for the exercise of their professional responsibilities, once they have completed training and any post-qualification supervision period. The requirement of clinical supervision is often used as the rationale for retaining primary accountability through professional line management structures. In fact, once practitioners have achieved independent practitioner status they are accountable to their professional bodies and the courts for the exercise of their professional responsibilities (and the legal responsibilities that these subsume). They should, nonetheless, have an effective relationship with a manager who will support, advise and, if necessary, constrain them to act in accordance with their acknowledged standards of their profession. That manager will themselves have a responsibility to do everything in their power to ensure that the people they manage act appropriately. This function should be distinct from support concerning personal or professional development, although it may be fulfilled by the same person. Practitioners should be able to seek support with their clinical work from whoever they judge to be most suitable.

2 *Operational management* occurs where a team manager has devolved responsibility for management tasks and can supervise the compliance of any discipline with operational policy. This form of accountability has strengthened with the development of management roles at team level.

It is important that practitioners are aware of the distinction between professional and legal responsibilities, as described above, and their responsibilities as employees of the managing authority. The management of their responsibilities as employees should be through a team manager to the employing authority. Should a management intervention be necessary then this would be the job of the team manager, seeking advice from others, including senior members of the relevant employee's own profession, as appropriate. The argument that only someone from within the same profession can exercise line management on behalf of the employer is no longer tenable, particularly since the introduction of clinical governance (Department of Health, 1998). As team managers are often at the interface of issues concerning operational and professional responsibilities, it is clear that they will require considerable skill and understanding of the demands of professional practice if they are to be credible to the people they manage.

3 *Peer consultation* is support and advice given within and across disciplines. Lack of formal accountability through 'supervision' does not render the support and advice given in clinical review meetings or through individual peer consultation useless. This peer consultation (both from within a profession and from others) is perhaps the core rationale for operating in a team. Individual peer consultation with a respected practitioner should be required of all practitioners, regardless of whether they require formal supervision or not. Aside from the importance of continuously developing the capabilities of practitioners, it may also be required to help practitioners recognise where they may be exceeding their competence. Those that fund teams need to ensure that time and resources for peer consultation (and clinical supervision for those that need it) are available and secure. We shall return to this critical issue when looking at how the team looks after itself in Chapter 8 and how quality is maintained in Chapter 9.

Management control versus practice autonomy

Practice autonomy, the practitioner's freedom to decide their own behaviour with regard to their work with individuals, is a strong signifier of professional status. Pilgrim and Rogers (1999) describe how professional groups vie for influence through demarcating specialist areas of practice with particular client groups, and exercise dominance over this domain as part of a process of professionalisation. It is also clear that practice autonomy is often claimed even when practitioners lack confidence in their abilities. As Cherniss (1995) observed of professionals in their first year of practice:

> The new professionals valued autonomy in part because it was linked to achieving a sense of competence. When others imposed restrictions on the new professionals, it not only limited their autonomy- it also called into question their ability. Competent professionals are supposed to enjoy a high degree of autonomy. So a lack of autonomy made the novices feel less competent (23; my italics).

As we shall see below, achieving a qualified autonomy for practitioners is not only important for their own sense of efficacy, it is also required for smooth running of the team. Practitioners need to be able to make a defined range of decisions for themselves, or else the team would spend all its time managing itself and never doing any clinical work. From the point of view of staff, autonomy is also important in terms of managing their own working lives. For example, Cooper *et al.* (1989) reported that the highest levels of satisfaction reported among general practitioners were associated with the amount of responsibility given, the freedom to choose working methods and the amount of variety in the job (see Chapter 8). But there needs to be checks and balances.

Morrall (1997) examined practice autonomy among ten CMHNs working in four CMHTs over two years, and found their practice to be arbitrary and unregulated. They were able to regulate the size of their caseload by choosing not to visit practices where referrals might be picked up. Almost a fifth of users on their caseloads were discharged after only a week suggesting that they could rapidly discharge people they deemed to be inappropriate. There was no systematic approach to assessment and there was very minimal discussion of clinical work with either CMHT colleagues or supervisors. Morrall concluded that although CMHNs in this context were operating with high levels of autonomy, this was by default rather than as a recognised emblem of their professionalism. Indeed it was clear that the psychiatrists and psychologists within the teams regarded the CMHNs as subordinates requiring improved monitoring and regulation.

Patmore and Weaver (1991a) were strong opponents of the exercise of professional autonomy within CMHTs and advocated strong operational management to restrain it (see above). Achieving an appropriate balance between professional discretion and operational management is a critical tension within CMHT leadership and management roles.

Team hierarchy and the problem of 'democracy'

Power relations will exist wherever two or more people come together. Often differences in power will be legitimate, based on experience, skill and knowledge. Sometimes they will be illegitimate, based upon the effects of social inequalities arising, for example from class, gender, race, and education.

The notion of 'democratic' teams is invoked to describe teams that are 'non-hierarchical', where everybody has an equal say on issues, and where decisions do not take place without majority rule. It is a highly socially valued description that in practice serves to prevent candid examination of legitimate and illegitimate power relations, and provides a defence against the intrusion of operational management roles into teams. Often teams claiming to be non-hierarchical are living a lie.

Lang's (1982) participant observation study of a team that claimed to be non-hierarchical found that hierarchical power relationships maintained nonetheless. The team aimed 'to restructure traditionally stratified professional role relationships in more democratic ways' (159) asserting an ideology in which professional workers were seen as equally able to work with any user of the team's services. The absence of stratification of authority was demonstrated through informal and non-deferential interactions and the fact that psychiatrists never challenged the competence of nurses. However, on closer examination stratification did emerge through the informal division of labour. The nurses placed greater value on duties that were seen as important in 'reaching out' to service users who might not otherwise engage with the service, such as phone contact to enquire about missed appointments, helping out with non-mental health problems, arranging child-care, providing transportation and home visiting. In contrast the doctors, 'believed that it was the task of mental health professionals to foster self-reliance, initiative and motivation in patients, and that over-solicitousness would undermine this goal' (162). Lang noted that low status positions, which bore a disproportionate amount of the 'dirty' work, were defined by persons in higher-status roles as being crucial. However, when allocating the *unwanted* tasks 'the intentions of democracy were undermined because of the persistent and unacknowledged fact that those who will accept expediting work are those who have been socialised to believe they "should"... the nurses whose professional and sex-role training had reinforced a broad notion of service' (164).

Baron's (1987) study of a day hospital that claimed to be non-hierarchical also revealed covert and oppressive power relationships based upon charismatic leadership and a psychodynamic group-based ideology that precluded the possibility of alternative interpretations of events. Similarly, Drolen's (1990) study of CMHC managers found that although most claimed to value management styles that encouraged participatory decision-making, over 78 per cent reported that senior management was the most important group in decision-making, and could identify no innovations that had originated with the clientele or other community members.

'Democracy' is not the same as participatory decision-making. The latter is clearly desirable and may indeed be more achievable where staff experience less role ambiguity because they are clear about where they sit in terms of power and authority within the team (Patmore and Weaver, 1991a). Hierarchy only becomes problematic when associated with a bureaucracy that emphasises top-down information flow, highly formalised rules, narrowly defined jobs, and norms that require obedience to official policy. In other words, exactly the opposite of the conditions for innovation described below.

Management and the containment of team anxiety

Whatever configuration is chosen, it is important to be mindful of the psychologically containing function of responsibility and accountability relationships, and the role of management and other supports as a whole.

The concept of 'containment' has widespread currency through the pioneering work of the Tavistock Clinic staff, who themselves draw upon the psychoanalytical works of Klein and Bion (see Foster and Roberts, 1998; and Obholzer and Roberts, 1994 for further background and application of this thinking). In essence, this approach assumes that people with severe and enduring mental health problems experience an inner chaos and fragmentation accompanied by feelings of intense anxiety. They have great difficulty 'containing' this within themselves and so use processes of projection to rid themselves of what feels unmanageable. Projection is a process by which those unwanted parts of ourselves are experienced as coming from outside. So, for example, the team may idealise itself while denigrating management or other agencies. Projective identification is a process whereby we identify with the projections of others into us. Foster and Roberts (1998) cite an example where adolescents split off and project either authoritarian or rebellious aspects of themselves onto staff who then, through a process of projective identification, themselves become either harsh and punitive or act out adolescent rebellion.

The importance of containment comes from the fact that these projections can be understood as a form of unconscious communication, but only where the recipient can tolerate the pain and anxiety that they convey. The seminal work of Menzies (1967) highlighted how the 'caring' environment can evolve to serve a defensive function against projected emotions. In order to cope with the strong feelings that the work invoked, the nursing task was fragmented so that nurses no longer had to relate to the patient as a whole person. This helped to defend against anxiety but also made the work feel meaningless, which then contributed to high drop-out rates.

In community mental health services there is a contradiction between an emphasis on record keeping and proceduralisation (as manifest in the more misguided approaches to implement the CPA; see North and Ritchie, 1993) which is evocative of the defensive systems described above, and the simultaneous emphasis on working with users as whole people with a range of needs. Given the emphasis on working through strong individual relationships between users and staff through intensive community treatment, this is an area that if neglected is likely to give rise to emotional withdrawal of staff from users, and a resulting sense of meaninglessness and dissatisfaction among staff (see Chapter 8).

Living on the boundaries of teams

Team managers have an important role in containing difficult team emotions. They sit on the boundaries of teams, facing outwards when representing the team or members of the team to management, other agencies, users, carers or other members of the public. They may also have a role in leading and presenting the finding of internal evaluations and audits. They also face inwards when acting as an agent of external management, communicating strategic goals, informing staff of developments at more senior and inter-agency levels, and ensuring clear lines of support, mentoring, supervision and accountability.

Living on the boundary can be a difficult and lonely place to be. Roberts (1998a) describes how an effective manager needs to be both in touch with the internal state of the team and the needs of its members, and looking outward to stay aware of the demands on the team as a whole. They often find themselves the receptacle of the group's projections, for example, the denigration of management as a whole, particularly in a context where structures are constantly evolving and frail, and there is no longer a robust institution to offer containment of these projections. In this context, the 'hate stays nearer home' (1998a: 56). They can neither entirely join the group nor distance themselves from it. Roberts (1998a) describes a need for managers to have good support from their own managers or the support of an external consultant or mentor to help them contain these projections. Teams need a manager who (citing Turquet, 1974: 57–8) can 'bear being used,... otherwise the negative projections go elsewhere: manager and staff may cling together and locate the blame with an external enemy – more senior managers, for example, or politicians; or the projections go ricocheting around the organisation, precipitating personalised conflicts among peers; or the negativity may be re-internalised in all its rawness, so that workers can no longer find meaning or pleasure in their work'.

Articulating a vision

Having clear aims and objectives is central to team effectiveness, and leaders and managers have a key role in articulating and communicating this vision.

Teams are open systems pulled around by the complex environment in which they are embedded. They need to be able to adapt to shifting patterns and intensity in demands while retaining a clear vision of the aims of the organisation.

The obscurity of team aims has been the focus of much criticism, particularly with respect to CMHCs, (for example, Galvin and McCarthy, 1994; Patmore and Weaver, 1991a; Sayce *et al.*, 1991). Sayce *et al.* (1991) found that the primary stated aims of CMHCs in the UK were defined very broadly. Examples cited included: 'To increase community awareness of mental health issues', 'To make services more accessible and less stigmatising', or even 'To operate a multidisciplinary team'. The latter was particularly emblematic of an emerging impression that CMHCs and subsequently CMHTs were emerging as an end in themselves rather than as a vehicle for improved outcomes for service users. This ambiguity in goal setting appeared to stem from interdisciplinary tensions that arose whenever the agreement of more precise objectives was attempted, rather than premeditated obfuscation. Since then the aims of CMHTs have become much more prescribed and there are many more models to draw on.

Clear aims and objectives are necessary for the practical realisation of a team's philosophy and ideology, and the evaluation of the work of the team as a whole. The aims of the service should be broken down into a statement of the overarching purpose of the service, and the more specific objectives which the service intends to meet along the way. These objectives should be framed in such a way as to be measurable. Gaining feedback on innovations is only useful if there is a standard against which results can be judged. Each aim and the associated objectives should be tested against the explicit underpinning values of the team.

Innovation is promoted within a work group that has a vision that is clear, negotiated, shared, evolving, valued and attainable (West and Farr, 1989). This requires that the team has a clear strategic role, as described in Chapter 4, and that individuals within the team 'sign up' to the teams organisational goals and vision.

One way of getting this 'sign' up is through the team developing an operational policy through a team training or review process (see Box 7). For this to be effective, the strategic parameters within which the team is operating must be clearly defined. For example, the client group of the team should be clearly stated and informed by local needs assessment and the work of other local providers.

Box 7 *A checklist of issues for the development of operational policy*

- Values
- Aims
- Objectives
- Client group
- Access
    - Agreed referral sources
    - How to refer
    - How referrals will be prioritised
    - Procedures for processing refused referrals
    - Agreed response times
- Assessment
    - Risk assessments
    - Initial interview process
    - Process for informing the referrer of the outcome of assessment
- Care coordination procedures
    - Identifying existing or arranging new care coordinators
    - Procedures for planning and reviewing care
    - Evidence-based interventions available and their application (for example, relapse prevention)
    - Statement on the involvement of carers
- Crisis response
    - Service available out of hours
    - Crisis response available
    - Processes for individual planning for future crisis response
- Record keeping and data-bases
    - How users and carers access
    - Policy on confidentiality
- Agree procedures for carrying and administering medication

- Staffing
  - Team composition
  - Roles
  - Safety procedures for staff (for example, what to do if a staff member fails to return from a visit)
  - Rotas, including out of hours
- Management and other non-clinical roles
- Accountability and reporting relationships
- Inter-agency relationships: primary care, voluntary sector, health-social services integration, other
- Meetings: purpose, duration, location, ground rules (for example, turning off pagers), chairing, recording
- Training
- Resources available to the team
- Quality assurance, audit and the participation of service users

Ideology and values

The starting point for describing a live operational policy that actually informs the way in which staff work with users is a statement of the values underpinning the aims and operation of the service. These values and beliefs concern what a service should be achieving for people, such as the much-quoted 'five accomplishments' (O'Brien and Lyle, 1988). Although the values statements should be developed in a way that promotes ownership by team members, it should also be informed, where possible, by similar statements made at a higher level (for example, health authority, local authority and PCT) or through a forum where people come together in partnership to plan local services (for example, the Local Implementation Team; see Box 8).

Hosking and Morley (1991) advocated caution when referring to groups as having 'shared values'. This assumes a rationalistic, consensual, managerialist perspective that does not place adequate emphasis on conflict and competition. It is safer to assert that teams displaying higher 'degrees of groupness' will have more shared values. Where shared values translate into clear superordinate goals that

Box 8 *The Avon Policy Development Group: An example of working with values*

A Policy Development Group had been established with the job of overseeing the work of more local planning groups and bringing a large new mental health service provider into being. It involved a diverse range of stakeholders who had never worked together like this before (including users, carers, the voluntary sector, the police, and senior managers and practitioners from health, social services and primary care).

The group recognised that this work needed to be based upon explicit values about what the mental health service should be achieving. In order to promote the participation of a large number of people, it was decided to use a directive, managed process to agree a shared set of values.

Twenty-four value statements were drawn together from national and local documents, the existing literature (such as the 'five accomplishments' of O'Brien and Lyle, 1988) and the group itself. Participants then rated these statements privately by stating 'how central to the aims of Avon Mental Health Services' they were, by placing them within a series of concentric circles where those nearer to the centre represented being 'completely central to our aims', and the outer circles represented 'Could be included but not very important'. Placing them outside the circles meant that participants did not feel the value to be relevant. Using this method the values could be prioritised numerically and fed back to the group.

In order to underline the importance and centrality of this work, the task was undertaken as part of the routine business of the group rather than at a special event. The findings provided a starting point for further lively discussion, amendment and whittling down till the following statements were agreed:

> In order to ensure that the mental health services in Avon are shaped by people's needs the service will:
>
> - Recognise that all users are citizens with rights and responsibilities, regardless of their culture, ethnicity, gender, age, sexuality, disability, involvement in the criminal justice system or housing status.

- Be shaped by the user's experience and concerns.
- Ensure that service users are helped to make their voice heard in order to give them the maximum control over the choices that are made.
- Communicate clearly and provide enough information to ensure that the right options are considered, informed consent is achieved, and the right to refuse treatment can be exercised where necessary.
- Involve users as far as possible in planning for those situations where services may have to take control in order to protect the user or other people.
- Provide resources across client groups and localities fairly according to need.
- Provide fair and prompt access to assistance when needed.
- Increase the independence and self-respect of users by increasing their ability to cope in natural community environments and relationships.
- Ensure that service users have opportunities to participate in the life of the community by supporting relationships with their families and others, where necessary helping them widen their network and supporting their actual physical presence in the same places as other citizens.
- Actively work to overcome the effects of social inequalities arising from, for example, ethnicity, gender, age and poverty.
- Use resources to achieve the greatest benefit by using research to inform what services do, and continually evaluate the outcomes of work with users.
- Involve carers wherever possible, and acknowledge that they will have their own needs.

the group members can identify with, it can be predicted that this will, in turn, enhance the degree of groupness felt by the team (Sherif, 1966), thereby establishing a virtuous cycle. As we saw from Chapter 5, teams that have clearer goals are more likely to have members that have a strong sense of team identification. In other words, belonging to the team will have greater social value. It is therefore more likely that the group members will act like a group in relation to a wider range of issues.

It is important not to underestimate the difficulties in establishing a shared ideology of care. Lang (1982) described how, in practice, psychiatrists and nurses adopted contrasting models for understanding users' experiences and how this impacted on their relationships with users. Her qualitative study of a CMHT examined attempts to realise an anti-'medical model' ideology in a team that aimed 'to replace traditional intra-psychic diagnostic and treatment models with more socially orientated ones' (159).

> The psychiatrists more routinely and comfortably used standard diagnostic categories – i.e. 'She sounds like a classic hysteric to me', or 'He is a real manic-depressive'. They were also more likely to cast a patient's behaviour in manipulative terms, against which strong, professional defences were urged. 'Be careful I think she is trying to use you.' 'She needs strong limits set, don't be too accessible'.
>
> The nurses on the other hand, more often described cases in ways that supported the plausibility of the patient's perspective. They presented cases in more behavioural than diagnostic terms, for example, describing a patient as 'feeling depressed' rather than as a 'depressive.' They tended to eschew imputations of hidden, symbolic or unconscious motivation and were more likely to cast their initial discussions in a framework of partnership, sympathy or empathy, making reference to the strengths or appeals of a particular patient. They did not usually initiate references to cynical or manipulative motivations of patients (Lang, 1982: 166).

Spindel and Nugent (1999) argue that there has been too much emphasis paid to 'models' of case management and ACT rather than a clearly articulated ideology of practice which challenges both the biomedical and social control aspects of community mental health work. They assert that this partly explains why so many models have been tried and subsequently abandoned as having little positive impact on the lives of users.

The team provides a vehicle for an ideology that promotes effective relationships between users and staff. This ideology needs to be well informed and realistic. If the values do not translate into achievable outcomes then the team risks disillusionment and loss of faith. It is important that the team as a whole inculcates among its members a realistic sense of what a valued outcome might be for the people it serves, and over what period. While advocates of a recovery approach have rightly underlined the possibility of full recovery of valued roles for people diagnosed with psychoses, and the importance of instilling hope and optimism (Carling and Allott, 2000), it is equally true that change is often very slow, and that crises, relapse and deterioration are also commonplace. If the team is too orientated towards notions of recovery that emphasise discharge, there is a danger that staff can become demoralised when, despite their efforts, the required change does not occur. To be effective allies of people with severe and long-term mental health problems, staff need to be able to support a person through the bad times as well as the good 'in order to help them to do the things they want and live the life they want to live' (Perkins and Repper, 1998: 27).

It will be important for the team's ideology of care to include an explicit position on the use of coercion in community care, the management of risk and a recognition of the importance of the effects of social inequalities on the incidence of mental health problems, and the ways in which they are responded to.

Issues concerning change to achieve a particular vision will be further explored in the final chapter.

Effective management day-to-day

A clear values-based vision counts for little if the team cannot run effectively day-to-day. Hence it is important to consider key procedural issues about how the team runs.

A summary of team management tasks is given in Box 9.

Developing operational policy

A key role in the above is the development of the team's operational policy. This should be informed by the care pathway of the user through the team. Ovretveit (1993) described the design of team process as a series of logical stages:

1 Deciding on acceptable referral sources, publicising the service accordingly and providing optimal means of access;
2 Receiving referrals in a way that allows the effective planning of assessment or an emergency response where necessary;
3 Determining criteria for acceptance for assessment;

Box 9 *Tasks of team management*

On-going development of operational policy

- Integrating purchasing imperatives and translating these into team operational policy with the support of other provider managers and planners.
- Developing the operational policy on the basis of an on-going evaluation of the team's work. There should never be a 'final draft' operational policy – it will always be a 'work in progress'.
- Ensuring that information on met and unmet needs, collected through individual service planning processes, is used to monitor the achievement of aims and objectives, and to inform future service development and training. This includes ensuring that CPA records and computerised information systems are operational, and feeding back summarised information to team members to inform their work.
- Informing purchasers and senior managers on service shortfalls that may not be obvious from individual service planning systems. This will include working with other key stakeholders to ensure that their views are heard.
- Organising regular reviews of the team's operations and practices.
- Voicing other team member concerns and constraints to provider management. This may be on behalf of the team as a whole or individuals.
- Disseminating the aims and practices of the service to the wider public and receiving feedback.

Managing the implementation of operational policy

- Establishing systems for prioritisation and caseload monitoring.
- Establishing record keeping and other information systems for clinical use (for example, integrated care coordination

assessment schedules and material for running reviews, risk management, informing others, and so on).

- Management of team meetings, including chairing, recording or supporting others in chairing.
- Operational management of care coordinating tasks. These tasks must be distinguished from the more specific tasks associated with particular professional and post-qualification training.
- Ensuring the care coordinating responsibility is allocated for all users on the team's caseload.
- Ensuring that processes for clinical support are available for team members. This may include clinical review meetings or more specific forums, alongside individual peer consultation, personal mentoring or supervision.
- Ensuring explicit mechanisms for conflict resolution within the team. This often takes the form of a series of progressive 'back-stops' starting within the team and involving others only where these steps fail.
- Coordinating annual leave and study leave.
- Managing team administration.
- Involvement in drafting job descriptions, short-listing job applicants, interviewing and appointing, induction, reviewing workload, appraising annual performance and personal development/training needs, and signing off expenses. These roles may be shared with other managers but the team manager will need to be heavily involved.

4. Allocating referrals for assessment;
5. Assessment;
6. Acceptance for longer-term work;
7. Allocation for longer-term work;
8. Intervention and/or monitoring;
9. Team review and
10. Closure.

The design of this process should be based upon an understanding of local users' pathways to and through CMHT provision. It should aim to achieve the optimal match between the team member's collective resources of knowledge, skills, experience and time, and the needs of their identified client group.

The priority and resources allocated to each stage will need to be agreed. These decisions should be informed by the aims of the team, which in turn are informed by local assessment of need and the availability of collateral services. For example, a crisis intervention team that was aiming to provide an alternative to admission may prioritise resources in order to achieve a rapid response to referrals, and effective assessment at the expense of longer-term work, on the grounds that other services are available locally to address the latter need.

Readers interested in further details of how these stages may be managed are referred to the many worked examples of team operations (for example, Onyett, 1998; and the Sainsbury Centre for Mental Health practice database, *www.scmh.org.uk.*)

Ensuring appropriate allocation of work

If the relationship between the user and the team member is critical to outcome then clearly issues of screening and appropriate allocation are central to the team process. Patmore and Weaver (1991a) stressed the importance of internal management in ensuring that referrals were appropriately screened and allocated as a way of ensuring that the needs of people with severe and long-term mental health problems were given priority. They saw deficits in this area as a key indicator of an internal management vacuum. Similarly, the allocation of cases to team practitioners was regarded by Ovretveit (1993) as the defining responsibility of team managers.

The aim of systematic allocation is that it should match users to workers according to the particular skills of workers, and their correspondence with the preferences and apparent needs of the individual referred. Patmore and Weaver's (1991a) study revealed a tendency for practitioners to self-allocate referrals according to how attractive they found the referral. Unpopular referrals, typically people with long-term problems and psychotic diagnosis, would be followed by long, tense silences, while those people who offered opportunities for psychotherapeutic work were more eagerly taken up. Patmore and Weaver found in their interviews with staff that those who had not yet volunteered in the course of a meeting, or were highlighted by the rest of the team as having the appropriate skills, complained of strong peer pressure to volunteer. As one worker put it, allocation of unpopular cases therefore was to: 'Whoever feels most guilty at not taking it' (21).

Lang (1982) also found that 'liking' or being 'interested' in particular referrals formed the common and accepted ground for selection of cases. This was associated with an apparently democratic and non-hierarchical team ideology that prohibited allocation on the basis of presumed competence. Patmore and Weaver (1990) found that some staff would argue that a minimal medication service was adequate for people on long-term caseloads, while the 'new clientele' was seen as having more challenging 'live' problems.

Patmore and Weaver (1991c) found that workers would tend to address the question: 'Can I personally help this person?' rather than whether the referral corresponded to the targeted client group of the team and whether the team had the skills and capacity to work effectively with the individual. Indeed, they highlighted that it would have been impossible for workers to make these judgements since the size and composition of each worker's caseload was often shrouded in secrecy. Some of the CMHCs studied could not even list the individuals being served by members of the team at any given time. This failure to internally manage the work of the team also resulted in large inequities in allocation with 'lonely and strenuous case management roles for those that volunteered for these less popular referrals' (1991c: 22). In effect, deciding that ones specialism was counselling would be more likely to result in smaller caseloads because of the competition for referrals. Deciding to specialise in work with people with severe and long-term mental health problems would predictably have the opposite effect.

As well as being emblematic of an internal management vacuum, self-allocation was also seen by Patmore and Weaver as indicative of a tendency to genericism and role blurring which itself made management of the team more difficult. They construed it as indicative of an unhelpful diminution of clear links between professional identity and particular roles. A collective belief that everyone essentially did the same job had been established in some of the CMHCs studied. This served to defend practitioners from explicit definition and scrutiny of their activities: 'alternatives to self-allocation could threaten team cohesion – such as teams or managers explicitly comparing the skills of workers from different professions in areas where all team members claim expertise' (Patmore and Weaver, 1991c: 20). Uncritical self-allocation was therefore seen as masking the inadequacy of skills within the team. Although workers claimed that self-allocation allowed them to work with users according to their skills, this could not be guaranteed, and there existed the danger of workers opting to work with people who presented difficulties that fell outside of their range of training, skills and experience.

Given the importance of managing allocation, what do we know about how it operates in mental health teams? The CMHT survey revealed that team managers or coordinators were reported as most responsible for allocating cases to team members in only 26 per cent of teams. Nearly half the teams (49 per cent) saw this as a task of the team as a whole. The team as a whole also dominated the decision-making regarding which referrals were accepted on a day-to-day basis.

Lack of clearly identified internal management responsibility has been implicated in the tendency of CMHTs to neglect people most in need of assistance, inequitable and inappropriate allocation of cases, and obfuscation of the skill mix within the team. Patmore and Weaver's work has underlined the need for someone to have the power to prioritise referrals, nominate assessors and subsequently ensure allocation of cases to care coordinators within the team. Among teams with low management they found that there was a consensus that greater authority needed to be invested in the team manager's role. Chapter 4 described how this process of prioritisation for allocation might be managed (Harrison, 2000; Job, 1999).

Managing workload

Tools for making workload explicit are helpful in alerting the team to inequitable and unrealistic workloads and also begin to provide a shared language for talking about the experience of working with particular clients. In Dorset, a caseload weighting scheme was developed drawing upon the framework of client definitions used in Chapter 4 and using a simple three-point weighting scale[1]. The numerical results of such weighting scales do not aim to establish a valid account of the experienced impact of working with particular clients. There are a host of other contributory factors (such as the amount of sleep that the clinician had the night before, the current state of their family relationships, and so on) that could never be captured in a tool for routine clinical use. However, such tools do help to open up discussion and can highlight gross inequalities in the work being undertaken by team members.

Achieving effective communication within the team

Effective communication achieves innovation: the introduction of ideas, processes, products or procedures that are designed to bring about improvement (West and Farr, 1989). It is the essence of what team-working is all about. We consider this last in this chapter because it should be the product of so much that has gone before. For example, effective communication requires clear aims, shared values and clarity over one's responsibilities and lines of accountability.

Communication in CMHTs needs to be centred on the user themselves and those people that they chose to involve. Communication for decision-making is a process where people come together with a clear understanding of the outcomes to be achieved, equally equipped with information about what is available to improve the situation. This requires that users come invested with enough authority by the other participants in the process to ensure they take a full and active role. This in turn demands that they have access to the right information and, where necessary, the support of an advocate in making their views and preferences known (see Chapter 6). It also requires flexibility about how their views are fed into the process. Some may chose to communicate their views on a one-to-one basis with their care coordinators while others, recognising the power and authority of others in the team, may wish to engage with a larger group of the people involved.

There are other preconditions for effective communication. First, there should be a recognised need to communicate. It should be seen as necessary to get the job done. Secondly, team members must have shared social reality about what they are doing, and a shared language with which to describe this reality. Building this shared reality should start with the experience of the user, and use language that promotes their inclusion. Thirdly, team members should be supported in being able to take the perspective of others into account in relation to both their emotional and cognitive position.

Often this is a characteristic of maturing teams with stable membership. In these circumstances, the team is better able to recognise the source of communication difficulties when they arise. Finally, there needs to be a recognisable and agreed process for communication and decision-making. It is important that decision-making is visible, inclusive and coherent, and that it is afforded time and substance.

Borrill *et al.* (2000) found that interaction frequency, frequency of meetings, attempts at integration within teams, and communication in meetings played very important parts in distinguishing between health care teams. They reported that: 'It was striking how poorly managed were many of the meetings we observed'.

The nature of psychiatric discourse itself creates problems in decision-making. Lang (1982) highlighted the paucity of theory and intellectual substance to be found in the content of interactions among practitioners stating that 'the intangibility of technique and achievements fosters a reliance upon experience, manner, and style to fill a void' (165). Lang lamented the high degree of responsibility that practitioners have over peoples' lives in mental health work while they operate with low degrees of theoretical sophistication. Her ethnographic study demonstrated how avoidance of substantive discussion served to mask structural inequalities within the team, and potential ideological conflicts.

Creating opportunities for reflecting on the team process, and work with individuals, groups and families is just part of creating, what Roberts (1998b) refers to as, 'the consultant in the system', a third party that alters the shape of the system from a two-person, user-worker bi-polar system to a triangular user-worker-consultant system. In the psychoanalytically-informed approach of Roberts (1998b), this triangular system forms a reflective space within which it becomes possible for projections to be acknowledged, owned and processed. It creates the possibility for us to observe ourselves in interaction with others and to see the situation from alternative perspectives. It also helps counter a tendency towards frenetic activity and doing (for example, another change in medication) rather than reflecting and staying with the user to better understand and respond to their experience.

Achieving this space requires that enough time is put aside for discussion, and that the space is defended and respected (for example, by turning off mobile phones or pagers). Managing the meetings requires highly developed facilitation skills. For each user being reviewed, someone will need to ensure that the discussion is divergent and inclusive enough for participants to truly understand the situation and generate new ideas. Teams must not become committed prematurely to ideas, which may be unhelpful, incomplete or too readily suggested by custom and practice. However, at some point in the discussion, it will need to shift from being divergent to convergent, narrowing down on some key actions to be taken forward.

Generating ideas and achieving commitment to action will be influenced by the team's expectation, approval and support of attempts to introduce new and improved ways of doing things. This aspect of team climate has been shown to be related to levels of innovation, alongside other factors such as a clear vision, a general team expectation that excellence will be achieved, and participative safety (West *et al.*, 1998). Support for innovation needs to entail verbal approval, and offers of cooperation, time and resources that are then demonstrated in practice.

Participative safety

'Participative safety' is another aspect of an innovative climate, and describes where team members feel free to participate and share ideas, even if those ideas are a little 'half-baked' (ibid.). It allows constructive controversy in pursuit of excellence. In order to make the social environment of the team safe enough to allow frequent efforts towards innovation, communication should be non-judgmental. If team members feel they can voice ideas within the group and receive a considered response, members achieve influence, higher levels of interaction and more sharing of information. This is promoted by collaborative, and participative leadership styles. The attendant devolution of decision-making promotes innovation through increased autonomy and commitment to the tasks at hand (ibid.).

Managing conflict

Rogers and Pilgrim (1996) describe the role relationships between disciplines as the outcome of successful bids for legitimacy on the part of particular disciplines rather than rationally determined roles that are self-evident from the knowledge and skills that a particular discipline brings. It is therefore not surprising that role relationships should provide a rich vein of conflict within teams (Anciano and Kirkpatrick, 1990; Galvin and McCarthy, 1994) as people defend their positions and perspectives.

Lang (1982) offers an example of how *lack* of conflict can reveal an attempt to create and maintain the illusion of egalitarianism within teams.

> Staff meetings and case disposition meetings, which could have served as the basis for more sustained and substantive interaction, were remarkably, even compulsively, devoid of substantive discussions which might bring forth indications of the workers' very different intellectual, social and professional levels. There was little in-depth discussion of cases, virtually no conflict over diagnoses or treatment recommendations, and rarely any discussion of issues drawn from the larger fields of psychiatry or mental health. In this instance the avoidance of substantive discussions and conflict can be viewed as a mechanism by which the reality of stratification was suppressed and prevented from interfering with the goal of equality (164).

Watts and Bennett (1983) also underlined the positive aspect of disagreements over clinical work: 'one of the problems that can afflict an over-cohesive team is a kind of "Groupthink" in which the team ceases to pay attention to information that conflicts with its general assumptions, and strong social pressures are brought to bear on any members who challenge these assumptions' (317–18). Without the expression of difference within teams, there is a danger that clinical meetings diminish the intellectual contribution of everyone present. It may also mean that the user's own representation of their situation is not taken fully into account as part of the clinical process (Opie, 1997).

West and Farr (1989) concluded that successful organisations manage rather than suppress or avoid conflict, and that responsibility for managing conflict should be seen as part of everybody's job rather than located with particular managers acting as referees or arbiters.

Resolving conflict is clearly easier where there are well-defined responsibilities and lines of accountability within the team, and where there is a shared understanding and agreement of who decides what, as described below. It may also be helpful to have a series of 'backstops' between team and other line managers agreed as part of operational policy. In the Early Intervention Service (Onyett, 1998), the team manager, a team support group and a management steering group comprised a mechanism for conflict resolution. There was agreement that the manager would first approach the conflicting team members and encourage them to make use of the support group. Where this was refused, inappropriate or ineffective, the manager had the authority to liaise with the appropriate line managers to attempt resolution. Where this failed, there was the possibility of then using the team's steering group, where key external managers and agencies were represented, to attempt resolution. Having clear mechanisms laid out in this way had the effect that there was only one occasion where issues had to be taken outside the team's support group. This appeared advantageous in promoting a sense of team identification and autonomy.

Who decides what?

Effective decision-making also requires that the team is clear about the type of decision to be made and who should make them. Four types of decision-making can be delineated (after Ovretveit, 1993).

1 *Decisions about work with an individual user within the user–staff member relationship.* This will include arrangements made with the team member and the user for how they will manage their work, such as when they will meet and where. It also includes profession-specific decisions that do not need wider consultation such as which profession-specific assessment to use (for example, for assessing activities of daily living skills, or vocational preferences), or which medication. By definition, the profession concerned would need to exercise these decisions without fear of being impeded by the team, otherwise they would find themselves unable to discharge their professional responsibilities. It nonetheless remains good practice to be constantly ready to seek advice and support that will inform and improve decision-making.
2 *Care coordination decisions concerning an individual user.* These decisions will be delegated to a care coordinator in partnership

with the user themselves and others involved. It is this group of people that constitute the team for the purposes of meeting the needs of the client. It is therefore in this domain that most team communication needs to take place. Care coordination decisions include, for example, who should be working together and how, what the objectives of different inputs to the care plan are, whether a new or different approach should be used, and whether other resources can be brought to bear to improve the situation. These decisions should be very visible and subject to regular review by the team as a whole, who should feel able to challenge the decisions and suggest alternatives. Indeed, the team as a whole and particularly the user himself or herself are a resource for thinking creatively about alternatives. In only rare cases will there be a prescribed team policy that will tell the practitioner everything they need to know.

3. *Policy or management* decisions about how the team serves all users, and how care coordination will be undertaken within the team. In order to promote sound policy and effective implementation, it will be important that all team members are involved in such decisions.
4. *Planning* decisions, for example, about the team's objectives, the assessed needs of the client group or substantial changes in operational policy. These decisions will extend to involve people outside the team but clearly should include team members in order to ensure the decisions are informed by practical experience and to ensure appropriate ownership of new ideas and effective implementation.

How does effective leadership happen?

This chapter has highlighted the importance of a transformational leadership style to enhance team performance and morale. This begs the question of how to develop this style of leadership. The traditional approach of using appraisal systems to provide managers with feedback does not place enough emphasis on how the values of the organisation are demonstrated in practice through the impact of the manager's behaviour. Their behaviour will affect how others feel about their work and perform in their roles. Multi-rater feedback (MRF) or 360-degree feedback provides an alternative that takes a more explicit, stakeholder-based view on the impact of leadership and management.

MRF involves managers rating themselves on a range of competency-based or attitudinal dimensions. Then, a number of other people, including their boss, peers and subordinates also undertake the ratings anonymously. The result is a report that shows the manager's self-ratings against the average ratings of their colleagues. In comparison with traditional appraisal methods the advantages to this approach include increased reliability, fairness and thus the acceptance of the ratings by the person rated; more valid feedback because it is received from people who are in close daily contact and on the 'receiving end' of a wider range of behaviours; and more enduring changes in the behaviour of the person rated (Alimo-Metcalfe, 1999).

Alimo-Metcalfe (1999) also stressed the need for aspects of effective leadership and management to form the basis of staff selection and promotion criteria. This is a significant challenge. For example, how does one assess integrity, or the ability to allow people to exercise power effectively? This has implications for how one selects and trains those people with responsibility for selection, and argues for the involvement of service users in the process. Users will be most aware of the human values that they would like to see modelled and inculcated among team members. Alimo-Metcalfe also underlines the important finding from both her own and other's research that women managers are consistently more likely than their male counterparts to adopt a predominantly transformational, rather than transactional approach to leadership. Given that many of the people designing selection and promotion criteria will be men who have achieved their current status through transactional management styles, it is clear that the challenge of effecting a culture change in leadership and management recruitment and development is not to be underestimated.

Conclusion

Effective leadership and management are the cornerstone of effective team processes, in the same way that effective relationships between users and staff are the cornerstone of effective clinical practice. Both are underpinned by basic human values concerned with respecting people's realities and the meaning they attach to their experiences, valuing people as whole individuals, building on their strengths, and being honest and explicit, particularly regarding the power relationships that exist between the parties involved.

The last four chapters have been about different aspects of team design and process, from the 'big' strategic decisions, through to operational issues such as a the services to be provided, individual practice in the team, and how it is all held together through effective leadership and management roles. It is possible to conclude (after Hosking and Morley, 1991) that effective team design requires:

- a social process which is organised to provide a recurring input of information and reasoning from the widest possible range of sources. This points to the need to involve users, carers and other significant 'stakeholders' in assessment and individual service planning and review, as part of the design of the team process itself.
- sufficient expertise and diversity of expertise.
- team members who are clear about their tasks and their place within the team.
- team norms and procedures that facilitate actively open-minded thinking. The process of decision-making must be visible, inclusive and coherent.
- that the team is not insulated but rather networks with other parts of the enterprise. While the history of case management highlights the failure of brokerage models that paid insufficient attention to the need for direct clinical work (Mueser *et al.*, 1998), it is also true that no single CMHT can hope to provide the range of services required by people with complex health and social care needs. Intensive inter-agency working is required.
- that the group is organised so that team members fulfil a variety of primary roles. In other words, no attempt is made to make everybody do the same thing, except regarding specific shared tasks and team operational policies that are concerned with the running of the team itself (for example, attendance at meetings, use of core assessments and record-keeping systems).
- a leader that takes responsibility for ensuring that the emergent group process has the desirable qualities outlined above.

One of the key characteristics of effective leaders and managers is the way in which they personally, and indirectly through the processes they establish, look after individual team members. It is these people whose work this book is about supporting. The next chapter will look at further ways in which they can be helped to be effective.

Note

1 Developed by Kate Schneider (2000). North Dorset Primary Care NHS Trust.

CHAPTER 8

Looking after team members

If effective long-term relationships with staff are important to the user's experience of mental health services then clearly he or she will need to be working with people who are likely to stay working in their current roles, and who have high morale, and low absenteeism. This chapter looks at how this can be achieved through understanding the importance and sources of both good and poor morale and implementing measures to increase the mental health of staff, principally through creating contexts in which they can be most effective.

The importance of staff morale

Unhappy staff are less effective. For example, Firth-Cozens' (1999) review highlighted the association between dissatisfied, stressed doctors and impaired patient care. Outcomes included higher prescription rates, less provision of information, lower patient satisfaction, higher non-attendance among users and lower compliance. Cronin-Stubbs and Brophy (1984) found that nurses with higher burnout scores tended to use drugs to calm patients and spent less time in direct contact with them. Qualitative research has also described a process of emotional disengagement from, or even blaming of service users as a result of chronic stress (Cherniss, 1995; Handy, 1990). This may effect up to one in four of staff (Hannigan *et al.*, 2000).

Low morale also has an indirect negative effect by impairing the ability of service systems to employ and retain good quality, functioning staff. The Institute of Employment Studies (1997) found that one in three nurses would leave the profession if they could.

What do we know about staff morale among mental health staff?

We saw in Chapter 1 that staff derive satisfaction from their work through feeling effective in their clinical practice. Barriers to feeling effective, such as work overload or bureaucracy constitute the biggest threats to morale. This was corroborated by a literature review that found increasing levels of stress and burnout among CMHT members and CMHNs resulting from increased workloads, administrative tasks and lack of resources (Edwards *et al.*, 2000).

There is some evidence that community staff have lower burnout than in-patient staff, particularly when implementing ACT (Boyer and Bond, 1992; Carson *et al.*, 1995; Harper and Minghella, 1997). A large-scale study of staff in newer and more innovative roles also found high levels of job satisfaction, particularly because of increased freedom and autonomy, the opportunity to manage their own caseload, and increased responsibility (Collins *et al.*, 2000). Other studies within the UK have also reported high levels of satisfaction among community staff (Knapp *et al.*, 1992; Onyett *et al.*, 1997), including those working specifically with people with the most severe and long-term mental health problems (Harper and Minghella, 1997; Oliver and Kuipers, 1996; Prosser *et al.*, 1996).

Several studies have found that job satisfaction can coexist with emotional exhaustion, the key indicator of burnout (Brown and Leary, 1995; Onyett *et al.*, 1997; Prosser *et al.*, 1996). How can this be?

Scheid (1996) argued that burnout should be distinguished from other forms of occupational stress because work in human services uniquely requires that staff engage in 'emotional labour which entails an investment of self into one's work in order to maintain a relationship with one's client(s)' (2). She describes emotional labour as deep rather than surface acting. In other words, mental health staff are required to *be* caring, rather than just to act in a caring way (for example, in the manner of airline stewards). People commit to their work emotionally because they perceive it to be meaningful and of social value. This intrinsic aspect of the job appears to be a source of satisfaction. Where the meaning that people derive from work is threatened by lack of resources, organisational constraints or an unsupportive social environment, making them ineffective, it has a very real impact on the personal identity of staff and can result in an inability to meet emotional demands (Cherniss, 1995). This inability forms the key component of burnout manifest as emotional exhaustion. In this formulation, a certain level of work commitment is a prerequisite to burnout and it is this commitment that can also be a source of job satisfaction. Honouring this commitment is about allocating resources so that staff with challenging clients are able to be effective, and designing, leading, managing and continuously improving team environments so that their work is properly supported over the long term.

Interventions to look after the mental health of staff

These interventions encompass both organisational-level and personal interventions. Many aspects are covered elsewhere in this book as part of the job of designing and running an effective team. As Firth-Cozens (1999) observes 'One of the most useful organisational interventions to improve mental health in the workplace appears to be by developing good teams: ones which have clear group and individual objectives, which meet regularly and which value the skills of individual members' (88). Payne and Firth-Cozens (1999) provide a comprehensive review of the literature on stress among health professionals and the efficacy of interventions. This discussion will focus on those aspects that are less well covered in the literature yet are key to maintaining the morale of CMHT staff.

Promoting role clarity

Clear team objectives promote effective team functioning and have a positive impact on the mental health of team members (Borrill *et al.*, 2000) and their job satisfaction (Onyett *et al.*, 1997). Clarity of team role is also associated with team identification, the extent to which people derive a positive sense of belonging from team membership (ibid.). Both team role clarity and team identification were associated with satisfaction with organisational design and relationships at work. Harper and Minghella (1997) found that the home treatment team in their sample had significantly higher team identification and team role clarity than other teams, and that this resulted in higher staff morale. This would be predicted from the more premediated design and narrow client group associated with this sort of team.

It will be difficult for team members to be clear about their work roles if the role of the team as a whole is obscure, and so it is unsurprising that team role clarity is associated with personal role clarity (Onyett *et al.*, 1997). The opposite of role clarity is role ambiguity. Revicki and May (1989) defined role ambiguity as 'when an individual is unclear about his or her job expectations and uncertain of the response to his or her behaviour' (32). Increased role ambiguity was associated with increased stress, depression and job dissatisfaction among nurses. It was reduced by supportive supervision and cohesive work group relations.

In order for staff to be clear about their role, and how it relates to the role of the team, there is also a need to establish a reflective space for practitioners to think about their work (Roberts, 1998b) and to receive effective mentoring or supervision as described later.

Creating manageable workloads

Work overload is often cited as a source of stress (Edwards *et al.*, 2000; Onyett *et al.*, 1995), although Onyett *et al.*, (1997) did not find that staff morale was significantly associated with caseload size, composition or the frequency of user contacts. Problems arise with excessively large caseloads of infrequently seen people. Consultant psychiatrists may be particularly vulnerable to this and experience particularly high burnout (ibid.). Consultant psychiatrists experience more emotional exhaustion and severe depression as a result of workload than either physicians or surgeons (Deary *et al.*, 1996), and this appears to be most profound among more junior psychiatrists (Guthrie *et al.*, 1999). Worryingly, they also feel less compassion for users compared with more experienced staff (ibid.).

The design of intensive community treatment teams has particularly stressed the need for limited caseloads in order for staff to stay effective (Department of Health, 2001a). This needs to be properly implemented and managed with systematic approaches to monitoring the impact of clinical work on staff (see Chapter 7). Another key consideration in designing work roles to avoid people becoming over-burdened is to ensure that people are not accountable for events that they cannot control or take responsibility for. This is a particular concern among psychiatrists when dealing with the management of clinical risk (Holloway *et al.*, 2000).

Keeping paperwork to a minimum

Perceptions of self-efficacy remained a central issue over the 12-year period of Cherniss's (1995) qualitative study of burnout among professionals. This was perhaps most evident in the first year of post-qualifying work when professionals encountered a 'crisis of competence' arising from a mismatch between the realities of their working lives and what their training had prepared them for. To quote: 'Sometimes, their work was not much more challenging or varied than clerical work. In fact, much of it *was* clerical work' (26, italics in original).

Bureaucracy has been a consistent concern of mental health staff, particularly since the introduction of the CPA (Edwards *et al.*, 2000; North and Ritchie, 1993; Onyett *et al.*, 1995). Some bureaucracy is clearly inescapable for the purposes of proper record keeping, communication and establishing explicit contracts with service users and their social networks. Procedures clearly need to be well designed and make maximum use of information technology to reduce paperwork.

Maintaining physical safety

Guthrie *et al.* (1999) found that fear of violence and difficulty working with violent users was a major source of stress among psychiatrists regardless of grade. This was also a major source of concern among CMHNs, particularly concerning having to visit unsafe areas (Brown and Leary, 1995; Edwards *et al.*, 2000). Staff need to have confidence in agreed operational policies for home visiting, working in pairs, use of mobile phones and alarms, and checking in with the team base to ensure personal safety. Aside from the welfare of staff, it is unlikely that staff will be able to achieve effective relationships and offer any sense of confidence and containment to service users if they are concerned about their personal safety.

Promoting contact among team members

Studies of community staff have found that working in a team and relationships with colleagues were rated as among the strongest sources of reward (Carson *et al.*, 1995; Knapp *et al.*, 1992; Onyett *et al.*, 1995). Knapp *et al.* (1992) particularly highlighted teamworking itself as a form of coping, and found that projects needed to establish support and review systems for staff to reduce the risks of isolation and burnout.

Allport (1954) described a *contact effect* whereby hostility between groups was reduced when there was prolonged exposure and the need for cooperative activity in pursuit of superordinate goals. Finding the time for contact with colleagues can be challenging. Newly qualified professionals in the Cherniss (1995) study had an expectation that that they would find stimulating and sympathetic colleagues who would help them to cope, learn and grow. This proved to be illusory, as colleagues' work pressure often precluded such support.

The amount of time team members spend with each other will also be influenced by operational features such as whether the team has a shared physical base, how much time they spend in meetings together and whether the team has a policy of joint working. Who the contact is with and the content of the interaction are also important. Hewstone and Brown, (1986) summarised the factors that promote the contact effect thus:

- Where there is equal status among participants (Allport, 1954).
- When an authority or the social climate are in favour of and promote the inter-group contact. Multidisciplinary teamworking is being promoted at the highest levels through social policy (see Chapter 2), although locally influential groups may militate against this.
- When the contact is pleasant or rewarding.
- When the members of interacting groups engage in functionally important activities or develop common goals that are higher ranking in importance than the individual goals of each of the

groups. At issue here is whether teamworking promotes the most valued interests of the participating disciplines. For example, psychiatrists may be ambivalent about their involvement in teams that plan to provide an alternative to admission for some users if they feel that their control of hospital beds is a source of power and influence.

Unfavourable conditions for the contact effect include:

- When the contact situation produces competition between the groups. Again, the need to describe clear, diverse and complementary roles within teams is underlined.
- When the contact is involuntary, unpleasant, or tension-laden. Staff that are reorganised into teams against their will are unlikely to be as positive about teamworking as those who are specifically recruited to work in them.
- When the prestige or status of one group is lowered as a result of the contact situation. This may be the case for higher status disciplines, such as clinical psychologists involved in CMHTs.
- When members of a group or the group as a whole are in a state of frustration. The concern about lack of resources for effective service provision expressed by staff provides a good example.
- When the groups in contact have moral or ethical standards that are objectionable to each other. This again underlines the need to work explicitly with teams on the values and ideologies that underpin their work. Starting with the experience of service users and involving them in working with the team in developing their working ideology is most likely to have an enduring impact.
- When the contact is of an intense rather than a casual nature. Leiter (1988) examined burnout in multidisciplinary mental health teams and its relationship to work-orientated interactions (for example, supervision, consultation, administration) and informal social support (for example, friendships, non-work orientated interaction). Burnout was associated with low job satisfaction and the maintenance of relatively few informal supportive contacts with co-workers. A high number of work-related contacts with co-workers increased feelings of accomplishment but also

contributed to emotional exhaustion. Informal contact was related both to higher levels of accomplishment and job satisfaction. The need for team members to have fun together should not be neglected.

Staying sensitive to gender issues

Women comprised 67 per cent of Borrill *et al.*'s (2000) sample of 1443 CMHT staff. As in their sample of primary health care team staff, it was only in the highest status group that men predominated (for example, psychiatrists). The only effect of gender on morale among CMHT staff in the Onyett *et al.* (1997) study was a finding that women reported less negative feelings towards service users as an aspect of burnout. However, a large-scale survey of stress in the NHS found particularly high levels of stress among women doctors and women managers (Hardy, 1997). Among clinical psychologists, Cushway and Taylor (1996) also found higher stress among women. Women were less likely to have partners than men, and a reduction in family and social support was found to be associated with increased stress.

Support from family members is a much-cited way of coping with stress. However, emotional investment with users at work can contribute to a need to avoid intense emotional contact at home, which may in turn have a deleterious effect on family relationships (Cronin-Stubbs and Brophy, 1984; Scheid, 1996). Women are more likely to be balancing multiple demands, as reflected in the fact that they are more likely to be working part-time. As Ray and Miller (1994) observed: 'Women-time generally means trying to integrate professional and personal life, while man-time traditionally involves using the personal as a support system for the professional' (357). Their study of nurses found that those with children, and those cohabiting but not married to their partners, were particularly vulnerable to burnout arising from the need to manage home and work pressures. Similarly, Cherniss (1995) found no gender differences with respect to professionals' experience of burnout except where women had children.

Borrill and Haynes' (1999) review suggested that women managers in the NHS were subject to a wider range of stressors than men, in addition to the home – work interface issues described above.

These included prejudice and discrimination, negative stereotyping and social isolation. Their study found that women managers particularly suffered from low levels of social support, lack of feedback on performance and lack of role clarity (Borrill *et al.*, 1998). They further suggested that women managers were more sensitive to the interactions between their staff in getting the job done, whereas males were more concerned with the demands of senior colleagues. This may have made them more vulnerable with respect to relationship problems at work and lack of cohesion among peers. However, it is also notable that these qualities may also have made them better managers (Alimo-Metcalfe, 1999). With the advent of an NHS Leadership Centre, we can hope that what constitutes effective management in mental health services will be more clearly articulated and implemented. Alongside anti-discriminatory practices this may result in a large proportion of women in leadership and management roles, which may in turn help eliminate some of the more negative experiences reported above.

Cherniss (1995) commented that, confronted by discrimination in terms of the opportunities and supports that women are offered in the workplace, 'placing less value on traditional career success may be a rational way for women to adjust to an unfortunate reality' (96). Clearly, employers need to ensure that this is not the reality and that their employment practices are family-friendly and do not discriminate against female workers.

The freedom and autonomy to control work and exercise discretion

Seniority, either as a manager or a clinician appears to offer reduced stress and increased job satisfaction, at least for men who disproportionately occupy such positions (Borrill and Haynes, 1999; Onyett *et al.*, 1995; Rees and Cooper, 1992). This is likely to be due to the effects of increased autonomy and power, not least in defining one's own role. For example, Ramirez *et al.* (1996) found autonomy and variety promoted job satisfaction and mental health among medical consultants. However, it is also true that with seniority comes the pressure of having to deal with continuous organisational change. Holloway *et al.* (2000) identified this as a particular issue for consultant psychiatrists and advocated greater training of psychiatrists in health service management, and their greater involvement in and influence over strategic development and operational management. Indeed for all NHS staff, Borrill *et al.* (1998) found that lack of influence was a major source of stress.

While it is important to acknowledge the benefits of autonomy for staff, this needs to be balanced against the negative effects on team effectiveness of an absence of clear leadership and management (Borrill *et al.*, 2000). In such a context, staff may chose to do what suits them with scant regard for local need or the objectives of the service (see Chapter 7, Morrall, 1997; Patmore and Weaver, 1991a). The aim is to define clear roles that are not so over specified and narrow that staff cannot enjoy reasonable levels of autonomy and variety within agreed parameters.

Promoting effective leadership and management

This and the previous chapter have argued that creating the right conditions for effective teamworking and the high morale of staff is largely the job of leaders and managers. Alimo-Metcalfe's (1999) review highlighted managing performance pressure, promoting autonomy and variety, clarifying roles and objectives, helping people identify with their job, promoting the social value of the job and providing high quality feedback as all crucial to maintaining staff morale, but found that managers seemed 'relatively unaware' of the role that they had in influencing these variables. She emphasised the need for staff to enjoy the greatest possible levels of autonomy and discretion, combined with the transactional management behaviours of ensuring clear goal setting and that all practitioners have proper access to the peer consultation and supervision that they require to properly exercise their role and develop in the job. Given the potential benefits of transformational leadership, particularly by women (see p. 201), it would be logical for organisations to focus on supporting leaders and managers so that they in their turn can support their own staff.

Achieving a personal focus

Guthrie *et al.* (1999) advocated greater awareness among senior psychiatrists about how personal difficulties may impinge upon the work of those that they are supervising or managing. This may require an in-depth exploration of the meaning of work for individuals, how it relates to their own personalities and sources of meaning and what attracted them to the work in the first place. Firth-Cozens' (1999) longitudinal study found that psychiatrists were more stressed and negative about their jobs than other doctors and that this difference emerged when they were students, and ten years later as qualified psychiatrists. She found psychiatrists to be particularly depressed and self-critical and suggested that some may have entered the specialty 'in order to explore their own distress more closely through the work of their patients' (85). She notes the paradox that these self-critical students chose a specialty in which the recipients of care are experienced as much less grateful and more critical than other patient groups.

Hardy and Barkham (1999) concluded that there is evidence for the effectiveness of workplace counselling and stress management training but that there needed to be clarity about who does what in delivering staff support, and recognition of when more intensive psychological interventions are required for people with significant mental distress. Team members need to be helped to recognise the indicators of their own poor mental health and be supported in seeking help. Given the harmful effects for users and staff of substance misuse as a way of coping, Firth-Cozens (1999) advocated making access to assistance easier and better publicised by, for example, establishing links with Alcoholics Anonymous or other helping agencies.

Peer consultation as a requirement

Individual peer consultation, mentoring, or supervision is essential to ensure best practice among staff. In Chapter 7, I differentiated between processes of 'supervision', where an accountability relationship existed between the supervisor and the supervisee, and processes of consultation or mentoring. However, most of the following is applicable to all support processes. I have not attempted to differentiate the role of consultant, from mentor, or from supervisor in this discussion. Each will have a different emphasis. For example, someone construing themselves as a mentor may place a greater emphasis on the provision of new information to inform new perspectives on the work; the supervisor may particularly attend to appropriate professional practice; and the consultant may emphasise sitting back and allowing the practitioner to set the agenda. However, these should be features of all the roles, however described, and the personal style of the individual providing support is likely to be more important than how they frame themselves. The key requirement is that the 'reflective space', or opportunities for 'reflexivity' as described earlier, are also experienced with respect to the individual practitioner's own behaviour, aside from the functioning of the team as a whole.

Morgan (1996) highlights the following key functions that need to be achieved through this supportive relationship:

- The maintenance and development of therapeutic competence.
- Monitoring the effectiveness of helping relationships.
- Overseeing the quality and quantity of workload responsibilities (including the size and composition of caseloads).
- Assisting with the effective management of time.
- Enabling continuing professional development, including accessing appropriate education and training.
- Planning future career development.
- Ensuring awareness and effective use of resources.
- Acknowledging the effective and successful use of knowledge, skills and experience.
- Sharing and exploring the emotional demands of other people's psychological difficulties.
- Helping to cope with stress, preventing burnout and addressing the negative aspects of work.
- Recognising and addressing personal needs and growth.

Morgan (1996) also stressed the importance of supporting the worker in deriving meaning from their work by realistic goal setting and recognising the importance of their work in the context of the life of the service user. Staff may also need help to stay conscious of how their own feelings of helplessness or feeling oppressed, perhaps by their own management, impacts on their efforts to support users in exercising power for themselves. Staff often have a powerful need to help users, and feel they must provide solutions and interventions. Not to do so threatens the practitioner's sense of self-efficacy, and may also serve to defend against feelings of powerlessness projected by users. Often such behaviour serves the interests of the staff more than the service user. Staff need to maintain awareness of their own need to take control of user's lives in order to be able to support users in achieving the right balance of dependence on and independence from formal sources of assistance.

The key features of maintaining an effective relationship described in Chapter 6 should form part of the standing agenda of sessions to support staff. A good consultant, mentor or supervisor will also help the team member stay conscious of the values underpinning their work, and help them to achieve congruence between these values and their practice. For example, staff may need a lot of support to stay close to the principle of user self-determination, particularly where they think the user is wrong on a particular issue and will regret their actions later.

Regardless of the professional status of the practitioner, without such support they risk becoming isolated, stale, rigid in attitudes towards their work, and defensive of poor practice. There is a danger that poor practice becomes ingrained, standards drop and reactions to queries or criticism of practice produce denial. The scope for such degraded practice cannot be overestimated. Witness, for example, the worryingly high incidence of sexual exploitation of users by therapists, and the fact that there may be a greater risk among more *senior* members of the professions (Garrett, 1998).

As with all other team meetings, group or individual peer consultation or supervision sessions should have an explicit function and boundary. Morgan (1996) advocates the use of contracts that specify the place and frequency of contacts, the functions that the sessions will address, the confidentiality of any spoken and written information, a process for appraising and reviewing the relationship, and procedures for resolving disagreements within the relationship. The latter again bears on the need to clarify the nature of the accountability relationship between the practitioner and their consultant, mentor or supervisor. The extent to which the relationship encompasses personal issues such as events outside of work, or remains focused on work practices themselves will be a core boundary issue to be clarified. In practice, personal issues such as one's past, current family relationships and the difficulties of maintaining a home-life in a high-pressure job are all relevant to the experience of work stress, fatigue or burnout. Therefore it will be helpful to encompass these within the relationship where possible. Sometimes staff cannot find anyone within the work setting that they can entrust such material to. This should be candidly acknowledged and the staff member should be encouraged, and practically supported, in finding this sort of relationship elsewhere.

Making team meetings work

Realistically the frequency of formal sessions will rarely meet the practitioner's needs for spontaneously sharing the personal impact of this demanding work. Morgan (1996) highlights the importance of a 'culture of support' in the team in addition to formal sessions. A key advantage of teamworking is that different people in the team are likely to be in tune with the emotional impact of working with particular people and can offer a 'sounding board' to each other. They can tactfully inquire about how a staff member is feeling and also encourage them to celebrate their achievements, and the achievements of users. Humour and a sense of fun have an important role to play here, and should be a highly valued part of the team experience. A reflexive team will however also be aware of the various functions that humour can serve in teams, including resisting the influence of powerful team members, building team identity at the expense of outgroups, establishing hierarchies, and denigrating users (Griffiths, 1998; Lang, 1982). Involving users in the team as providers, with a specific role in helping the team stay reflexive, can be invaluable in this respect (for example, as in the Bradford Home Treatment Team; Bracken and Cohen, 1999).

The team can proactively reproduce some of the key features of effective support described above in clinical review meetings, or meetings specifically dedicated to staff support. Clinical review meetings are the heart of effective teamworking and the experience of them should demonstrate the key values underpinning the work (for example, in implementing the recovery approach or a strengths-based model). They should therefore (after Morgan, 1996) generate:

- *Hope*: inculcating a view of service users as whole people with futures and valuable roles to play;
- *Affirmation*: the recognition of the work being undertaken;
- *Information*: the sharing and clarification of details;

- *Ideas*: generating new options, and
- *Fun*: to ensure colleagues in the team are enjoying their work.

The process should be personal and in the here and now, rather than deviating into abstract concepts, or an over-professionalised discourse that does not result in a clear way forward. Morgan (1996) also stressed actively listening to colleagues, valuing different opinions and viewpoints and brainstorming ideas concerning a particular clinical situation. Brainstorming demonstrates participative safety, generates creativity and contributes to the fun of teamworking.

Implementing integrated education and training

Education and training opportunities should be in place to continually enhance the effectiveness of staff. A skilled workforce will be required to implement improved practices, and the clinical governance framework places considerable emphasis on lifelong learning through continuous professional and medical development (CPD/CMD). If well implemented, this has the potential to improve the recruitment, retention and motivation of the workforce (Holloway *et al.*, 2000). CPD and CMD programmes, as well as curriculum development for pre-qualification education and development is being increasingly influenced by agreed occupational standards. However, it is expected that programmes will be managed locally in order to meet local service needs. CPD/CMD therefore needs to have strong links with strategy development, audit programmes, interventions to increase clinical effectiveness and research and development.

Personal Development Plans should be developed by individual practitioners in consultation with colleagues as part of the implementation of clinical governance (Department of Health, 1998). They should include preferred methods of learning (such as peer-group or individual learning, team and on-the-job training) and should inform, and be informed by an organisation-wide development plan.

In implementing training, it is again important to maintain integrity with staff about its aims and implications. Training implies change, which will have a personal impact on staff in terms of their employment status, job satisfaction and self-esteem. For example,

Krupa *et al.* (1992), in describing their experience of implementing training in rehabilitation within a hospital setting, stressed the need for honesty with staff about the implications of change. It clearly should not be assumed that trainees will be willing and eager recipients and Krupa *et al.* recommended explicitly stating the benefits for individuals and the system, integrating old with new knowledge, and facilitating open discussion and debate. Involving enthusiastic and credible advocates of change can be helpful, as well as involving users in the training in order to ensure that it is fully grounded in the experience of being on the receiving end of provision (see below).

Conclusion

At the end of Cherniss' (1995) longitudinal study there were some practitioners who had been able to remain compassionate towards difficult users. They were characterised as 'having the appropriate tools' in terms of a supportive work environment, appropriate training and a realistic perspective on the time required to achieve meaningful change. Their work environment provided good feedback and approaches to evaluation that highlighted small but significant improvements. This allowed practitioners to maintain a sense of meaning in their work. It kept them aware of why they were drawn to the job in the first place. Intrinsic rewards like challenge, stimulation and opportunities to use valued skills continued to be important, and in some cases more important than the extrinsic rewards of pay and status.

This review concludes that in order to maintain the mental health of team members it is important to focus on the organisational context of the team, particularly the clarity of its aims, the clarity of team members' roles in pursuit of these aims, and the material resources needed to be effective in one's work. Leadership, management, supervisory or mentoring relationships must also supply useful feedback, increased role clarity and a positive sense of belonging to the team. They also need to provide support in the way that work and home demands are managed through 'family friendly' employment practices.

It is clear that the mental health of staff will be enhanced by ensuring that they feel personally effective in their work. This is more likely when the team in which they work is able to remain effective over the long term. This is the subject of the final chapter.

CHAPTER 9

Staying Effective over the Long Term

Team development is a continuous process of learning from experience rather than a one-shot affair. This chapter develops the emphasis on the dynamic nature of team leadership and management from Chapter 7 by exploring change to achieve better outcomes as part of a continuous quality improvement process. It focuses on the importance of getting the team to reflect on its own operations, outcomes and contexts, and will conclude by reiterating the central role of users in the continuous development of high-quality services.

Change for survival

Teams need to be able to change and adapt to continually shifting circumstances in order to flourish, while holding true to their core vision. Staying effective is therefore, to a large extent, about how to manage change effectively.

Senge *et al.* (1999) make the stark point that most change initiatives fail. Within the health service, we have seen repeated reorganisations that appear to have had little impact on the lives of users and carers. We are not alone. Senge (1999) describes how some companies create their own jargon to lampoon their own scepticism about the next change initiative. At Harley-Davidson, the management's latest, greatest ideas were greeted with the phrase 'AFP' or 'Another fine programme'.

Senge *et al.* (1999) eschew the notion that change is brought about by expert advice, more committed management, or expensive consultants. Instead they urge us to think less like managers and more like biologists; something that should be easy for those of us in the health service with a scientific background. They highlight the natural pattern for anything that grows in nature. Organisms from humans to beetles accelerate in growth for a time, and then grow slowly until full adult size is reached. Growth in nature occurs because of *reinforcing* growth processes and *limiting* growth processes: 'As Chilean biologist Humberto Maturana puts it, "Every movement is being inhibited as it occurs". This is nature's way. We can either work with it or against it' (Senge *et al.*, 1999: 10).

Senge uses the metaphor of a tree. The seed has potential to grow into a tree and realises that potential through emergent reinforcing growth processes. The seed sends out small feelers which draw in water and nutrients leading the roots to grow further, drawing in more water and nutrients, leading to further expansion of the root system and more water and nutrients, and so on. This growth is, however, subject to a number of limits including the availability of water, nutrients, space to expand and warmth. As the tree expands beyond the surface, other limits become important such as light, insects and pollution. When growth stops prematurely, it is because it has encountered constraints, but constraints that are not inevitable.

So what are the implications for change management of this sort of thinking? People participating in or leading change need to understand and focus on those limiting processes that slow or stop change, and those reinforcing growth processes that promote it. However, the emphasis needs to be on working on relaxing the limits to growth. Merely pushing harder on the processes that promote growth may be counterproductive as this merely pushes harder against the limits.

Other implications of failing to take account of limiting factors include:

- *An over-valued belief in the redeeming qualities of hero-leaders.* You cannot make change happen through strategies that focus solely on vigorous and skilled leadership. If there is not the potential for growth then there is little that any leader or gee-whizz manager can do about it. As Senge observes, that would be like the gardener standing over the seed saying, 'Grow! Try harder! You can do it!'. This tendency to believe in hero-leaders represents a strong cultural myth which inhibits the development of leadership *capacity* within the organisation. It creates the impression that the common people do not have the capacity to bring about change whereas, in fact, change cannot happen without them. Senge highlights some of the subtle ways in which this idea that management is the source of change can become reinforced through organisational initiatives such as surveys, and focus groups, which serve as ways of giving information to management without diffusing responsibility and authority for addressing the issues. Projects that are driven by top-level management usually just require compliance with their recommendations rather than heartfelt commitment. The patchy introduction of the CPA in the UK is one such innovation. Where clinicians have seen it as adding meaning to their lives by improving the work they do with users, it has flourished. Where it has been seen as a top-down management tool aimed at regulating and administering practice it has tended to fail.

- *Starting an ambitious project with easy change, or those things that we feel we have the tools to fix, and then getting disheartened as the tasks become more and more difficult to address.* One example is an organisation's tendency to 'fix' a given team without looking at its role within the wider service system. This may be addressing the symptoms of a problem rather than the underlying causes. The whole-system perspective would require a radical reappraisal of the function of different parts of the local service system and the need to introduce adequate referral, assessment and allocation processes to ensure that people get the right kind of help. This whole-systems approach is needed to avoid new service models being 'bolted on' to existing services with all the discontinuity and bad feeling that this can engender. This tendency can also be exacerbated by the fashion for always aiming for 'early wins'. While this may well be appropriate to boost morale and demonstrate a way of working as part of a larger change project, it should be avoided where it serves to avoid tackling fundamental issues.
- *No-go areas that are deemed too risky and therefore cannot be discussed.* This is often related to the problem of managers or other powerful people, such as consultant psychiatrists being committed to change as long as it does not affect them. I was

asked to do some work with senior and middle managers concerned with the strategic development of their service and was told that if I wanted to get anywhere I should specifically avoid examining the performance of their long-standing crisis service. Previous attempts had caused bad feeling and defensiveness, particularly with the consultant that led the service. In fact, it soon became clear that this service was having a major distorting effect on the whole design of the local mental health service. Indeed focusing on the work of this team seemed to be the key to unlocking problems with the wider service system.

- *Lack of reflexivity*. Much of the foregoing highlights that a major limiting growth process is the ability of a range of people to develop the reflection and enquiry skills that will allow them to talk openly about complex, conflictual issues without becoming defensive. West (1996) stressed the importance of 'reflexivity': 'the extent to which team members collectively reflect upon the team's objectives, strategies and processes, as well as the wider organisation and environment, and adapt them accordingly'. This bears on the need to promote 'participative safety' to promote innovation (see Chapter 7).

Leading change

While individual leaders should not be regarded as hero-innovators bringing about change through lone crusades, there is role for a range of people in leadership roles concerned with helping to create and maintain cultures where the capacity of the whole system to achieve positive change is enhanced. Chapter 7 described these reinforcing growth processes, such as articulating a vision, having a personal concern for the welfare of others, the provision of models of effective ways of behaving and creating effective partnership working conditions.

Senge *et al.* (1999) stressed the need for people to see and deal with interdependences, and the deeper causes of change problems. This requires skills in developing 'systems thinking'. This involves understanding how change is either promoted or limited by interdependency, the way people construct the reality in which they work, and add meaning and social value to their work.

Hosking and Morley (1991), draw their formulations on leadership and management from their review of the social psychology of organising. They define organising as:

> a process in which interdependent persons and groups mobilise value to influence actual or potential changes in the status quo. Actors [actual or potential stakeholders] may give or withhold help; actors may be more or less successful in adding value to their lives and the lives of others (127).

Note the emphasis on changing the values among people involved in change. This emphasis on the values of individuals as part of a system has much in common with Senge's (1999) notion of 'profound change' as:

> organisational change that combines inner shifts in people's values, aspirations and behaviours with 'outer' shifts in processes, strategies, practices, and systems.... In profound change there is learning. The organisation doesn't just do something new; it builds its capacity to do things in a new way – indeed it builds capacity for on-going change... It is not enough to change strategies, structures and systems, unless the thinking that produced those strategies, structures and systems also changes.

Hosking and Morley (1991) rejected the notion that there are competencies for leadership that are found in managers but not among non-managers. They construed leaders as anyone who comes to be expected to contribute to the structuring of processes in an acceptable way. It is a process through which 'actors', in other words potential or actual stakeholders in the change, 'create cultures which may be more or less helpful' (249). This cultural change is also reflected in Senge's definition of leadership:

> The capacity of a human community to shape its future, and specifically to sustain the significant processes of change required to do so (1999: 16).

Leadership has a *creative* dimension that helps people make sense of their social worlds, and a *political* dimension concerned with valuing possible lines of action in different ways. Constructions of the 'current reality' are dependent upon people's valuation of the status quo, and the vision for change will have different implications for different people dependent upon these valuations. The management of these tensions is inevitably political, and issues of negotiation and the management of influence become critical.

In creating the right processes for change, those with particular responsibility for managing the process should work to ensure that participants experience the emerging processes as:

- *legible* – where equivocation among participants can be understood and reduced in recognisable and agreeable ways,
- *coherent* – where the right people are involved in an integrated structure throughout the process, and
- *open-ended* – entailing flexible relationships that can create and accommodate change as required.

Getting started on a change project

Hosking and Morley (1991) identify four elements essential to the appreciation of organising. Inasmuch as their definition of organising is very much about changing the status quo, they also provide a useful starting point for creating change.

1. '*Identify the actors and their valuations in relation to an identified actual or potential change project*'. Valuations describe their commitments to particular activities, relationships, and descriptions of how things are.
2. '*Understand to what extent, and in what ways, the change constitutes an issue for each actor, individual or group*'. How big a stake do the stakeholders have in the project?
3. '*Examine relations, particularly those of interdependence, between actors and between projects*'.
4. '*Appreciate the political processes through which actors influence the structure and processes of change, and in so doing, create and support certain sorts of setting or organisational "culture"*'. To what degree do they protect and promote particular projects?

Changing the status quo therefore requires consideration of the *valuations* to which actors are committed in their activities and relationships, and the *implications* of change for them. This will

	Advantages	Disadvantages
Change		
No change		

Figure 6 *A two-by-two matrix looking at the advantages and disadvantages of change and no change*

influence the ways in which they can be supported in changing. As a clinical approach, motivational interviewing respects the ambivalences that users have about change by looking at their readiness and confidence in changing, as well as the importance they attach to the change. The same analysis can be applied to participants in a change process.

One simple way of thinking about the valuations and implications of changing and not changing for particular groups or individuals is to map them in a matrix such as Figure 6.

Achieving teams with attitude

Reflexive teams have an awareness of, and communicate about, their organisational context and the barriers they face. The team adapts to these barriers but also attempts to modify them: 'Effective teams reflect upon and communicate about their working and their work environment – they revolutionise their organisations by clamouring persistently and coherently for the organisational conditions and supports which enable effective communication and team working' (West, 1996: 16). The notion of reinforcing and limiting growth processes described above (Senge *et al.*, 1999) provides a useful way of thinking about the extent to which teams are promoted or held back by their environment. West *et al.* (1998) cites the social psychology of minority dissent to understand how teams can influence their environment (Moscovici *et al.*, 1985). Where a team (the minority) is dissenting from the views of the majority in the wider organisational context (for example, other providers, parts of the system or the management of the host organisations), it can bring about enduring change in attitudes through sustained debate or even conflict. This has the effect of

Box 10 *An example of beginning to think about the actors involved in a change project*

If the proposed change is the development of ACT, the skilled change agent will need to examine the implications for a range of local stakeholders, such as consultant psychiatrists, existing CMHT members, colleagues in social services, local users and carers. This will require good understanding of how they currently see things, what they do and the relationships between them (step 1, p. 225).

It will then be important to examine the extent to which the proposed change constitutes an issue for them and in what ways (step 2). For example, colleagues in social services may have little support from their managers in seeking out new people to drain their already overstretched budgets.

If the service is specifically aiming to reduce the pressure on in-patient beds then there is clearly an interdependency between the new ACT team and local consultants who control the beds (step 3).

If local consultants see their power base as highly dependent upon the number of in-patient beds that they control then they may have little investment in championing the proposed development. They may then seek to undermine the project by failing to attend meetings to discuss it, forming their own tighter and parallel group for strategy development through the Division of Psychiatry, or denigrating the perspectives of other stakeholders as being ill-informed by evidence from research or local needs assessment (step 4).

Thinking systemically about such a change problem might lead change agents to consider how the local consultants could come to feel that their power and influence was less dependent on the beds that they control, or promoting ownership of the evidence for the need to change by having 'one of their own' leading the development of proposals for change.

influencing decision-making as a result of the cognitive or social conflict caused by the minority's consistent and coherent dissent from the dominant view. It makes the organisational majority examine the issues and problems more thoroughly, communicate, and think more creatively around the topic. It creates more divergent thinking and can change the private thoughts of the majority. The minority influence literature would suggest that, for the team to be effective, it would need to be clear, committed and consensual about the innovation in question; consistent and confident in the presentation of its arguments; and persistent (Nemeth and Owens, 1996). The team will also need to be aware of the social and political context in which it is operating.

Working with complex systems

A theme of this book has been the multiple stakeholders involved in teamworking and their diverse valuations, motivations and actions. As such, we are all working within complex adaptive systems, which Plsek and Greenhalgh (2001) defined as 'a collection of individual agents with freedom to act in ways that are not always totally predictable, and whose actions are interconnected so that one agent's actions changes the context for other agents'.

We have seen how people are parts of different interconnecting systems. The psychiatrist is both a team member and a doctor. She may also be part of a family system that involves her having to pick up her children from school at a certain time, which in turn has implications for the hours she can work. Each system has its own rules, which shape the behaviour of its members, which may not be understood or comprehensible to other actors. However, because actors can change, a complex system can evolve over time, and different systems that may be connected, or embedded one in the other, can evolve and co-evolve. Plsek and Greenhalgh (2001) described how the evolution of one system influences and is influenced by that of other systems. For example, the campaigning agendas of the user movement and the more general societal concerns with risk have come to influence mental health social policy in different ways. Consequently, this influences practice in ways that lead to tensions and paradoxes that can never be fully resolved. These complex and irresolvable tensions influence the interactions among actors, which can produce unpredictable and creative new behaviours. This emergent innovation from human interaction, including teamwork, is difficult to describe and predict through reductionist thinking that focuses merely on the interacting actors and the rules they use. The implication of this is that the system can only really be better understood by observing it, and seeing what works best over time.

Most of the time it is not clear what to do next in seeking improvement. In mental health services, as in many other contexts, there are varying levels of certainty and agreement about what should be done. The certainty–agreement diagram in Figure 7 describes this 'zone of complexity' where most work is conducted most of the time (Plsek and Greenhalgh, 2001). While it is not obvious what to do, as in the simple zone, there is not so much disagreement and uncertainty as to throw the whole system into chaos. The development of standards and guidelines, approaches to the spread of best practice and team-based training and educational interventions can all be thought of as ways of moving the system away from chaos towards a situation where the need for certain planned action is more evident and achievable. As Fraser and Greenhalgh (2001) noted, however, 'checklist driven' approaches to clinical care such as critical appraisal, clinical guidelines and the implementation of care pathways are important tools but only useful once the issues have been understood. Working in the zone of complexity places a higher value on intuition and imagination. It requires multiple approaches that make effective use of experience, experimentation, freedom to innovate and working at the edge of knowledge and experience. The use of action learning (Smith, 2001) and the plan-do-study-act cycle of quality improvement (Berwick, 1998) are two examples. Other tips for working with complexity include using only minimum specifications that allow maximum freedom for creativity, grouping the issues to be addressed so that just one or two problems are addressed initially, using metaphor to more effectively communicate the complexity of the situation, and using provocative questioning that challenges core beliefs and assumptions, thereby creating new mental models for what is going on (see again Figure 4 in Chapter 6). See Wilson *et al.* (2001) and Stacey (2000) for further tips on working with complexity.

Fraser and Greenhalgh (2001) further describe a range of education and training interventions aimed at developing the system's capability to improve. These interventions should be self directed, team focused, and based upon story telling and other narratives, particularly from users of the service.

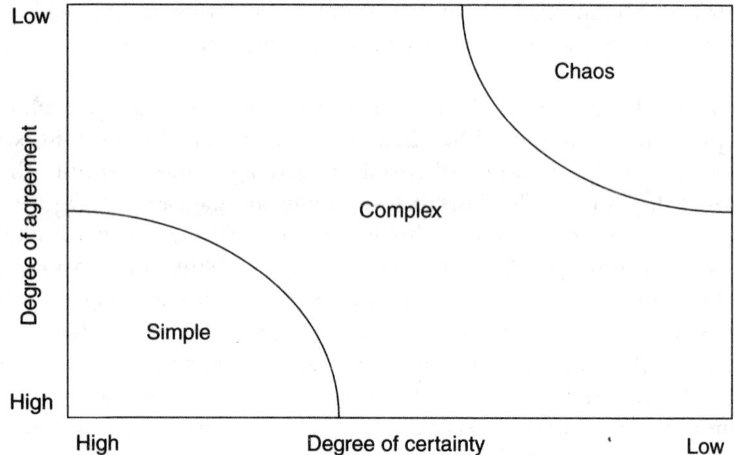

Figure 7 *The certainty–agreement diagram*

Keeping users at the centre

We have said that teams should be built around users, their networks and their needs and aspirations. Working with complex systems and pathways requires that the diverse stakeholders involved are grounded in the shared reality that stems from hearing about how services are experienced. Without this shared starting point, it is unlikely that they will be able to undertake the change journey together.

We shall conclude this book by looking at cycles of continuous quality improvement. Before exploring the lessons learnt from these initiatives, it is important to stress that however good the technological aspects of your quality assurance processes, it is ultimately the value judgements that are made about provision that are critical. Someone has to decide what is good enough and what is not. Having the right people making those judgements on the best available information is therefore of paramount importance. However, this is only part of the picture. If users are only involved in monitoring and evaluating poor services then the barn door can truly be said to have been shut long after the horse has bolted.

User participation in the monitoring, researching and evaluation of services

The National Framework for Assessing Performance in the NHS (Department of Health, 1998) includes as one of its six key elements the need to base provision on user and carer perspectives on the delivery of services. This includes their evaluation of:

- responsiveness to individual needs and preferences;
- the skill, care and continuity of service provision;
- user involvement, information and choice;
- accessibility and waiting times;
- the physical environment and the organisation and courtesy of administrative arrangements.

User commentaries on the services they receive have long been achieved through mechanisms such as local user groups, and Patient's Councils. Their influence has been variable and the explicit role of such bodies in service improvement has not always been clear. They often rely on there being some physical point of reference within which users can come together and identify shared concerns, such as a ward environment or a day service. They also suffer from arguably being of most value to those people who find it comparatively easy to express themselves in groups, thus attracting the criticism from local sceptics that they fail to represent those people who are most distressed, or find it least easy to find a voice.

The Sainsbury Centre for Mental Health has championed a complementary approach called User Focused Monitoring (Rose *et al.*, 1998), which explicitly seeks out those most distressed users who would find it difficult to attend groups. It trains local service users to draw out the views of other service users on their experience of local services and uses instruments that can be adapted to local circumstances and concerns.

Users are becoming increasingly involved in more formal research and audit processes. One positive aspect of this development is that such activities are socially valued and so enhance the role of users within the organisation generally. The research also benefits by being more obviously grounded in the issues and experiences of those on the receiving end of provision.

User participation in the planning of services

Hutchison (2000) proposed the following steps to guarantee that user involvement in planning services goes beyond mere tokenism. Ensure that:

- there is more than one user involved in the meeting or committee.
- all user-members are familiar with the workings of committees, and provide training if not.
- all user-members have access to the same information as all other committee members.
- this information is clear and jargon-free, or that any jargon is explained.
- user-members have access to any support that they may require.
- users are paid for their involvement unless they receive payment from another source.
- you are clear and honest about the nature and boundaries on the participation of user-members, for example any areas or issues that they cannot influence. Such boundaries would need to be justified and understood.

User participation in training and staff development

Hutchison (2000) highlights the advantages of involving users in training. These include enabling those responsible for service delivery to gain an insight into what it is like to be on the receiving end of their services thereby challenging some of the myths around mental health problems. This allows users and staff to discuss potential dilemmas and provides a safe but informed environment for controversial issues to be explored.

As an experienced trainer herself, Hutchison highlights the need for user input to be integrated within the training as a whole, rather than just as a slot on a programme. The course coordinator needs to ensure that trainees give adequate and equal attention to user input. As with all other forms of user participation, user-trainers need to be given all the information and support they need and be given fair payment for their contribution.

Users certainly have a role in staff development that goes beyond training. They should also be involved in staff recruitment through being involved in the drawing up of job descriptions, designing selection processes and taking part in those processes as an equal member. It is important that, like others involved in selection, users are trained for the role, including the application of Equal Opportunities Policies.

User participation in providing services

Employing users as staff has been very positively evaluated (see Chapter 5). There are an increasing number of model, user-run services such as Anam Cara in Birmingham. Often, they are framed as an alternative to mainstream mental health services, and benefit from a voluntary-sector ethos of valuing independence from statutory providers, flexibility and responsiveness to the needs of their users. Flexibility is a particular asset when developing out-of-hours services such as helplines, or crisis houses.

Employing users as staff members provides effective role models for both users and staff on how to demonstrate a positive, value-based service in action. They therefore have an important leadership function.

Access to provider roles for users needs to be supported by effective and ongoing training that is accessible to people from a wide variety of backgrounds. The Certificate in Community Mental Health Care developed by the Mental Health Foundation is a shining example of such training and is being taken up in a variety of sites around the UK.

Continuous quality improvement cycles

This book uses a very simple definition of quality: a high quality service is one that makes the best possible use of resources to achieve the best possible outcomes for service users. It is therefore about promoting the reinforcing growth properties referred to earlier while working to remove, lessen or reduce the impact of limiting factors.

Senge *et al.* (1999) described 'quality' as all the things that matter to a customer, which in this context primarily means service users. The NSF and clinical governance (Department of Health, 1998, 1999) emphasises the need to continually improve the overall standard of clinical care, and reduce unacceptable variations in practice.

Quality assurance systems require the establishment of standards set within a clear framework. The *framework* divides the organisation or services that are being evaluated into meaningful and manageable parts based upon a model of what constitutes good quality. For example, the Excellence Model uses nine headings covering such issues as leadership, staff issues, measuring user satisfaction and performance results (EFQM and the British Quality Foundation, 1999). The *standards* are explicit statements of what the service or organisation aims to achieve. A clear description of processes for achieving those standards and reviewing and evaluating this achievement is essential. Standards vary in terms of whether they describe a basic minimum performance or are more aspirational. This is important *as whatever system is in place ultimately needs to be evaluated against basic value statements about what the service should be achieving for people.*

There have never been such clear standards for the achievement of a high quality mental health service. They are embodied within the NSF, the NHS Plan, and the Mental Health Service Policy Implementation Guide (Department of Health, 1999, 2000, 2001a). There is, however, a danger that the level of specification can work against creativity. Plsek and Wilson (2001: 746) observed that,

> current organisational thinking is built largely on the assumption that plans for progress must provide the 'best' way, completely specified in great detail, and consistently implemented in that same level of detail across the board. This thinking, often reflected in the NHS in such things as national service frameworks or detailed guidelines with newly specified standards, fails to take advantage of the natural creativity embedded in the organisation, and fails to allow for the inevitable unpredictability of events.

Many local stakeholders, in implementation, report a sense of having their innovation and creativity stifled by such over-specification. However, this does need to be balanced against the need to communicate a clear expectation of what users can expect from mental health services. Managing this paradox is just another example of what the skilled leader has to undertake in helping change participants improve their local services as part of complex systems.

Onyett (1998) described quality assurance processes using the stages of the care coordination process (engagement, assessment, planning, intervention, monitoring and review), but applied to the organisation as a whole rather than individual service users. Such cyclical processes characterise most quality assurance processes and so serve as a useful and familiar template for clinicians when thinking about initiatives aimed at service improvement.

Such cycles of learning can operate at different levels, corresponding to different orders of change. Argyris and Schön (1996) describe three levels of learning:

1 **Single loop learning** is concerned with the detection and correction of errors. A good example of this is the classic audit cycle whereby existing practice is compared against agreed standards. While this is invaluable it also leaves the organisational objectives and processes largely unchanged.
2 **Double-loop learning** begins to more fundamentally question the nature of usual practice and the feedback loops used to maintain that practice. This more sophisticated learning allows for the possibility of the redefinition of the organisation's goals, norms, policies, procedures or even structures. Bottom-up redesign of the whole service or the introduction of new service models is an example of such double-loop learning. It requires new information to be introduced to the cycle, for example by placing a greater emphasis on user perspectives. This may reveal that the original standards against which services were being audited are not as central to users' concerns as other aspects of care.
3 A final level of learning concerns how the organisation reflects on its own ability to learn. It is learning about learning, or '**meta-learning**'. The organisation builds on its experience of learning, or failing to learn, and develops and tests new learning strategies accordingly. For example, a model of team-based, multidisciplinary collaborative learning has been pioneered within the NHS with respect to reducing waiting lists (see *www.modernnhs.nhs.uk*). A number of organisations have adopted a similar approach to explore the potential to learn about other areas of clinical concern such as the quality of the in-patient environment.

In order for the organisation to be able to learn from its own experience i/t will also have to demonstrate tolerance of mistakes. This does not imply a low expectation of excellence but rather requires that the inevitable failures within complex systems are learned from, rather than merely provoking blame or scapegoating.

Unlearning is also required to bring about meaningful change beyond single-loop learning. Profound change requires a fundamental questioning of existing custom and practice. For example, Davies and Nutley (2000) cite the challenge of moving services from secondary to primary care and the ways this may question deeply held assumptions about the roles of specialists. This unlearning may be particularly difficult because of the personal investments that people have in their current competencies. This goes some way to explain why, despite radical policy reforms, continuity rather than change remains the dominant theme.

Learning the lessons of quality assurance

Wakeling (2000) describes the industrial origins of public sector quality assurance initiatives and some of the key lessons learnt. Quality assurance systems should:

- *demonstrate that the service is doing what it is meant to do.* A basic tenet of one of the longest established quality systems, ISI 9000, is that you should 'say what you do . . . and then do what you say'. This is not such a modest achievement for many mental health services. The intended benefits and outcomes of what they provide may not be explicitly stated, and where they are, their activities may not obviously reflect their stated mission.
- *consider improvements rather than only correcting deficits.* Otherwise the same problems will be repeated.
- *aim to achieve good performance from the outset.* When faced with the requirement to implement quality improvements, staff are often deterred by the time and resources required, instead of the cost of *not* doing it right first time.
- *involve front-line staff as key players.* Bottom-up approaches that value the unique contribution of front-line staff and build on their commitment are advocated. Clinical governance (Department of Health, 1998) requires that all clinicians and managers understand their individual and collective responsibilities for

assuring high quality care. The process should be inclusive and multidisciplinary.

- *focus on building the capacity of staff to become more effective.* This includes the use of Personal Development Plans that address their needs both for personal support and training. It also involves positive employment practices that take seriously the resources that practitioners need in order to be effective in their roles, and the flexibility to ensure that they are fully supported in managing the integration of competing demands of their work and family life.
- *involve users at all levels of the quality assurance process.* Smith (1992) drew parallels between approaches to quality assurance in industry and the application of similar models to human services. She concluded that the failure to implement effective quality assurance strategies stemmed from an over-emphasis on monitoring and inspection, rather than an emphasis on partnership with users, and workers exerting control over quality-related activities. Pilgrim (1999) also expressed concern about the failure to base quality assurance processes on those aspects of change that are most valued by service users (such as improved quality of life), and a bias towards randomised controlled trials as the basis for evidence-based practice. Such methods usually fail to represent the experience of service users and require practices that are a poor analogue of usual practice. There are now well-established approaches to service evaluation, such as User Focused Monitoring (Rose *et al.*, 1998) which employ users to talk to other users about their experience of services using specific protocols.

Endnote: towards a future of effective teamworking

This book has attempted to describe teamworking within the context of a mental health service that is shaped by the imperatives and perceptions of a wide range of stakeholders. Differences between these perceptions have created major and enduring contradictions and tensions. What is an acceptable level of risk? To what extent should services be shaped by the user's or professional's perspective of need? How do absolute levels of resources impact on the nature of the services and the extent to which they are crisis-driven? Should people with severe and long-term health and social care needs be prioritised and, if so, how can we make this happen?

This book will not have resolved all these tensions. Hopefully, it will have helped to highlight them, and it has described the complex contexts in which such tensions are contested. Happily, this is a context in which traditional demarcations between stakeholders are becoming increasingly blurred. Health and social care are becoming more integrated. The same could be said of primary and specialist care. Differences between disciplines within teams endure but there is increasingly a shared platform of ideology and knowledge of what works that promotes a common language for team members. The user and carer campaigning agendas have also appeared to converge over the years with an increased emphasis on the importance of valued social roles such as employment. Finally, and perhaps most encouragingly, the roles of user and provider, receiver and giver of care, are also becoming intermingled. With clear leadership that models those values that are close to the hearts of people that use services, there is a very real hope for a future for teamworking in mental health that is increasingly accountable to users, planned around users' needs and aspirations, user-led in implementation and, thus, ultimately more effective.

References

Albert, S. and Whetten, D. A. (1985). Organisational identity. In L. L. Cummings and B. M. Staw (eds). *Research in Organisational Behaviour.* Vol. 7, 263–95. Greenwich, CT: JAI Press.

Alimo-Metcalfe, B. (1999). Leadership in the NHS: what are the competencies and qualities needed and how can they be developed? In Annabelle, L. M. and Dopson, S. (eds). *Organisational Behaviour in Health Care.* Basingstoke: Macmillan Business – now Palgrave Macmillan.

Allport, G. W. (1954). *The Nature of Prejudice.* Cambridge, Mass: Addison Wesley.

Anciano, D. and Kirkpatrick, A. (1990). CMHTs and clinical psychology: the death of a profession? *Clinical Psychology Forum,* **26**, 9–12.

Anthony, W. A., Rogers, E. S., Cohen, M. *et al.* (1995). Relationships between psychiatric symptomatology, work skills, and future vocational performance. *Psychiatric Services,* **46**, 353–7.

Argyris, C. (1990). *Overcoming Organizational Defences: Facilitating Organizational Learning.* Needham, MA: Allyn & Bacon.

Argyris, C. and Schön, D. A. (1996). *Organizational Learning II.* Reading, MA: Addison Wesley.

Atkinson, J. M. (1996). The community of strangers: Supervision and the New Right. *Health and Social Care in the Community,* **4(2)**, 122–5.

Audini, B., Marks, I. M., Lawrence, R. E., Connolly, J. and Watts, V. (1994). Home-based versus out-patient/in-patient care for people with serious mental illness. Phase II of a controlled study. *British Journal of Psychiatry,* **165**, 204–10.

Audit Commission (1986). *Making a Reality of Community Care.* London: HMSO.

Audit Commission (1994). *Finding a Place.* London: HMSO.

Axelrod, S. and Wetzler, S. (1989). Factors associated with better compliance with psychiatric aftercare. *Hospital and Community Psychiatry,* **40(4)**, 397–401.

Barker, P. and Baldwin, S. (1991) (eds). *Ethical Issues in Mental Health.* London: Chapman and Hall.

Baron, C. (1987). *Asylum to Anarchy.* London: Free Association Press.

Barr, W. (2000). Characteristics of severely mentally ill patients in and out of contact with community mental health services. *Journal of Advanced Nursing,* **31(5)**, 1189–98.

Bass, B. M. (1997). *Transformational Leadership.* Lawrence Erlbaum Associates.

Beeforth, M., Conlon, E., and Graley, R. (1994). *Have We Got Views for You.* London: SCMH.

Belbin, M. (1981). *Management Teams: Why they Succeed or Fail.* London: Heinemann.

Berridge, V. and Thom, B. (1996). Research and policy: what determines the relationship? *Policy Studies,* **17(1)**, 23–34.

Berwick, D. M. (1998). Developing and testing changes in delivery of care. *Annals of International Medicine,* **128**, 651–6.

Bindman, J., Beck, A., Glover, G., Thornicroft, G., Knapp, M., Leese, M. and Szmukler, G. (1999). Evaluating mental health policy in England: Care programme approach and supervision registers. *British Journal of Psychiatry,* **175**, 327–30.

Birchwood, M. (1998). New directions in the psychosocial approach to psychoses. *Journal of Mental Health,* **7, 2**, 111–14.

Birchwood, M., Smith, J., Macmillan, F. and McGovern, D. (1998). Early intervention in psychotic relapse. In Brooker, C. and Repper, J. (eds). *Serious Mental Health Problems in the Community: Policy, Practice and Research.* London. Bailliere Tindall Limited.

Bond, G. R., Drake, R. E., Mueser, K. T. *et al.* (1997). An up-date on supported employment for people with severe mental illness. *Psychiatric Services,* **48**, 335–57.

Bond, G. R., McCrew, J. H. and Fekete, D. M. (1995). Assertive outreach for frequent users of psychiatric hospitals: A meta-analysis. *Journal of Mental Health Administration,* **22(1)**, 4–16.

Bond, G. R., Miller, L. D., Krumveid, R. D. and Ward, R. S. (1988). Assertive case management in three CMHCs: A controlled study. *Hospital and Community Psychiatry,* **39(4)**, 411–18.

Borrill, C. and Haynes, C. (1999). Health service managers. In Payne and Firth-Cozens (eds) *Stress in Health Professionals.* Chichester: Wiley.

Borrill, C. S., Carletta, J., Carter, A. J., Dawson, J. F., Garrod, S., Rees, A., Richards, A., Shapiro, D. and West, M. A. (2000). *The Effectiveness of Health-care Teams in the National Health* Service. Birmingham: Aston University.

Borrill, C. S., Wall, T. D., West, M. A., Hardy, G. E., Carter, A. J., Haynes, C. E., Shapiro, D. A., Stride, C. and Wood, D. (1998). *Stress among NHS Staff: Final Report.* Institute of Work Psychology, University of Sheffield.

Boyer, S. L. and Bond, G. R. (1992). A comparison of assertive community treatment on burnout and job satisfaction. *Outlook,* **2(2)**, 13–15.

Bracken, P. and Cohen, B. (1999). Home treatment in Bradford. *Psychiatric Bulletin,* **23**, 349–52.

Bright, J. I., Baker, K. D. and Neimeyer, R. A. (1999). Professional and paraprofessional group treatments for depression: A comparison of cognitive-behavioural and mutual support interventions. *Journal of Consulting and Clinical Psychology,* **67(4)**, 491–501.

British Psychological Society (2000). *Understanding Mental Illness and Psychotic Experiences: A Report by the British Psychological Society Division of Clinical Psychology*. Leicester: BPS.

British Psychological Society (2001). *Working in Teams*. Leicester: BPS.

Brooker, C., Falloon, I., Butterworth, A., Goldberg, D., Graham-Hole, V. and Hillier, V. (1994). The outcome of training community psychiatric nurses to deliver psychosocial intervention. *British Journal of Psychiatry*, **165**, 222–30.

Brown, B., Crawford, P. and Darongkamas, J. (2000). Blurred roles and permeable boundaries: the experience of multidisciplinary working in community mental health. *Health and Social Care in the Community*, **8(6)**, 425–35.

Brown, D. and Leary, J. (1995). Findings from the Claybury study for psychiatric nurses. In J. Carson, L. Fagin, and S. Ritter (eds). *Stress and Coping in Mental Health Nursing*. London: Chapman and Hall.

Brown, P. (1985). *Transfer of Care*. London: Routledge Kegan Paul.

Brown, R. and Wade, G. (1987). Superordinate goals and intergroup behaviour: The effect of role ambiguity and status on intergroup attitudes and task performance. *European Journal of Social Psychology*, **17**, 131–42.

Burns, T. and Firn, M. (2002). *Assertive Outreach in Mental Health: A Manual for Practitioners*. Oxford University Press.

Burns, T. and Guest, L. (1999). Running an assertive community treatment team. *Advances in Psychiatric Treatment*, **5**, 348–56.

Burns, T., Beadsmoore, A., Bhat, A. V., Oliver, A. and Mathers, C. (1993a). A controlled trial of home-based acute psychiatric services I: Clinical and social outcome. *British Journal of Psychiatry*, **163**, 49–54.

Burns, T., Raftery, J., Beadsmoore, A., McGuigan, S. and Dickson, M. (1993b). A controlled trial of home-based acute psychiatric services II: Treatment pattern and costs. *British Journal of Psychiatry*, **163**, 55–61.

Busfield, J. (1996). *Men, Women and Madness: Understanding Gender and Mental Disorder*. London: Macmillan – now Palgrave Macmillan.

Caldicott, F. (1994). Supervision registers: The College's response. *Psychiatric Bulletin*, **18**, 385–8.

Cantwell, R., Brewin, J., Glazebrook, C., Dalkin, T., Fox, R., Medley, I. and Harrison, G. (1999). Prevalence of substance misuse in first-episode psychosis. *British Journal of Psychiatry*, **174**, 150–3.

Carling, P. and Allott, P. (2000). *Core Vision and Values for a Modern Mental Health System*. Directional paper 1. Birmingham: NHS West Midlands Region.

Carpenter, J. and Sbaraini, S. (1997). *Choice, Information and Dignity: Involving Users and Carers in Care Management in Mental Health*. Bristol: Policy Press/ Joseph Rowntree Foundation/Community Care.

Carpenter, M. (1994). *Normality is Hard Work*. London. Lawrence & Wishart.

Carson, J., Fagin, L. and Ritter, S. (eds) (1995). *Stress and Coping in Mental Health Nursing.* London: Chapman & Hall.

Challis, D. J. and Davies, B. P. (1986). *Case Management in Community Care.* Aldershot: Gower.

Chandler, D., Meisel, J., McGowen, M., Mintz, J. and Madison, K. (1996). Client outcomes in two model capitated integrated service agencies. *Psychiatric Services,* **47**, 175–80.

Charman, T. and Clifford, P. (1989). *Staff Training Issues in the Move towards Community Care: The First Year of the Daily Living Programme.* Unpublished report. London: NUPRD.

Cherniss, C. (1995). *Beyond Burnout.* London: Routledge.

Christensen, A., and Jacobson, N. S. (1994). Who (or what) can do psychotherapy: The status and challenge of non-professional therapies. *Psychological Science,* **5(1)**, 8–14.

Cm 849 (1989). *Caring for People.* London: HMSO.

Cm 4386 (1999). *Our Healthier Nation.* London: DOH.

Collins, K., Jones, M. L., McDonnell, A., Read, S., Jones, R. and Cameron, A. (2000). Do new roles contribute to job satisfaction and retention of staff in nursing and professions allied to medicine? *Journal of Nursing Management,* **8**, 3–12.

Confidential Inquiry into Homicides and Suicides by Mentally Ill People (1996). *Report of the Confidential Inquiry into Homicides and Suicides by Mentally Ill People.* London. Royal College of Psychiatrists.

Cooper, C. L., Rout, U. and Faragher, B. (1989). Mental health, job satisfaction, and job stress among general practitioners. *British Medical Journal,* **298**, 366–70.

Covey, S. R. (1992). *The Seven Habits of Highly Effective People.* London: Simon and Schuster.

Cronin-Stubbs, D. and Brophy, E. B. (1984). Burnout: Can social support save the psychiatric nurse? *Journal of Psychosocial Nursing and Mental Health Services,* **23**, 8–13.

Crowther, R., Marshall, M., Bond, G. and Huxley, P. (2001). Vocational rehabilitation for people with severe mental illness (Cochrane review). In: *The Cochrane Library,* Issue 4, Oxford: Update Software.

Cushway, D. and Taylor, P. (1996). Stress in clinical psychologists. *International Journal of Social Psychiatry,* **42**, 141–9.

Davies, H. T. O. and Nutley, S. (2000). Developing learning organisations in the new NHS. *British Medical Journal,* **320**, 990–1001.

Day, E., Arcelius, J. and Kahn, A. (1999). Perceived role of psychiatrists in the management of substance misuse. *Psychiatric Bulletin,* **23**, 667–70.

Dean, C., Phillips, E. M., Gadd, E. M., Joseph, M. and England, S. (1993). Comparison of community-based service with hospital based service for people with acute, severe psychiatric illness. *British Medical Journal,* **307**, 473–6.

Deary, I. H., Agius, R. M. and Sadler, A. (1996). Personality and stress in consultant psychiatrists. *International Journal of Social Psychiatry*, **42**, 112–13.

Deci, P. A., Santos, A. B., Hiott, D. W., Schoenwald, S. and Dias, J. K. (1995). Dissemination of assertive community treatment programs. *Psychiatric Services*, **46(7)**, 676–8.

Department of Health (1990). *Community Care in the Next Decade and Beyond.* London: HMSO.

Department of Health (1994a). *Health of the Nation Key Area Handbook. Mental illness* (2nd edn). London: HMSO.

Department of Health (1994b). *Hospital Discharge Workbook: A manual on hospital discharge practice.* London: HMSO.

Department of Health (1994c). Legislation planned to provide for supervised discharge of Psychiatic Patients. Press release, 12 August 1994, H93/908.

Department of Health (1995a). *Building Bridges: A guide to arrangements for inter-agency working for the care and protection of severely mentally ill people.* London: HMSO.

Department of Health, Working Group (1995b). *Practical Guidance on Joint Commissioning.* London: DoH.

Department of Health (1996). *The Spectrum of Care: Local Services for People with Mental Health Problems.* London. DoH.

Department of Health (1998a). *A First Class Service.* London: HMSO.

Department of Health (1998b). *A First Class Service: Quality in the New NHS.* London: DoH.

Department of Health (1999). *National Service Framework for Mental Health: Modern Standards and Service Models.* London: DoH.

Department of Health (2000). *The NHS Plan.* London: DoH.

Department of Health (2001a). *Mental Health Policy Implementation Guide.* London: DoH.

Department of Health (2001b). *An Audit Pack for Monitoring the Care Programme Approach.* London: DoH.

Department of Health (2001c). *Shifting the Balance of Power within the NHS.* London: DoH.

Department of Health (2001d). *Mental Health National Service Framework (and the NHS Plan). Workforce Planning, Education and Training Underpinning Programme: Adult Mental Health Services. Final Report by the Workforce Action Team.* London: DoH.

Department of Health (2002a). *Mental Health Policy Implementation Guide: Community Mental Health Teams.* London: DoH.

Department of Health (2002b). *Mental Health Policy Implementation Guide: Adult Acute In-patient Care Provision.* London: DoH.

Department of Health (2002c). *Mental Health Policy Implementation Guide: Dual Diagnosis Good Practice Guide.* London: DoH.

Department of Health & Social Security (DHSS) (1980). *Organisational and Management Problems of Psychiatric Hospitals.* London: HMSO.

Department of Health/Home Office (2000). *Reforming the Mental Health Act.* London: HMSO.

Department of Health/Social Services Inspectorate (1991). *Care Management and Assessment: Managers Guide.* London: HMSO.

Deschamps, J. and Brown, R. (1983). Superordinate goals and intergroup conflict. *British Journal of Social Psychology*, **22**, 189–95.

Diamond, R. J. (1996). Coercion and tenacious treatment in the community: Applications to the real world. In Dennis, D. L. and Monahan, J. (eds) *Coercion and Aggressive Community Treatment. A new frontier in mental health law.* Plenum Press. New York.

Dowell, A. and Ciarlo, J. A. (1983). Overview of Community Mental Health Centres Program from an Evaluation Perspective. *Community Mental Health Journal*, **19(2)**, 95–125.

Drake, R. E. and Noordsy, D. L. (1994). Case management for people with coexisting severe mental disorder and substance use disorder. *Psychiatric Annals*, **24**, 427–31.

Drake, R. J., Haley, C. J., Akhtar, S. and Lewis, S. (2000). Causes and consequences of duration of untreated psychosis in schizophrenia. *British Journal of Psychiatry*, **177**, 511–15.

Drolen, C. S. (1990). Current community mental health centre operations: entrepreneurship or business as usual? *Community Mental Health Journal*, **26(6)**, 547–58.

Dvoskin, J. A. and Steadman, H. J. (1994). Using intensive case management to reduce violence by mentally ill persons in the community. *Hospital and Community Psychiatry*, **45(7)**, 679–84.

Edwards, D., Burnard, P., Coyle, D., Fothergill, A. and Hannigan, B. (2000). Stress and burnout in community mental health nursing: A review of the literature. *Journal of Psychiatric and Mental Health Nursing*, **7**, 7–14.

EFQM and the British Quality Foundation (1999). *The European Foundation for Quality Management Excellence Model 1999: Public and Voluntary Sector.* Belgium: EFQM.

Falloon, I. R. H., Shanahan, W., Laporta, M. and Krekorian, H. A. R. (1990). Integrated family, general practice and mental health care in the management of schizophrenia. *Journal of the Royal Society of Medicine*, **83**, 225–8.

Faulkner, A. (2000). Strategies for living with mental distress. In Basset, T. (ed.). *Looking to the Future: Key Issues for Contemporary Mental Health Services.* Pavilion Publishing/Mental Health Foundation.

Faust, D. and Zlotnick, C. (1995). Another dodo bird verdict? Revisiting the comparative effectiveness of professional and paraprofessional therapists. *Clinical Psychology and Psychotherapy*, **2(3)**, 157–67.

Firth-Cozens, J. (1999). The psychological problems of doctors. In Payne, R. and Firth-Cozens, J. (eds) *Stress in Health Professionals.* Chichester: Wiley.

Ford, R., Beadsmore, A., Ryan, P., Repper, J., Craig, T. and Muijen, M. (1995). Providing the safety net: Case management for people with a serious mental illness. *Journal of Mental Health,* **1**, 91–7.

Foster, A. (1998). Integration or fragmentation: The challenge facing community mental health teams. In. Foster, A., and Roberts, V. Z. *Managing Mental Health in the Community: Chaos and Containment.* London: Routledge.

Foster, A., and Roberts, V. Z. (1998) (eds). *Managing Mental Health in the Community: Chaos and Containment.* London: Routledge.

Francis, E., David, J., Johnson, N. and Sashidharan, S. P. (1989). Black people and psychiatry in the UK. *Psychiatric Bulletin,* **13**, 482–5.

Frank, A. F. and Gunderson, J. G. (1990). The role of the therapeutic alliance in the treatment of schizophrenia. *Archives of General Psychiatry,* **47**, 228–36.

Franklin, J. L., Solovitz, B., Mason, M., Clemons, J. R. and Miller, G. (1987). An evaluation of case management. *American Journal of Public Health,* **77**, 674–8.

Fraser, S. W. and Greenhalgh, T. (2001). Coping with complexity: educating for capability. *British Medical Journal,* **323**, 799–803.

Fuller, L. (2000). Anti-racist practice in mental health assessment. In Basset, T. (ed). *Looking to the Future: Key Issues for Contemporary Mental Health Services.* Pavilion Publishing/Mental Health Foundation.

Galvin, S. W. and McCarthy, S. (1994). Multi-disciplinary community teams: Clinging to the wreckage. *Journal of Mental Health,* **3**, 167–74.

Garety, P. and Jolley, S. (2000). Early intervention in psychosis. *Psychiatric Bulletin,* **24**, 321–3.

Garrett, T. (1998). Sexual contact between patients and psychologists. *The Psychologist,* **11(5)**, 227–30.

Gask, L., Rogers, A., Roland, M. and Morris, D. (2000). *Improving Quality in Primary Care: A Practical Guide to the National Service Framework for Mental Health.* University of Manchester: National Primary Care Research and Development Centre.

Gauntlett, N., Ford, R. and Muijen, M. (1996). *Teamwork: Models of Outreach in an Urban Multi-cultural Setting.* London: SCMH.

Gehrs, M. and Goering, P. (1994). The relationship between the working alliance and rehabilitation outcomes of schizophrenia. *Psychosocial Rehabilitation Journal,* **18**, 43–54.

Gitlin, M. J., Swendsen, J., Heller, T. L. and Hammen, C. (1995). Relapse and impairment in bipolar disorder. *American Journal of Psychiatry,* **152(11)**, 1635–40.

Goater, N., King, M., Cole, E., Leavey, G., Johnson-Sabine, E., Blizard, R. and Hoar, A. (1999). Ethnicity and outcome in psychosis. *British Journal of Psychiatry,* **175**, 34–42.

Goffman, E. (1961). *Asylums.* Harmondsworth: Penguin.

Gournay, K. (1999). Assertive community treatment – why isn't it working? *Journal of Mental Health,* **8**, 427–9.

Gournay, K., Sandford, T., Johnson, S. and Thornicroft, G. (1997). Dual diagnosis of severe mental health problems and substance abuse/dependence: A major priority for mental health nursing. *Journal of Psychiatric and Mental Health Nursing,* **4(2)**, 89–95.

Gowdy, E. and Rapp, C. A. (1989). Managerial behaviour: The common denominator of effective community-based programs. *Psychosocial Rehabilitation Journal,* **13(2)**, 31–51.

Griffiths, L. (1998). Humour as resistance to professional dominance in community mental health teams. *Sociology of Health and Illness,* **20(6)**, 874–95.

Gunn, J. and Fahy, T. (1990). Police admissions to a psychiatric hospital. Demographic and clinical differences between ethnic groups. *British Journal of Psychiatry,* **156**, 373–8.

Guthrie, E., Tattam, T., Williams, E., Black, D. and Baciocotti, H. (1999). Sources of stress, psychological distress and burnout in psychiatrists. *Psychiatric Bulletin,* **23**, 207–12.

Hackman, J. R. (1990). *Groups that Work (and Those that Don't).* San Francisco: Jossey-Bass.

Haddock, G., Tarrier, N., Spaulding, W., Yusopoff, L., Kinney, C. and McCarthy, E. (1998). Individual cognitive-behaviour therapy in the treatment of hallucinations and delusions: A review. *Clinical Psychology Review,* **18**, 821–38.

Hagan, T. (1990). Accessible and acceptable services. In Huxley, P. *Effective Community Mental Health Services.* Aldershot: Avebury/Gower.

Handy, J. (1988). Theoretical and methodological problems within occupational stress and burnout research. *Human Relations,* **41(5)**, 355–69.

Handy, J. (1990). *Occupational Health in a Caring Profession.* Aldershot: Avebury.

Hannigan, B., Edwards, D., Coyle, D., Fothergill, A. and Burnard, P. (2000). Burnout in community mental health nurses: Findings from the all-Wales stress study. *Journal of Psychiatric and Mental Health Nursing,* **7**, 127–34.

Hardy, B., Turrell, A. and Wistow, G. (1992). *Innovations in Community Care Management.* Avebury. Aldershot.

Hardy, G. E. (1997). *The Mental Health of the NHS Workforce: A Report from the NHS Workforce Project. Proceedings of the Annual Meeting of the Royal College of Psychiatrists.* London: RCP.

Hardy, G. E. and Barkham, M. (1999). Psychotherapeutic interventions for work stress. In Payne and Firth-Cozens (eds) *Stress in Health Professionals.* Chichester: Wiley.

Harper, H. and Minghella, E. (1997). Pressures and rewards of working in community mental health teams. *Mental Health Care,* **1(1)**, 18–21.

Harrison, G., Holton, A., Neilson, D., Owens, D., Boot, D. and Cooper, J. (1989). Severe mental disorder in Afro-Caribbean patients: Some social, demographic and service factors. *Psychological Medicine*, **19**, 683–96.

Harrison, J. (2000). Prioritising referrals to a community mental health team. *British Journal of General Practice*, **50**, 194–8.

Harrison, K. (1994). *Mind's Response to the Department of Health's Guidance on Supervision Registers and on Hospital Discharge.* London: Mind.

Hayes, N. (1993). Social representation and organisational diversity. Paper presented at the British Psychological Society Occupational Psychology Conference, 1993. University of Huddersfield. Huddersfield.

Heim, E. (1991). Job stressors and coping in health professions. *Psychotherapy and Psychosomatics*, **55**, 90–9.

Herzberg, F., Mausner, B. and Synderman, B. B. (1959). *The Motivation to Work* (2nd edn). New York: John Wiley.

Hewstone, M. and Brown, R. (1986). Contact is not enough: An intergroup perspective on the 'Contact hypothesis'. In M. Hewstone and R. Brown (eds) *Contact and Conflict in Intergroup Encounters.* Oxford: Blackwell.

Hiday, V. A. (1996). Outpatient commitment: Official coercion in the community. In Dennis, D. L. and Monahan, J. (eds). *Coercion and Aggressive Community Treatment: A New Frontier in Mental Health Law.* Plenum Press. New York.

Hine, C. E. and Bachman, M. O. (1997). What does locality commissioning in Avon offer? Retrospective descriptive evaluation. *British Medical Journal*, **314(7089)**. 1246–50.

Holloway, F. and Carson, J. (1998). Intensive case management for the severely mentally ill: Controlled trial. *British Journal of Psychiatry*, **172**, 19–22.

Holloway, F., Szmukler, G. and Carson, J. (2000). Support systems. 1. Introduction. *Advances in Psychiatric Treatment*, **6**, 226–35.

Hosking, D.-M. and Morley, I. (1991). *A Social Psychology of Organising: People, Processes and Contexts.* Hemel Hempstead: Harvester Wheatsheaf.

Hoult, J. (1986). Community care of the acutely mentally ill. *British Journal of Psychiatry*, **149**, 137–44.

Hoult, J., Reynolds, I., Charbonneau-Powis, M., Weekes, P. and Briggs, J. (1983). Psychiatric hospital versus community treatment: The results of a randomised controlled trial. *Australian and New Zealand Journal of Psychiatry*, **17**, 160–7.

Hudson, B. (1996). Care management: Is it working? *Community Care Management and Planning*, **4(3)**, 77–84.

Hutchison, M. (1999). Still singing the same old blues. *Health Matters*, **34**, 16–17.

Hutchison, M. (2000). Issues around empowerment. In Basset, T. (ed.). *Looking to the Future: Key Issues for Contemporary Mental Health Services.* Pavilion Publishing/Mental Health Foundation.

Huxley, P. (1991). Effective case management for mentally ill people: The relevance of recent evidence from the USA for case management services in the United Kingdom. *Social Work and Social Sciences Review*, **3(1)**, 192–203.

Huxley, P. (1996). *Community Mental Health Teams in North West England: Results of a Regional Survey*. Warrington: North West Regional Office of NHS Executive.

Institute of Employment Studies (1997). *Taking Part: Registered Nurses and the Labour Market in 1997*. Report No. 338. Brighton: IES.

Intagliata, J. (1982). Improving the quality of care for the chronically mentally disabled: The role of case management. *Schizophrenia Bulletin*, **8(4)**, 655–73.

Isaacs, A. D. and Bebbington, P. E. (1991). Strategies for the management of severe psychiatric illness in the community. *International Review of Psychiatry*, **3**, 71–82.

Jabitsky, I. M. (1988). Psychiatric teams and the psychiatrist's authority in the New York State mental health system. *New York State Journal of Medicine*, **88(11)**, 577–81.

Jackson, G., Gater, R., Goldberg, D., Tantam, D., Loftus, L. and Taylor, H. (1993). A new community mental health team based in primary care. *British Journal of Psychiatry*, **162**, 375–84.

Job, T. (1999). A system for determining the priority of referrals within a multidisciplinary community mental health team. *British Journal of Occupational Therapy*, **62(1)**, 486–90.

Johnston, S., Salkeld, G., Sanderson, K., Issakidis, C., Teeson, M. and Buhrich, N. (1998). Intensive case management in Australia: A randomised controlled trial, *Australian and New Zealand Journal of Psychiatry*, **32**, 551–9.

Joseph Rowntree Foundation (1995). *Inquiry into Income and Wealth*. London: JRF.

Joy, C. B., Adams, C. E. and Rice, K. (2001). Crisis intervention for those with severe mental illness. In *The Cochrane Library*, Issue 4, Oxford: Update Software.

Kemp, R., Kirov, G., Everitt, B., Hayward, P. and David, A. (1998). Randomised controlled trial of compliance therapy – 18-month follow-up. *British Journal of Psychiatry*, **172**, 413–19.

Kendrick, T., Burns, T. and Freeling, P. (1995). Randomised controlled trial of teaching general practitioners to carry out structured assessments of their long term mentally ill patients. *British Medical Journal*, **311**, 93–8.

King, M., Coker, E., Leavey, G., Hoare, A. and Johnson-Sabine, E. (1994). Incidence of psychotic illness in London: Comparison of ethnic groups. *British Medical Journal*. **309**, 1115–19.

Kingsland, J., Williams, R. and Gibbs, T. (1999). Registration of serious mental illness in primary care. *Community Mental Health*, **2(3)**, 18–19.

Knapp, M., Beecham, J., Koutsogeorgopoulou, V., Hallam, A., Fenyo, A., Marks, I. M., Connolly, J., Audini, B. and Muijen, M. (1994). Service use and costs of home-based versus hospital-based care for people with serious mental illness. *British Journal of Psychiatry*, **165**, 195–203.

Knapp, M., Cambridge, P., Thomason, C., Allen, C., Beecham, J. and Darton, R. (1992). *Care in the Community: Challenge and Demonstration.* Aldershot: Gower.

Koelbel, P. W., Fuller, S. G. and Misener, T. R. (1991). An explanatory model of nurse practitioner job satisfaction. *Journal of the American Academy of Nurse Practitioners*, **3(1)**, 17–24.

Krupa, T., Eastabrook, S., Blake, P. and Goering, P. (1992). Lessons learned: Introducing psychiatric rehabilitation in a multidisciplinary hospital. *Psychosocial Rehabilitation Journal*, **15(3)**, 29–36.

Kuipers, E. (1996). The management of difficult to treat patients with schizophrenia, using non-drug therapies. *British Journal of Psychiatry*, **169** (suppl. 31), 41–51.

Lachance, K. R. and Santos, A. B. (1995). Modifying the PACT model: Preserving critical elements. *Psychiatric Services*, **46(6)**, 601–4.

Lamb, H. R. (1980). Therapist case-managers: More than just brokers of services. *Hospital and Community Psychiatry*, **31(11)**, 762–3.

Lang, C. L. (1982). The resolution of status and ideological conflicts in a community mental health setting. *Psychiatry*, **45**, 159–71.

Le Grand, J. and Robinson, R. (1981). *The Economics of Social Problems.* London: Macmillan – now Palgrave Macmillan.

Lehman, A. F. and Dixon, L. B. (eds) (1995). *Double Jeopardy: Chronic Mental Illness and Substance Use Disorders.* Basel: Harwood.

Leiter, M. P. (1988). Burnout as a function of communication patterns: A study of a multidisciplinary mental health team. *Group and Organisational Studies*, **13(1)**, 111–28.

Lelliott, P., Wing, J. K. and Clifford, P. (1994). A national audit of new long-stay psychiatric in-patients I: Method and description of the cohort. *British Journal of Psychiatry*, **165**, 160–9.

Leong, G. B. (1982). Psychiatrists and community mental health centres: can their relationship be salvaged? *Hospital and Community Psychiatry*, **33(4)**, 309–10.

Link, B. G., Rahav, M., Phelan, J. C. *et al.* (1997). On stigma and its consequences: Evidence from a longitudinal study of men with dual diagnosis of mental illness and substance abuse. *Journal of Health and Social Behaviour*, **38**, 177–90.

Links, P. S., Kirkpatrick, H. and Whelton, C. (1994). Psychosocial rehabilitation and the role of the psychiatrist. *Psychosocial Rehabilitation Journal*, **18(1)**, 121–30.

Lucksted, A. and Coursey, R. D. (1995). Consumer perceptions of pressure and force in psychiatric treatments. *Psychiatric Services*, **46**, 146–52.

Mahy, G. E., Mallett, R., Leff, J. and Bhugra, D. (1999). First-contact incidence rate of schizophrenia on Barbados. *British Journal of Psychiatry*, **175**, 28–33.

Marks, I. M., Connolly, J., Muijen, M., Audini, B., McNamee, G. and Lawrence, R. E. (1994). Home-based versus hospital-based care for people with serious mental illnesses. *British Journal of Psychiatry*, **165**, 179–94.

Marriott, S., Malone, S., Onyett, S. and Tyrer, P. (1993). The consequences of an open referral system to a community mental health service. *Acta Psychiatrica Scandinavica*, **88**, 93–7.

Marshall, M. (1996). Case management: A dubious practice. *British Medical Journal*, **312**, 523–4.

Marshall, M. (1999). Modernising mental health services: Time to define the boundaries of psychiatric care. *British Medical Journal*, **318**, 3–4.

Marshall, M. and Lockwood, A. (1998). Assertive community treatment for people with severe mental disorders (Cochrane review). In *The Cochrane Library*, Issue 4, Oxford: Update Software.

Marshall, M., Lockwood, A. and Gath, D. (1995). Social services case-management for long-term mental disorders: A randomised controlled trial. *The Lancet*, **345**, 409–12.

Marshall, M., Lockwood, A. and Green, R. (1998). Case management for people with severe mental disorders (Cochrane review). In *The Cochrane Library*, Issue 4, Oxford: Update Software.

Marshall, M., Bond, G., Stein, L. I., Shepherd, G., McGrew, J., Hoult, J., Rosen, A., Huxley, P., Diamond, R., Warner, R., Olsen, M., Latimer, E., Goering, P., Craig, T. K., Meisler, N. and Test, M. A. (1999). PRiSM Psychosis Study: Design limitations, questionable conclusions. *British Journal of Psychiatry*, **175**, 501–3.

Maslow, A. H. (1954). *Motivation and Personality*. New York: Harper & Row.

McAusland, T. (1985). *Planning and Monitoring Community Mental Health Centres*. London: Kings Fund Centre.

McAusland, T. and Wibaut, A. (1988). *Mental Health Matters. Evaluation of the Tiverton Community Mental Health Team*. Exeter: Exeter Health Authority.

McDonel, E. C., Bond, G. R., Salyers, M., Fekete, D., Chen, A., McGrew, J. H. and Miller, L. (1997). Implementing assertive community treatment programmes in rural settings. *Administration and Policy in Mental Health*, **25(2)**, 153–73.

McGrew, J. H., Wilson, R. G. and Bond, G. R. (1996). Client perspectives on helpful ingredients of assertive community treatment. *Psychiatric Rehabilitation Journal*, **19(3)**, 13–21.

McGrew, J. H., Bond, G. R., Dietzen, L., McKasson, M. and Miller, L. D. (1995). A multisite study of client outcomes in Assertive Community Treatment. *Psychiatric Services*, **46(7)**, 696–701.

Mechanic, D. (1996). Emerging issues in international mental health services research. *Psychiatric Services*, **47(4)**, 371–5.

Mellor-Clark, J. (2000). *Counselling in Primary Care in the Context of the NHS Quality Agenda: The Facts.* Rugby: British Association for Counselling and Psychotherapy.

Menezes, P. R., Johnson, S., Thornicroft, G., Marshall, J., Prosser, D., Bebbington, P. *et al.* (1996). Drug and alcohol problems among individuals with severe mental illness in South London. *British Journal of Psychiatry*, **168**, 612–9.

Mental Health Nursing Review Team (1994). *Working in Partnership: A Collaborative Approach to Care.* London. HMSO.

Menzies, I. (1967). *The Functioning of Social Systems as a Defence Against Anxiety.* London: Tavistock.

Merelman, R. M. (1989). On culture and politics in America: A perspective from cultural anthropology. *British Journal of Political Science*, **19**, 465–95.

Merson, S., Tyrer, P., Onyett, S., Lack, S., Birkett, P., Lynch, S. and Johnson, T. (1992). Early intervention in psychiatric emergencies: A controlled clinical trial. *The Lancet*, **339**, 1311–14.

Minghella, E., Ford, R., Freeman, T., Hoult, J., McGlynn, P. and O'Halloran, P. (1998). *Open All Hours: 24 Hours Response for People with Mental Health Emergencies.* London: SCMH.

Mohrman, S. A., Cohen, S. G. and Mohrman, A. M. (1995). *Designing Team-based Organisations.* San Francisco: Jossey Bass.

Morgan, H. G. (1997). Management of suicide risk. *Psychiatric Bulletin*, **21**, 214–16.

Morgan, S. (1996). *Helping Relationships in Mental Health.* Cheltenham: Stanley Thornes.

Morgan, S. (2000a). Risk and safety. In Basset, T. (ed.). *Looking to the Future: Key Issues for Contemporary Mental Health Services.* Pavilion Publishing/ Mental Health Foundation.

Morgan, S. (2000b). *Clinical Risk Management: A Clinical Tool and Practitioner Manual.* London: SCMH.

Morgan, S. and Akbar-Khan, S. (2000). Individual care planning in the UK. In Basset, T. (ed.). *Looking to the Future: Key Issues for Contemporary Mental Health Services.* Pavilion Publishing/Mental Health Foundation.

Morrall, P. A. (1997). Professionalism and community psychiatric nursing: A case study of four mental health teams. *Journal of Advanced Nursing*, **25**, 1133–37.

Morris. D. and Davidson, L. (1992). Community mental health centres in a changing environment. *Journal of Mental Health*, **1**, 295–9.

Moscovici, S., Mugny, G., van Avermaet, E. (eds) (1985). *Perspectives on Minority Influence.* Cambridge: Cambridge University Press.

Mossman, D. (1997). Deinstitutionalisation, homelessness and the myth of psychiatric abandonment: A structural anthropological perspective. *Social Science and Medicine*, **44(1)**, 71–83.

Mueser, K. T., Bond, G. R., Drake, R. E. and Resnick, G. (1998). Models of community care for severe mental illness: A review of research on case management. *Schizophrenia Bulletin*, **24(1)**, 38–73.

Muijen, M., Cooney, M., Strathdee, G., Bell, R. and Hudson, A. (1994). Community psychiatric nurse teams: Intensive support versus generic care. *British Journal of Psychiatry*, **165**, 211–17.

Munro, E. and Rumgay, J. (2000). Role of risk assessment in reducing homicides by people with mental illness. *British Journal of Psychiatry*, **176**, 116–20.

Murray, A., Shepherd, G., Onyett, S. R. and Muijen, M. (1997). *More than a friend: The Role of Support Workers in Community Mental Health Services.* London: SCMH.

National Schizophrenia Fellowship (1995). *The Silent Partners: The Needs and Experiences of People Who Provide Informal Care to People with a Severe Mental Illness.* London. NSF.

Nazareth, I., King, M. and Davies, S. (1995). Care of schizophrenia in general practice: The general practitioner and the patient. *British Journal of General Practice*, **45**, 343–7.

Nemeth, C. and Owens, J. (1996). Value of minority dissent. In West M. A. *Handbook of Work Group Psychology.* Chichester: Wiley.

Newnes, C. (1996). The development of clinical psychology and its values. *Clinical Psychology Forum*, **95**, 29–34.

NHS Centre for Review and Dissemination (2000). *Effective Health Care: Psychosocial Interventions for Schizophrenia*, **6(3)**.

NHS Executive (2001). *Making it Happen: A Guide to Delivering Mental Health Promotion.* London: DH 23821.

NHS Management Executive (1994a). *Introduction of Supervision Registers for Mentally Ill People from 1 April 1994.* HSG(94)5. HMSO.

NHS Management Executive (1994b). *Guidance on the Discharge of Mentally Disordered People and their Continuing Care in the Community.* HSG(94)27. HMSO.

NHSE/SSI (1999). *Effective Care Coordination in Mental Health Services: Modernising the care programme approach.* DH 16736.

Nikkel, R. E., Smith, G. and Edwards, D. (1992). A consumer-operated case management project. *Hospital and Community Psychiatry*, **43(6)**, 577–9.

Noonan, W. C. and Moyers, T. B. (1997). Motivational interviewing. *Journal of Substance Misuse*, **2**, 8–16.

Norman, I. J. and Peck, E. (1999). Working together in adult community mental health services: An inter-professional dialogue. *Journal of Mental Health*, **8, 3**, 217–30.

North, C. and Ritchie, J. (1993). *Factors Influencing the Implementation of the Care Programme Approach.* London: HMSO.

O'Brien, J. and Lyle, C. (1988). *Framework for Accomplishment.* Atlanta, Georgia: Responsive Systems Associated.

Obholzer, A. and Roberts, V. Z. (1994) (eds). *The Unconscious at Work.* London: Routledge.

Obholzer, A. (1994). Authority, power and leadership. In Obholzer, A. and Roberts, V. Z. (eds). *The Unconscious at Work.* London: Routledge.

Office of National Statistics (1998). *Labour Force Survey 1997/8.* London: ONS.

Oliver, N. and Kuipers, E. (1996). Stress and its relationship to expressed emotion in community mental health workers. *International Journal of Social Psychiatry*, **42(2)**, 150–9.

Onyett, S. R. (1995). Responsibility and accountability in community mental health teams. *Psychiatric Bulletin*, **19**, 281–5.

Onyett, S. R. (1998). *Case Management in Mental Health.* Cheltenham: Stanley Thornes.

Onyett, S. R. and Ford, R. (1996). Community mental health teams – Where's the wreckage? *Journal of Mental Health*, **5(1)**, 47–55.

Onyett, S. R. and Henderson, G. (1996). *The Riverside Project: Building on Good Multi-disciplinary Practice.* London: Centre for Mental Health Services Development.

Onyett, S. R., Heppleston, T. and Bushnell, D. (1994). A national survey of community mental health teams. *Journal of Mental Health*, **3**, 175–94.

Onyett, S. R., Heppleston, T. and Muijen, M. (1995). *Making Community Mental Health Teams Work.* London: SCMH.

Onyett, S. R., Pillinger, T. and Muijen, M. (1997). Job satisfaction and burnout among members of community mental health teams. *Journal of Mental Health*, **6, 1**, 55–66.

Onyett, S. R., Tyrer, P., Connolly, J., Malone, S., Rennison, J., Parslow, S., Davey, T., Lynch, S. and Merson, S. (1990). The Early Intervention Service: The first 18 months of an inner London demonstration project. *Psychiatric Bulletin*, **14**, 267–9.

Opie, A. (1997). Thinking teams thinking clients; issues of discourse and representation in the work of health care teams. *Sociology of Health and Illness*, **19(3)**, 259–80.

Orlinsky, D. E. and Howard, K. I. (1986). Process and outcome in psychotherapy. In S. L. Garfield and Bergin (eds). *Handbook of Psychotherapy and Behaviour Change*, 3rd edn, New York: Wiley.

Ovretveit, J. (1986). *Organisation of Multidisciplinary Community Teams.* BIOSS Working paper. Uxbridge: Brunel University.

Ovretveit, J. (1993). *Coordinating Community Care: Multidisciplinary Teams and Care Management.* Buckingham: Open University Press.

Ovretveit, J. (1997). Leadership in multiprofessional teams. *Health and Social Care in the Community,* **5(4)**, 276–83.

Owens, R. G. and Ashcroft, J. B. (1982). Functional analysis in applied psychology. *British Journal of Clinical Psychology,* **21**, 181–9.

Patmore, C. and Weaver, T. (1990). Rafts on an open sea. *Health Service Journal,* **100, 5222** (11 October), 1510–12.

Patmore, C. and Weaver, T. (1991a). *Community Mental Health Teams: Lessons for Planners and Managers.* London: Good Practices in Mental Health.

Patmore, C. and Weaver, T. (1991b). Strength in numbers. *Health Service Journal,* **101**, 5274 (17 October), 24–5.

Patmore, C. and Weaver, T. (1991c). Unnatural selection. *Health Service Journal,* **101:5273** (10 October), 20–2.

Paxton, R. (1995). Goodbye community mental health teams – at last. *Journal of Mental Health,* **3**, 331–4.

Payne, R. and Firth-Cozens, J. (1999). *Stress in Health Professionals.* Chichester: Wiley.

Peck, E. (1994). Community mental health centres: Challenges to the new orthodoxy. *Journal of Mental Health,* **3**, 151–6.

Peck, E. (1995). On the team. *Health Service Journal,* **105, 5447**, 28–9.

Peck, E. and Parker, E. (1998). Mental health in the NHS: Policy and practice 1979–1998. *Journal of Mental Health,* **7, 3**, 241–59.

Pekkala, E. and Merinder, L. (2000). Psychoeducational interventions for schizophrenia and other severe mental illnesses (Cochrane Review). *The Cochrane Library,* Issue 3. Oxford: Update Software.

Pelican, C. (1991). A marriage of convenience? *Community Care.* 19 September.

Pelosi, A. and Jackson, G. A. (2000). Home treatment – enigmas and fantasies. *British Medical Journal,* **320**, 305–9.

Perkins, R. and Repper, J. M. (1998). Principles of working with people who experience serious mental health problems. In Brooker, C. and Repper, J. *Serious Mental Health Problems in the Community: Policy, Practice and Research.* London. Bailliere Tindall Limited.

Perkins, R. and Repper, J. M. (1999). Compliance or informed choice. *Journal of Mental Health,* **8**, **2**, 117–29.

Perkins, R., Buckfield, R. and Choy, D. (1997). Access to employment: A supported employment project to enable mental health service users to obtain jobs within mental health teams. *Journal of Mental Health,* **6**, 307–18.

Pettigrew, A., Mackee, L. and Ferlie, E. (1988). Understanding change in the NHS. *Public Administration,* **66(3)**, 297–317.

Pharoah, F., Mari, J. and Streiner, D. (2000). Family intervention for schizophrenia (Cochrane Review). *The Cochrane Library*, Issue 3. Oxford: Update Software.

Pilgrim, D. (1999). Making the best of clinical governance. *Journal of Mental Health*, **8, 1**, 1–2.

Pilgrim, D. and Rogers, A. (1996). Two notions of risk in mental health debates. In Heller, T., Reynolds, J., Gomm, R., Muston, R. and Pattison, S. (eds). *Mental Health Matters: A Reader*. Basingstoke: Macmillan Press – now Palgrave Macmillan.

Pilgrim, D. and Rogers, A. (1999). *A Sociology of Mental Health and Illness* (2nd edn). Buckingham: Open University Press.

Pincus, H. A., Henderson, B., Blackwood, D. and Dial, T. (1993). Trend in research in two general psychiatric journals in 1969–1990: Research on research. *American Journal of Psychiatry*, **150**, 135–42.

Plsek, P. E. and Greenhalgh, T. (2001). The challenge of complexity in healthcare. *British Medical Journal*, **323**, 625–8.

Plsek, P. E. and Wilson, T. (2001). Complexity, leadership and management in healthcare organisations. *British Medical Journal*, **323**, 746–9.

Poxton, R. (1999). *Partnerships in Primary and Social Care*. London: King's Fund.

Pratt, P. (1998). The administration and monitoring of neuroleptic medication. In Brooker, C. and Repper, J. *Serious Mental Health Problems in the Community: Policy, Practice and Research*. London: Bailliere Tindall Limited.

Prosser, D., Johnson, S., Kuipers, E., Szmukler, G., Bebbington, P. and Thornicroft, G. (1996). Mental health, 'burnout' and job satisfaction among hospital and community-based mental health staff. *British Journal of Psychiatry*, **169**, 334–7.

Provan, K. G. and Milward, H. B. (1995). A preliminary theory of inter-organisational network effectiveness: A comparative study of four community mental health systems. *Administrative Science Quarterly*, **40**, 1–33.

Ramirez, A., Graham, J., Richards, M. A., Cull, A. and Gregory, W. M. (1996). Mental health of hospital consultants: The effects of stress and satisfaction at work. *Lancet*, **347**, 724–8.

Rapp, C. A. and Wintersteen, R. (1989). The strengths model of case management: Results from twelve demonstrations. *Psychosocial Rehabilitation Journal*, **13(1)**, 23–32.

Ray, E. B. and Miller, K. L. (1994). Social support, home/work stress, and burnout: Who can help? *Journal of Applied Behavioural Science*, **30(3)**, 357–73.

Read, J. and Baker, S. (1996). *Not Just Sticks and Stones. A Survey of the Stigma, Taboos and Discrimination Experienced by People with Mental Health Problems*. London: Mind.

Rees, D. and Cooper, C. (1992). Occupational stress in health service workers in the UK. *Stress Medicine*, **8**, 79–90.

Repper, J., Ford, R. and Cooke, A. (1994). How can nurses build relationships with people who have severe and long-term mental health problems? Experience of case managers and their clients. *Journal of Advanced Nursing*, **19**, 1096–1104.

Revicki, D. A. and May, H. J. (1989). Organizational characteristics, occupational stress and mental health in nurses. *Behavioural Medicine*, **15(1)**, 30–6.

Richards, A. and Rees, A. (1998). Developing criteria to measure the effectiveness of community mental health teams. *Mental Health Care*, **21, 1**, 14–17.

Ridgely, M. S., Morrissey, J. P., Paulson, R. I., Goldman, H. and Calloway, M. O. (1996). Characteristics and activities of case managers in the RWJ Foundation Program on Chronic Mental Illness. *Psychiatric Services*, **47(7)**, 737–43.

Roberts, V. Z. (1998a). Is authority a dirty word? In Foster, A. and Roberts, V. Z. *Managing Mental Health in the Community: Chaos and Containment.* London: Routledge.

Roberts, V. Z. (1998b). Psychotic processes and community care. In Foster, A. and Roberts, V. Z. *Managing Mental Health in the Community: Chaos and Containment.* London: Routledge.

Rogers, A. (1993). Coercion and voluntary admissions: An examination of a psychiatric patient's view. *Behavioural Science and the Law*, **11(3)**, 259–67.

Rogers, A. and Pilgrim, D. (1993). Mental health service users' views of medical practitioners. *Journal of Interprofessional Care*, **7(2)**, 167–76.

Rogers, A. and Pilgrim, D. (1996). *Mental Health Policy in Britain.* Basingstoke: Macmillan Press – now Palgrave Macmillan.

Rogers, A., Pilgrim, D. and Lacey, R. (1993). *Experiencing Psychiatry: Users Views of Services.* Hampshire: Macmillan/Mind.

Rogers, A., Day, J., Wood, P., Randall, F., Healy, D. and Bentall, R. P. (1998). Subjective experience of neuroleptic medication: a view from the other side. *Social Science and Medicine*, **47**, 1212–1323.

Rollnick, S. and Miller, W. R. (1995). What is motivational interviewing? *Behavioural and Cognitive Psychotherapy*, **23**, 325–34.

Rollnick, S., Mason, P. and Butler, C. (1999). *Health Behaviour Change: A Guide for Practitioners.* Edinburgh: Churchill Livingstone.

Rose, D., Ford, R., Lindley, P. and Gawith, L. (1998). *In our Experience.* London: SCMH.

Rose, N. (1996a). The death of the social? Re-figuring the territory of government. *Economy and Society*, **25(3)**, 327–56.

Rose, N. (1996b). Psychiatry as a political science: Advanced liberalism and the administration of risk. *History of the Human Sciences*, **9(2)**, 1–23.

Sainsbury Centre for Mental Health (1997). *Pulling Together. The Future Role and Training of Mental Health Staff.* London: SCMH.

Sainsbury Centre for Mental Health (1998a). *Keys to Engagement.* London: SCMH.

Sainsbury Centre for Mental Health (1998b). *Acute Problems: A Survey of the Quality of Care in Acute Psychiatric Wards.* London: SCMH.

Sainsbury Centre for Mental Health (2000a). *Taking your Partners.* London: SCMH.

Sainsbury Centre for Mental Health (2000b). *The Capable Practitioner.* London: SCMH.

Santos, A. B., Deci, P. A., Lachance, K. R., Dias, J. K., Sloop, T. B., Hiers, T. G. and Bevilacqua, J. J. (1993). Providing assertive community treatment for severely mentally ill patients in a rural area. *Hospital and Community Psychiatry*, **44**, 34–9.

Sashidharan, S. P., Smyth, M. and Owen, A. (1999). PRiSM Psychosis Study: Thro' a glass darkly: A distorted appraisal of community care, *British Journal of Psychiatry*, **175**, 504–7.

Sayce, L. (1990). *Waiting for Community Care: Implications of Government Policy for 1991.* London: Mind.

Sayce, L. and Measey, L. (1999). Strategies to reduce social inclusion for people with mental health problems. *Psychiatric Bulletin*, **23**, 65–7.

Sayce, L. and Wilmot. J. (1997). *Gaining Respect: A Guide to Preventing and Tackling Community Opposition to Mental Health Services.* London: Mind.

Sayce, L., Craig, T. K. J. and Boardman, A. P. (1991). The development of community mental health centres in the UK. *Social Psychiatry and Psychiatric Epidemiology*, **26**, 14–20.

Scheid, T. L. (1996). Burned out emotional labourers: An analysis of emotional labour, work identity and burnout. Paper presented at the American Sociological Association Meeting, New York.

Searle, R. T. (1991). Community mental health teams: Fact or fiction. *Clinical Psychology Forum*, **31**, 15–17.

Segal, S. P., Bola, J. R. and Watson, M. A. (1996). Race, quality of care, and antipsychotic prescribing practices in psychiatric emergency services. *Psychiatric Services*, **47(3)**, 282–5.

Senge, P., Roberts, C., Ross, R., Smith, B., Roth, G. and Kleiner, A. (1999). *The Dance of Change.* London: Nicholas Brealey.

Shea, G. P. and Guzzo, R. A. (1987). Groups as human resources. *Research in Personnel and Human Resources Management*, **5**, 323–56.

Shepherd, G. (1999). *Review of Specialist Mental Health Rehabilitation Services. Avon and Western Mental Health Trust.* London: Health Advisory Service 2000.

Shepherd, G., Muijen, M., Dean, C. and Cooney, M. (1996). Residential care in hospital and in the community – quality of care and quality of life. *British Journal of Psychiatry*, **168**, 448–56.

Shepherd, G., Murray, A. and Muijen, M. (1994). *Relative Values.* London: SCMH.

Sheppard, D. (1996). *Learning the Lessons*, 2nd edn. London: The Zito Trust.

Shergill, S. S., Murray, R. and McGuire, P. K. (1998). Auditory hallucinations: A review of psychological treatments. *Schizophrenia Research*, **32**, 137–50.

Sherif, M. (1966). *Group Conflict and Co-operation: Their Social Psychology*. London: Routledge & Kegan Paul.

Sherlock, J. (1994). *Through the Rural Magnifying Glass*. London: Good Practices in Mental Health.

Sherman, P. S. and Porter, R. (1991). Mental health consumers as case management aides. *Hospital and Community Psychiatry*, **42(5)**, 494–8.

Simmonds, S., Coid, J., Joseph, P., Marriott, S. and Tyrer, P. (2001). Community mental health team management in severe mental illness: A systematic review. *British Journal of Psychiatry*, **178**, 497–502 .

Slade, M. (1994). Needs assessment. *British Journal of Psychiatry*, **165**, 293–6.

Smail, D. (1989). Clinical psychology, managerialism and power. *Clinical Psychology Forum*, **20**, 10–12.

Smith, H. (1992). Quality in community care: Moving beyond mediocrity. *Journal of Mental Health*, **1**, 207–17.

Smith, H. (1998). Needs assessment in mental health services: The DISC framework. *Journal of Public Health Medicine*, **20(2)**, 154–60.

Smith, J. A., Hughes, I. and Budd, R. J. (1999b). Non-compliance with antipsychotic depot medication: Users' views on advantages and disadvantages. *Journal of Mental Health*, **8, 3**, 287–96.

Smith, M., Coleman, R., Allott, P. and Koberstein, J. (1999a). Assertive outreach: A step backward. *Nursing Times*, 28 July–3 August; **95(30)**, 46–7.

Smith, P. A. C. (2001). Action Learning and Reflective Practice in Project Environments that are related to Leadership Development. *Management Learning*, **32(1)**, 31–48.

Smyth, M. G. and Hoult, J. (2000). Home treatment enigmas. *British Medical Journal*, **320**, 305–9.

Solomon, P. and Draine, J. (1995a). One-year outcomes of a randomised trial of case management with seriously mentally ill users leaving jails. *Evaluation Review*, **19(3)**, 256–73.

Solomon, P. and Draine, J. (1995b). The efficacy of a consumer case management team: 2-year outcomes of a randomised trial. *Journal of Mental Health Administration*, **22(2)**, 135–45.

Solomon, P., Draine, J. and Delaney, M. A. (1995). The working alliance and consumer case management. *Journal of Mental Health Administration*, **22(2)**, 126–34.

Spindel, P. and Nugent, J. A. (1999). The Trouble with PACT: Questioning the increasing use of assertive community treatment teams in community mental health. http://www.madnation.cc/documents/spindel.htm

Stacey, R. D. (2000). *Strategic Management and Organisational Dynamics* (3rd edn). Harlow: Pearson Education Limited.

Steadman, H. J., Monahan, J. and Appelbaum, P. S. (1994). Designing a new generation of risk assessment research. In Monahan, J. and Steadman, H. J. (eds). *Violence and Mental Disorder: Developments in Risk Assessment.* Chicago: University of Chicago Press.

Stein, L. I. (1992). On the abolishment of the case manager. *Health Affairs,* Fall, 172–7.

Stein, L. I. and Santos, A. B. (1998). *Assertive Community Treatment of Persons with Severe Mental Illness.* New York and London: W. W. Norton.

Stein, L. I. and Test, M. A. (1980). Alternative to mental hospital treatment I. *Archives of General Psychiatry,* **37**, 392–7.

Strakowski, M., Shelton, R. C. and Kolbrener, M. L. (1993). The effects of race and comorbidity on clinical diagnosis in-patients with psychosis. *Journal of Clinical Psychiatry,* **54**, 96–102.

Stroul, B. (1989). Community support programmes for people with long-term mental illness: a conceptual framework. *Psychosocial Rehabilitation Journal,* **12(3)**, 9–26.

Tajfel, H. and Turner, J. C. (1979). An integrative theory of social conflict. In W. Austin and S. Worchel (eds). *The Social Psychology of Intergroup Relations.* Monterey: Brooks/Cole.

Tannenbaum, S. I., Salas, E. and Cannon-Bowers, J. A. (1996). Promoting team effectiveness. In West, M. A. (ed.). *Handbook of Work Group Psychology.* Chichester: John Wiley and Sons Ltd.

Taylor, M. B. (1997). Compassion: Its neglect and importance. *British Journal of General Practice,* **47**, 521–3.

Taylor, P. J. and Gunn, J. (1999). Homicides by people with mental illness: Myth and reality. *British Journal of Psychiatry,* **174**, 9–14.

Teague, G. B., Bond, G. R., and Drake, M. D. (1998). Program fidelity in assertive community treatment: Development and use of a measure. *American Journal of Orthopsychiatry,* **68(2)**, 216–32.

Thomas, C. S., Stone, K., Osborn, M., Thomas, P. F. and Fisher, M. (1993). Psychiatric morbidity and compulsory admission among UK-born Europeans, Afro-Caribbeans and Asians in central Manchester. *British Journal of Psychiatry,* **163**, 91–9.

Thomas, P., Romme, M. and Hamelijnk, J. (1996). Psychiatry and the politics of the underclass. *British Journal of Psychiatry,* **169**, 401–4.

Thomas, R. V. R. and Corney, R. H. (1993). Working with community mental health professionals: A survey among general practitioners. *British Journal of General Practice,* **43**, 417–21.

Thornicroft, G., Becker, T., Holloway, F., Johnson, S., Leese, M., McCrone, P., Szmukler, G., Taylor, R. and Wykes, T. (1999). Community mental health teams: evidence or belief? *British Journal of Psychiatry*, **175**, 508–13.

Tomson, D. (2000). *Primary care and specialist mental health care – working at the interface.* Unpublished report commissioned by the SCMH.

Turner, J. C. (1982). Towards a cognitive redefinition of the social group. In Tajfel, H. (ed.). *Social Identity and Intergroup Relations.* Cambridge: Cambridge University Press.

Turquet, P. (1974). Leadership: The individual and the group. In Colman, A. D. and Geller, M. H. (eds). *Group Relations Reader 2.* Washington DC: A. K. Rice Institute Series.

Tyrer, P. (1998a). Cost-effective or profligate community psychiatry? *British Journal of Psychiatry*, **172**, 1–3.

Tyrer, P. (1998b). Whither community care? *British Journal of Psychiatry*, **173**, 359–60.

Tyrer, P. (2000). Effectiveness of intensive treatment in severe mental illness. *British Journal of Psychiatry*, **176**, 492–3.

Tyrer, P. Simmonds, S., Coid, J., Mariott, S. and Joseph, P. (2001). A defence of community mental health teams (letter). *British Journal of Psychiatry*, **179**, 268.

Tyrer, P., Morgan, J., Van Horn, E., Jayakody, M., Evans, K., Brummell, R., White, T., Baldwin, D., Harrison-Read, P. and Johnson, T. (1995). A randomised controlled study of close monitoring of vulnerable psychiatric patients. *The Lancet*, **345**, 756–9.

Vaughan, P. J. The supervision register: One year on. *Psychiatric Bulletin*, **20**, 143–5.

Verhaak, P. F. M. (1993). Analysis of referrals of mental health problems by general practitioners. *British Journal of General Practice*, **43**, 203–8.

Wakeling, D. (2000). Building quality mental health services. In Basset, T. (ed.). *Looking to the Future: Key Issues for Contemporary Mental Health Services.* Pavilion Publishing/Mental Health Foundation.

Waldron, G. (1981). Picking up the pieces. *Health and Social Service Journal*, June 12, 708–10.

Ward, M. F., Armstrong, C., Lelliott, P. and Davies, M. (1999). Training, skills and caseloads of community mental health support workers in case management: Evaluation from the initial UK demonstration sites. *Journal of Psychiatric and Mental Health Nursing*, **6**, 187–97.

Warner, R. (1985). *Recovery from Schizophrenia.* Boston: Routledge & Kegan Paul.

Warner, R. W., Gater, R., Jackson, M. G. and Goldberg, D. (1993). Effects of a community mental health service on the practice and attitudes of general practitioners. *British Journal of General Practice*, **43**, 507–11.

Watts, F. and Bennett, D. (1983). Management of the staff team. In F. N. Watts and D. H. Bennett. *Theory and Practice of Psychiatric Rehabilitation.* Chichester: Wiley.

Weaver, T. and Patmore, C. (1990). United fronts. *Health Service Journal*, **100, 5223** (18 October), 1554–5.

Weaver, T., Renton, A., Stimson, G. and Tyrer, P. (1999). Severe mental illness and substance misuse. *British Medical Journal*, **318**, 137–8.

West, M. A. (1994). *Effective Teamwork*. Leicester: BPS.

West, M. A. (1996). Reflexivity and work group effectiveness: A conceptual integration. In West, M. A. (ed.). *Handbook of Work Group Psychology*. Chichester: John Wiley & Sons Ltd.

West, M. A. and Farr, J. L. (1989). Innovation at work: Psychological perspectives. *Social Behaviour*, **4**, 15–30.

West, M. A. and Hennessy, J. (1999). Intergroup behaviour in organisations. A field test of social identity theory. *Small Group Research*, **30(3)**, 361–82.

West, M. A., Borrill, C. S. and Unsworth, K. L. (1998). Team effectiveness in organisations. In Cooper, C. L. and Robertson, I. T. (eds). *International Review of Industrial and Organisational Psychology*. Chichester: John Wiley and Sons Ltd.

White, E. and Brooker, C. (1990). The future of community psychiatric nursing: What might the care programme approach mean for practice and education. *Community Psychiatric Nursing Journal*, **10(6)**, 27–30.

Williams, J. (ed.) (1996). Social inequalities and mental health: Implications for service provision. *Journal of Community and Applied Social Psychology*, **6** (Special Issue).

Williams, J. and Watson, G. (1988). Sexual inequality, family life and family therapy. In E. Street and W. Dryden (eds). *Family Therapy in Britain*. Milton Keynes: Open University Press.

Williams, M. L., Forster, P., McCarthy, G. D. and Hargreaves, W. A. (1994). Managing case management: What makes it work? *Psychosocial Rehabilitation Journal*, **18(1)**, 49–60.

Wilson, T., Holt, T. and Greenhalgh, T. (2001). Complexity and clinical care. *British Medical Journal*, **323**, 685–8.

Wing, J. K. (1992). *Epidemiologically Based Mental Health Needs Assessments*. London: Department of Health.

Witheridge, T. F. and Dincin, J. (1985). The Bridge: An assertive outreach program in an urban setting. *New Directions for Mental Health Services*, **26**, 65–76.

Index

Bold page numbers denote main reference to the subject

D

I

J

K

L

M